WITH EYES TO SEE

Walbert Bühlmann

WITH EYES TO SEE

Church and World in the Third Millennium

Translated from the German by
Robert R. Barr

 St Paul Publications

Original title: *Wer Augen hat zu sehen...: Was Gott heute mit uns Christen vorhat,* © 1989 Verlag Styria

St Paul Publications
Middlegreen, Slough SL3 6BT, United Kingdom

First published in U.S.A. by Orbis Books, Maryknoll, NY 10545
English translation © 1990 by Orbis Books and St Paul Publications

ISBN 085439 342 0

Printed by Billing & Sons, Worcester

St Paul Publications is an activity of the priests and brothers
of the Society of St Paul who proclaim the Gospel through the
media of social communication

Contents

PART 1
INTRODUCING A NEW CONSTELLATION OF WORLD FORCES

One World and a World Church   **3**
    At Last: One World   3
    At Last: A World Church   6
    A New Decalogue for the Third Millennium   11

PART 2
THE "NEW" TEN COMMANDMENTS OF GOD:
A DECALOGUE BASED ON THE SIGNS OF THE TIMES

1. You Will Allow Common Sense To Prevail   **19**
    Autonomy of the Sciences

2. You Will Take Yourselves Seriously as People of God   **33**
    The Laity in the Church

3. You Will Extend Your Hand to Your Fellow Christians   **50**
    Ecumenism

4. You Will Take Sides with the Poor   **62**
    Justice in Latin America

5. You Will Wonder at the Breadth of the Creator   **78**
    Inculturation in Africa

6. You Will Acknowledge That the "I Am Here" Is Present   **89**
    among All Peoples
    Dialogue with the Religions of Asia

7. You Will Accompany Religious Nomads   **102**
    Secularization in Euramerica

8. You Will Swell the Ranks of the Peacemakers   **114**
    Justice and Peace

9. **You Will Make the Earth a Paradise**   124
   Ecology and Eschatology

10. **You Will Encounter the God of History**   134
    Spirituality and Politics

PART 3
REFLECTIONS ON THE NEW FUTURE

The Church on the Way to the Third Millennium   143
   Three Millennial Turning Points   143
   The Actual Situation of the Church Today   144
   Building a "Church of Conscience"   149
   Summary   156

Notes   158

PART 1

Introducing
a New Constellation
of World Forces

One World and a World Church

AT LAST: ONE WORLD

Our planet plays a very humble, but far from meaningless, role in God's world. Earth is the world of human beings. The story of its formation, like that of its exploration, is a very long one. For untold ages, every tribe, every people, thought that it lived at the center of the world, not only geographically, but in every other respect as well. Each nation, each tribe, believed it was the measure of all things. Thus it could contemn other nations and tribes, make war on them, plunder them, and enslave them. Each group also thought that it enjoyed a special relationship with its own tutelary deity—that it had that divinity's special protection and was its chosen people. The gods reverenced by other peoples, then, were false gods. This way of thinking, which is far from having disappeared today, is called "ethnocentrism." Each tribe (Gk., *ethnos*) made itself the center of all things, and looked down on all other tribes by reason of their origin, color, language, or religion.

The biblical world fit this general human experience exactly. The "earth" was coextensive with one people's field of vision. Only familiar persons and groups counted as part of the world. Thus the great flood was said to have covered "the whole earth" (Gen. 7:18-23), and famine to have prevailed not only in Egypt, but "throughout the world" (Gen. 41:57). Darius, king of the Medes, made his proclamation "throughout the earth" (Dan. 6:26), to all peoples and nations, to speakers of all tongues.

True, in its exordium as in its conclusion, the Bible bursts the bonds of this narrow purview, and descries, as through a telescope, the distant "ends" of a far broader earth. The first eleven chapters of Genesis constantly speak of *ha-Adam*—the human being, humanity. God was making history by way of the whole of humanity, then. God's first love was the whole human race.

As holy scripture closes, however, it looks back no longer on our first beginnings. Now its gaze is directed upon humanity's future—nor indeed its gaze alone, but its commission as well: "Go! Proclaim! Heal! Deliver human beings from the powers of darkness," and this "to the ends of the earth" (Acts 1:8). And by the "ends of the earth" were meant not merely the geographical limits of the known world of the time, but the absolute

3

limits of the world of any future time. As these limits expanded, then, so would the task and commission.

While the biblical world embraced the entire world only in retrospect and prospect, the boundaries of the Roman world comprised, even in those ancient days, an astonishingly broad space. Rome not only knew, but subjugated and colonized, the lands of the East to the Persian Gulf and the Caspian Sea, of the North to today's southwest Germany and England, of the West to Spain, and of the South to north Africa and Egypt. In their diplomatic wisdom, the Romans sought to hold the reins of freedom of the individual populations as loosely as possible, and keep the bands of unity only as taut as necessary. The old Christmas martyrology opened with the proclamation that, under Caesar Augustus, "the whole world being at peace [*tota orbe terrarum in pace composita*], Jesus Christ, the Savior of the world, was born. . . . " Even today we are astonished at how long such a far-flung hegemony endured, in the poor conditions of transportation and communication of those days. The decline set in with the degeneration of the upper classes, whose comportment set the tone for the rest of the people. Despite financial incentives for the generation of offspring, these classes died out, and folk from the provinces crept into the army and the administration, until the great processions of the peoples finally sounded the death knell of the Roman Empire.

From the ruins of the Roman Empire sprang the Western world—Christendom. Charlemagne regarded himself as the new David, and actually had his throne in Aachen modeled after the biblical throne of the first David. The little flock of Jesus' disciples had become a great church and a Christian empire. At the twin pinnacles of this Christendom sat pope and emperor, acknowledging each other's right to wield, respectively, spiritual and secular power. In the eleventh century, their competition was resolved in the outright hegemony of the papal over the imperial might. Once eschatological hope had been the hallmark of a strong, young church, but the church now shifted its focus to the kingdom of this world; the next world was important for only two reasons—it was the site of the resolution of the individual's ultimate destiny after death and it was the source of the fear of hell.

If you lived in this Christendom, you paid pope and emperor unconditional fealty. If you dared rattle the cage of your Catholic faith, you were regarded as an enemy of the empire, and were dealt with accordingly. Beyond the confines of the empire were only barbarity and the kingdom of Satan, with which there was no tolerance, only struggle. To carry salvation to the ends of the earth meant to extend the frontiers of the empire, and then to incorporate these strangers into the empire and the church.

This medieval empire was coextensive with what its leaders viewed as the civilized world of the time. To the west lay only the ocean, with its seemingly impenetrable frontier. To the south and east stretched the lofty wall of Islam, and the crusaders sought to breach it in vain.

Midway through this second Christian millennium, suddenly, powerfully, the Western world exploded in every direction. Portuguese seafarers pressed ever further southward along the coast of Africa, finally circumnavigating the cape and reaching the Indies. In 1492 Christopher Columbus crossed the ocean and landed in the New World, which was thereupon subjugated, colonized, and missionized with astonishing rapidity. Henceforth this broadened world could be called the European world: Europe held all the reins of world politics and world trade firmly in hand, and drew a sharp distinction between metropolis and periphery, colonial power and colony, church and mission. Without so much as a by-your-leave, these other peoples were now under the "protectorate" of Europe, and in its shadow. Now they were the white male's training field. Given this Eurocentric, triumphalistic colonial and missionary history, it is surely understandable that since the 1950s Asians, Africans, and Latin Americans have begun to write their own history, and to rub our noses in it until we begin to have some idea of what it was like for them to feel and suffer our presence.

The zenith and demise of European hegemony came simultaneously, with World War II. Colonial nations still rallied to the European cause, but immediately thereafter filed their claims for indemnification in the form of demands for national independence. Within two decades, practically all of Asia and Africa were decolonialized. Today these new nation states hold a two-thirds majority in the world forum of the United Nations.

So one after another the tribal world, the biblical world, the Roman world, and the Western world have seen their day. The worldwide world is here. The story of its maturation has been a long one, but its hour has struck. The day of a mature world community of all peoples, founded on the bedrock of equal rights, has dawned. The United Nations gave expression to this new sense of ours on December 10, 1948, in its Universal Declaration of Human Rights.

We feel that we are "all in the same boat" now, the same spaceship earth. Europe no longer lies at the center of the geography of our globe. Now the central nation of the world is every land and no land. The Italians describe the new lifestyle this new situation has summoned into being as *vivere la mondialità* (living on the horizon of the world). The well-being and suffering of every person must be in our mind and heart now. Thanks to our new technology of transportation and communication, we have become a small world. Economically and politically, we have become a single community, bound together in a single destiny. We have new tasks now, of continental and global proportions.

The second Christian millennium was still powerfully marked by nationalism. We have only to see the monuments to the heroes of the past that adorn the great squares of the capitals of Europe. How often we read on their pedestals: "They Served Their People." But they did so by making war on their neighbors and subjugating them, so as to be able to build a colonial realm about their homeland. We no longer have need of heroes of this sort. What we need today are heroes of universalism, who will throw in their lot with humanity and help build "one house, the world."

When and where will these visions have their prophets? Solomon the Wise said, "A people without visions comes to dust" (Prov. 29:18), and in his reflection, as in a prelude, we hear the strains of the first theme of this book: church and state alike need prophets—persons capable of transcending the myopia and narrow-mindedness of the everyday, persons who will reach out, in the Spirit of God, to proclaim, and to realize, all that God has in mind for humanity.

The church has had its developmental history just as humanity has. The first communities to grow out of the Jesus event were the Jewish communities who believed in Jesus but who still felt bound by the Mosaic Law. Then the Apostle Paul—with a praxis rooted in his courageous doctrine that faith in Jesus Christ is all that matters—carried the gospel to the Greco-Roman world. Thereupon, in a missionary history that fills volumes, first the Roman Empire, then the Germanic tribes, then the newly discovered continents, were Christianized—albeit with missionary methods that are due considerable criticism. Following on that Christianization and following on the rise and fall of the Jewish, the Greek, the Roman, the Germanic, and the Western church, we now for the first time have the world church before us: in nearly all of the nations of the earth, there is at least a minimal presence of Christian communities and structures. Beginning with my *The Coming of the Third Church* (1976), I have endeavored time and again to call attention to this historic turning point.

AT LAST: A WORLD CHURCH

In 1900, 85 percent of all Christians, and 77 percent of all Catholics, lived in the Western, or Northern, world—Europe and North America. Over the last few decades, however, this historical situation has changed radically. With the baby boom and new conversions in Latin America, Africa, Asia, and Oceania, by 1970 51.86 percent of Catholics lived in the third world. Based on this trend, I predicted at that time that by the year 2000 some 70 percent of Catholics would be living in the third world. By 1985 the proportion had already risen to 59.80 percent, an increase of 7.94 percent. Were this rate of increase to hold steady over the next fifteen years, the proportion would be 67.74 percent by the year 2000. Correcting for some probable acceleration, the actual figure will indeed doubtless be around 70 percent. Thus my risky hypothesis has hardened into an actual thesis.

By continent:

1985	Number of Catholics (in thousands)[1]	
Africa	72,658	(8.53%)
America: North America	64,475	(7.57%)
Latin America	358,188	(42.04%)
Asia	72,141	(8.47%)
Europe	278,047	(32.63%)
Oceania	6,444	(0.76%)
Total	851,953	(100.00%)

World population: 4,817,560,000
Catholic percentage of world population: 17.68%

It is a fact, then: the church of Latin America has dethroned the church of Europe from its role as quantitative leader. We may easily imagine that this will not be without consequences for the future of the church. Because Orthodox Christians and Protestants are far from being as numerous in Latin America as Catholics, the center of gravity of the Orthodox and Protestant confessions is not as strikingly shifting to the third world. For Christianity as a whole, the proportions are as follows:

Christians	1900	1970	1980	2000
Northern World	85%	57.4%	51%	39.8%
Third World	15%	42.6%	49%	60.2%

Almost unconsciously, then, we have become the witnesses of a mighty historical process within the church. A Western church, with its world hegemony, has become a world church, comprised of six continental churches (counting the Americas as two continents), all endowed with equal rights.

The third world church is taking the lead not only quantitatively (the proportion of third world representatives being the same in the Roman Bishops' Synod as in the United Nations: approximately two-thirds), but qualitatively, as well. Ever since the 1974 Synod of Bishops on "evangelization in today's world," one readily gathers the impression that the most important ideas and inspirations come to the church as a whole from the church of the third world. Paul VI, in *Evangelii Nuntiandi,* the final document of that 1974 synod, exalts the great task of the third world bishops.

Were we to divide the history of the church into millennia, we might say — grossly oversimplifying, admittedly: The first Christian millennium was under the hegemony of the Eastern church, with the first eight councils all being held in the East. The second millennium, unquestionably, has been ruled by the second church, the Western church — our church. In the coming third millennium, it is the third church, just now coming into existence, that apparently will take over the leadership, while at the same time remaining in union with the Catholic, Western church. After all, the Eastern church plus the Western church plus the "Southern" (third world) church now form, together, the world church. (By which, for our present purposes, I mean my own church, the Catholic church, although my global interest is in all Christian churches as a unit, as I shall explain more clearly in chapter 3.)

Thus we have entered the first phase of the age of the world church. That phase will determine the image of the church for all future time.

> To put it simply: the Catholic church no longer simply *has* a third world church, it now *is* a third world church — with Western and European origins. The Catholic church stands at a caesura in its history, perhaps the deepest-reaching since primitive Christian times: from a culturally more or less unitary, therefore culturally monocentric, church of Europe and North America, it is on its way to being a culturally multi-rooted, and in this sense a culturally polycentric, world church.[2]

Nothing would be more malapropos than to understand the expression "world church" in a triumphalistic sense. Catholics make up roughly only 18 percent of the world population. All Christians together make up 32 percent. World-renowned, we nonetheless remain a world minority. Even before Vatican II, Karl Rahner wrote of our "planetary diaspora." In many countries of the third world, Christianity seems little more than an insignificant sect, and even in the West the age of the "Christian nations" is a thing of the past — however little certain circles may have relinquished their dream of a homogeneous Christian West, or, especially, come to the realization that we are becoming a Christianity of free choice instead of a Christianity that "just grows."[3]

Despite this reservation, we live in the age of the world church. Providence has decreed that this new era of the church should be inaugurated by a council that must go down in history as the first council of the world church. Let us not deceive ourselves: of the twenty-one councils reckoned as "ecumenical" (embracing the entire inhabited world) by Catholic tally, all except Vatican II were actually no more than continental synods. The first eight were held in the East, each with several hundred bishops from the Eastern churches and only a handful of visiting bishops from the Roman church. Then all of the subsequent councils but the last — from Lateran I to Vatican I—were gatherings of bishops from the Western church alone. Only with Vatican II was there finally a council of all of the (Catholic) churches of all the continents. During the three-and-one-half years of preparation for the council, the appointment of African and Asian bishops was intentionally accelerated, so that the council might really be seen to represent a world church. The council fathers and their theologians—while unaware of the church's shift to the third world, which was still *in fieri*—proceeded to establish guidelines that were indeed drawn on a world-church format. In the earlier councils, the church had taken a strongly introverted stance, busying itself with itself—concerning itself with dogmas, morals, and discipline. Now Vatican II threw open the windows and doors wide to the laity, to our fellow Christians, to non-Christians, and to the secular world.

Vatican I had dealt exclusively with the one, holy, catholic, and apostolic church. It had defined the dogmas of papal infallibility and universal jurisdiction (immediate papal jurisdiction over all the local churches), thereby endowing the church with a strong central government. Now Vatican II, by way of complementarity, and appealing to the practice of the ancient church, developed the theology of the episcopate, exalting the local church and insisting that the pope is obliged to exercise his supreme power "in collegiality"—in consort with the bishops. A diocese is not a mere branch office of Roman headquarters. It has a bishop who, as a successor of the apostles, is the actual shepherd of his church. This should have entailed a certain decentralization. It should have dismantled some of the centralism that had been so emphasized since the days of Vatican I. As examples of such decentralization in the civil realm, we might cite the Federal Republic of Germany or Austria, with their eleven and nine federal *Länder* or states, respectively; in those countries each *Land*, each subsidiary region of the nation, maintains its own legislative and executive governmental powers, much as do the states of the United States. Civil society appreciates the impossibility of doing justice to such diverse cultural, economic, political, and religious circumstances from a center like Bonn or Vienna or Washington. How much more will this be verified in the case of a church that reaches the ends of the earth!

From the principles of subsidiarity and collegiality, a further principle, logically enough, then followed: that of inculturation. Concretely, inculturation will appear in a legitimate pluriformity in theology, liturgy, and discipline. Until the very moment of the council, Rome had still been insisting on absolute uniformity, right down to the last details, including the Latin liturgy on every continent in the world. Now the attitude of the administrators yielded to the theologians' insight that since Jesus had not been a "universal" person, but an altogether concrete one, a Jew of Palestine, of such and such an era, of such and such a family matrix, of such and such a synagogal formation, and so on—certain practical conclusions should follow. In virtue of the principle of incarnation—as likewise in function of the incredible diversity of creation—the gospel ought to be expressed in many languages, ought to take flesh and form again and again in the multiplicity of cultures. Consequently, the form of Christianity that has made its appearance in the course of Western history is not the only conceivable one—although, of course, as the concrete path the church has followed up to the present point it will scarcely be without its significance for the other continents as well. And by way of a final conclusion: Africa, Asia, and Latin America need not be mere replicas of the Roman stereotype, but may produce an "African church," an "Asian church," and a "Latin American church." Each continent would have its "own" continental church.

Vatican II expressed these ideas only very cautiously. After all, it was the first time they had been expressed. Ten years later, in his *Evangelii Nuntiandi*, Paul VI formulated them far more forthrightly: not only *may* all of this happen, it *ought to* happen. We hear the present pontiff, as well, urging the same thing in his many addresses on these continents.

But now a strange thing occurs. For all the emphasis on all of this in theory, it is simply not permitted in practice. The moment bishops or bishops' conferences begin to take concrete steps in the direction of actually becoming a local or regional church, the voice of Rome is suddenly heard loud and clear: Halt, in the name of unity! *Non licet tibi!* Rome still confuses unity with uniformity. And so, instead of becoming the motive and model of a legitimate pluriformity, the principle of a world church suddenly becomes a brake: one may do only what is already done on the level of the world church! But that cancels all of these beautiful principles. It cancels them in practice. Bishops will have to strike a far more vigorous dialogue with Rome if they hope to further their legitimate particular interests and give their local churches the peculiar character that is theirs by right.

And here we have the second leitmotif, or theme, of this book: the contradiction between theory and praxis, between documents and deeds, between the impulses of the council and a crimping, crippling postconciliar legislation. Stimulating conciliar documents, which point the way to the third millennium, are purged. Curial positions calculated to entrench the church in the status quo, for example in the areas of birth control, celibacy, or women's ordination, are everywhere imposed. Herein, to a large extent, consists the malaise of our time in the church.

Vatican Council II, then, with its prophetic outlook, created the real structural framework for a world church. There can be no question about this. Not that one should regard the conciliar documents as some kind of great, cold monolith, or sealed volume of lore. We demonstrate our loyalty to the council to the extent that we develop the substance of that council. The gospel underwent a development in its very inception. What a difference between Mark and John in ecclesiology, or christology! Just so, the whole of Christian history has been the story of the church's dogmatic development—or conciliar development, we might say. Time has never stood still, even for a moment. Theological insights and pastoral postulates thrust the development ever onward. From this viewpoint, it was incorrect of Cardinal Josef Ratzinger to call the texts of Vatican II the "church's today." I should prefer to call them the "church's yesterday"—in the sense of something good, of course: in the sense of an authentic church tradition, with priceless significance for today and tomorrow.

Meanwhile the majority of the council fathers have passed from the world scene. But the church lives on, thinks on, and develops further. The bishops underwent a prodigious learning process in the course of the three years that the council was in session—for example, in the areas of religious freedom, or the non-Christian religions—accepting things by the close of the council that would have seemed tantamount to heresy when the council began. But had the council continued for twenty-three years, as did the Council of Trent (with two prolonged interruptions), what an ongoing assimilation we should have witnessed—what an assimilation of the new ideas and situations constantly presenting themselves in the church and the world! We ourselves, then, must see to this—we the postconciliar church. The council must be realized and applied anew, ever and again. Otherwise it may simply be filed away in the archives and sink into oblivion, away from the eyes and ears and hearts of the current generation.

John XXIII gave the council its slogan: *aggiornamento*. The council was to "update" the church—literally, make the church a "today" church. It was to "throw open the windows, and allow a fresh breeze to waft through the stuffy rooms of history." The council fathers accepted the challenge, and constantly spoke of the "signs of the times" as an expression of the will of God (*Unitatis Redintegratio,* no. 4; *Apostolicam Actuositatem,* no. 14; *Gaudium et Spes,* nos. 4, 11; *Presbyterorum Ordinis,* no. 9). Not that the church must blindly adapt to the world. Far from it. The church retains its critical function vis-à-vis society. But it should not allow itself to cling desperately to antiquated forms. The "signs of the times" constituted by new mental attitudes and movements, new historical trends, can in turn be designated by slogans: the modern human being is "for" equality, fellowship, collegiality, for subsidiarity and participation, for overture, ecumenism, and tolerance. The modern human being is "against" discrimination, authoritarianism, and institutionalism.

All too often, sad to say, in history as in the postconciliar present, the church has failed to recognize the "signs of the times." Hence the third theme of this book: missed opportunities. It is a theme that we shall encounter, in the course of this book, more often than we should like.

A NEW DECALOGUE FOR THE THIRD MILLENNIUM

This new constellation—the worldwide world and the worldwide church—now calls for a new world order. It would be worth the effort, then, to ask ourselves what God is seeking to proclaim to us today by way of the "signs of the times." Is God really so "changeless" as only to be able to hammer on the old Decalogue, the old Ten Commandments, for our instruction after these three thousand years? For new situations, will God not call for new accents, and urge Ten "new" Commandments—not to replace the old commandments, but to complement them?

In defense of the traditional Decalogue,[4] let us observe that even in ancient days God did not impose law for law's sake, simply to test the people's blind obedience. In issuing the Ten Commandments, God had the genuine welfare of the people of Israel at heart. The preamble to the Decalogue of Sinai states this very clearly: "I am Yahweh, your God, who has led you out of Egypt, out of the house of servitude. Therefore you shall . . ." (Exod. 20:2). In other words, these Ten Commandments were handed down in order that their observance would preserve the people from falling back into spiritual and political slavery. And they still stand today, for us Christians, as beacons and signposts along our way, lest we become lost on our journey and have to suffer the consequences.

Events today in Central Europe are proceeding at a pace that reminds us once again of the value and classic nature of the ancient Decalogue. The more that *glasnost* and political changes give us insight into the formerly so-called "Second World," the more clearly we see that contemporary ideologies need a critique from the perennial wisdom of the Decalogue. Modernity seems badly lacking a moral rudder.

The Decalogue is timeless, then. It is eternally valid. But it is not a sacred cow. It is not something that can never be touched. In fact the notion and some of the content of such a code were not even the exclusive possession of the people of Israel: at the moment of the granting of the Decalogue to Moses—indeed, even earlier—Israel's neighbors possessed similar codes of rules for living. The twin tablets of the Law were scarcely dictated verbatim, then, or "revealed," in the fundamentalistic sense of the word, to Moses on Sinai. Rather, this greatest lawgiver of his time compiled "his" insights, as dictated to him by his common sense, in the form of a brief compendium of the fundamental rules of a religious orientation (the first, second, and third commandments) and a moral life in society (the remaining seven). Subsequently, we may grant, this was all expressly sanctioned by God on Sinai, and brought into connection with the covenant that God had offered the chosen people. Thereby the Decalogue acquired a religious sense to accompany its moral signification, and was now to be lived by the people in an exemplary fashion. The New Testament refers to these commandments in a number of places, but, especially, reduces them to a double commandment of unconditional love for God and neighbor. All the other commandments are to proceed from this indissoluble pair. Thus, for example, Jesus relativized the sabbath commandment—not "breaking" it, but interpreting it in such a way as to prevent it from being used to contradict human need.

In our traditional prayer books, under "confession" or "penance," we frequently find the Ten Commandments reduced to a neat little list of children's sins. Many Christians have simply gone through life repeating these formulae. In today's penance celebrations, the examination of conscience conducted in common is much more enlightening as to what sin really means in life today. For example, drinking and driving violates the commandment, "Thou shalt not kill." Speculation in real estate at inflated prices that will eventually have to be paid by families living in overpriced houses is an infraction of the commandment, "Thou shalt not steal." But even all this cosmetic correction, all this moral updating, falls short of what is really needed. We really ought to be translating the church's new outlook on its behavior in and with the world into concrete "new" commandments. Thus we should measure the success of Vatican II not by the internal ecclesial viewpoint of an increase or decrease in attendance at Sunday Mass, but by a Christian commitment to the world, which has surely seen a remarkable increase since, and owing to, the council.

In function of these preliminary considerations, the formulation of the "new" Ten Commandments will differ from that of the "old" Ten Commandments in three ways:

1. Most of the "old" Ten Commandments were formulated as prohibitions: "You shall not. . . ." In today's one world, we must regrettably confess, commandments like, "You shall not torture, you shall not sell arms, you shall not exploit," and so on, would make precious little impression on the malicious persons who perpetrate these atrocities. Instead, then, we must encourage persons of good will to join forces for good, and to regard sins of omission, which are so frequent, as seriously as those of commission. This is why we express the "new" Ten Commandments in positive, "encouraging," formulations.

2. The cry of the Lord's Prayer, "Thy will be done," should not be uttered as a prayer simply for something to happen. It should be a plea for the grace to make it happen. We must contribute actively to the implementation of God's salvific plan for the world. The "old" Ten Commandments were addressed to the individual: "Thou shalt not. . . ." The individual, normal, "pious" life is surely not to be belittled. Structural change will always presuppose the conversion of the individual. At the same time, individuals, even large numbers of individuals, will be incapable of exerting the public pressure needed to effect change in conditions in the church and the world. Accordingly, I formulate the "new" Ten Commandments in the plural — "You (pl.) . . ." We must join forces, organize, demonstrate — courageously and purposefully employ all democratic means to effect something new under the sun.

3. Our modern Bibles still say: "You shall . . ." Hebrew employed three imperative forms. The strongest was the infinitive (as in German, for example, in military commands: "*Aufstehen! Schiessen!*"). This is the form used in the third commandment, concerning the Sabbath. The other commandments employ a milder imperative form, identical with the future indicative of our Western languages: "You will not kill." In order to stress impera-

tiveness, this verb is conventionally translated into English with the word "shall." But here we may well ask ourselves whether God would use this same tone with men and women of today, with their enhanced consciousness of their moral autonomy. Would God not rather make suggestions, recommendations, intimations? On the basis of this consideration, as well as in view of the use of the future indicative in the Hebrew text, I propose to formulate the new commandments thus: "You (pl.) will . . ." This would mean something like: "If you take me, the deliverer, and yourselves, the delivered, seriously, then you 'will' surely do such and so. You owe it to me, as well as to yourselves, to behave in such and such a way." God does not compel. God attracts. God encourages us, and we, as mature women and men, will understand the divine language.

So much for the form of the "new" Ten Commandments. Let us now see their actual content.

A. Church Problems

1. You Will Allow Common Sense to Prevail: Autonomy of the Sciences
2. You Will Take Yourselves Seriously as People of God: The Laity in the Church
3. You Will Extend Your Hand to Your Fellow Christians: Ecumenism

B. Continental Problems

4. You Will Take Sides with the Poor: Justice in Latin America
5. You Will Wonder at the Breadth of the Creator: Inculturation in Africa
6. You Will Acknowledge That the "I Am Here" Is Present among All Peoples: Dialogue with the Religions of Asia
7. You Will Accompany Religious Nomads: Secularization in Euramerica

C. World Problems

8. You Will Swell the Ranks of the Peacemakers: Justice and Peace
9. You Will Make the Earth a Paradise: Ecology and Eschatology
10. You Will Encounter the God of History: Spirituality and Politics

As we see, there are two ways of acquiring wisdom. One is to read the Bible and seek to apply its teachings in our daily lives. The other is to keep open our inner and outer eye, which are given to us to see and to notice what is needful. Far from being mutually exclusive, these two approaches are complementary. But the second has the advantage of serving not only churchgoers, but those, too, who are beyond the reach of religion or ideology. Thus, as many persons as possible will be helped to assimilate the minimal categorical imperatives of a world ethic, the attitudes and efforts postulated by our "spaceship culture" (E. Y. Meyer)—a new phase of cultural history for the third millennium. Christians will then have the task of underpinning all of this from the gospel, giving all of it its ultimate sense in the dimension of depth—the religious dimension—and especially, on the basis of this religious view of the enterprise, seeing to the needed thrust of the whole.

PART 2

The "New" Ten Commandments of God: A Decalogue Based on the Signs of the Times

1

You Will Allow Common Sense To Prevail

Autonomy of the Sciences

It may come as a surprise that the first of the "new" Ten Commandments of God does not even refer to God. Instead, it speaks of something called common sense. Today's human beings are no longer willing to be inundated by the idea of God the minute they start to think. They are determined to take themselves seriously first. Of course, whether they know it or not, they are created in the image of God. That is, they have the gift of reason, together with self-awareness, a spirit of inquiry, and a sense of God. And this is why, sooner or later, after much musing, and a great deal of life experience, they will reach the goal of their long journey: God. But that is just the point: faith is the goal, the end of the journey. Faith and revelation are no longer simple premises, to be taken for granted—especially since all this "supernatural" business will more than likely have left a bad taste in people's mouths. Too long has our common sense been whipped into line by so-called faith.

I shall not take a theoretical, scholarly approach to the problem of revelation and reason, the problem of faith and science. Instead, I shall report that problem as it is actually experienced in life—first in a general setting of the Northern world, then in a context of the local churches—that we may see how common sense has gradually fought free of its subjugation by faith, or rather by church authority in the name of faith, and what a difficult victory this has been.

Let us begin with a consideration of the work of the dean of medieval scholastic theologians, Thomas Aquinas. Here is a teacher whose work permeated theology for hundreds of years. His influence is unrivaled. He certainly filled his writings with reason—an enormous quantity of it, especially in his *Summa Theologiae.* Nor had he any qualms about appealing to Greek and Arab philosophers—"pagan" philosophers, then—despite the resistance of so many of his contemporaries. His imitators employed considerably lesser amounts of reason than he did. Instead of harking back to the old philosophers and complementing them with new thinking, as Thomas had done—filling out a received theological tradition with a dialogue with the wonderful developments of the new, modern sciences, and thereby creating new syntheses in keeping with the times—later theologians were content to preserve and hand on the accomplishments of the past, and simply propounded "eternal truths," without making any attempt to link them with the current age. Even the neoscholasticism of the nineteenth and twentieth centuries was still largely bogged down in tradition. Original theologians, who had the courage to give up their stubborn viewpoints and flow with the current of history, like M. J. Scheeben or John Henry Newman, were exceptions, and were for all practical purposes on the sidelines as far as official Catholic theology was concerned.

Writing of those bygone days, Hans Küng says:

> More and more threatened by modern spiritual and political currents, with its back to the wall now, this medieval, counter-Reform [theological] paradigm, with the help of theology and politics, textbooks and editions, encyclicals and Inquisition, was refurbished time and again in Catholic countries of the nineteenth century. Outwardly modernized by way of still more rational analysis and still less biblical theology, it was finally officially sanctioned, dogmatically in Vatican I (1870) and juridically in the *Codex Juris Canonici* (1918).[1]

The aim was not a "new theology," but a "theology of yesteryear" (J. Kleutgen). One simply did not feel oneself in a position to connect with the modern age.

Küng grew up with this theology, as did I, as did generations of priests before Vatican Council II. This was doctrine. It was solid as a rock, and crystal-clear. No one had the slightest doubt of the soundness of its argumentation. When all was said and done, you knew: this was the way it was, and this was the way it was going to be. We lived in the unshakable conviction that theology was "queen of the sciences." As faith was above reason, grace above nature, and the pope over the emperor, so also was theology above the other sciences. This was the way it had to be.

The Roman church countenanced no exception to this integralist monolith. We need not cite the example of the Inquisition, or the "Galileo case." We need only look at events under the Popes Pius of the past hundred years. Pius IX, in his *Syllabus of Errors* (1864), condemned the new ideas that came from the secular world: precisely eighty "errors of our time," like rationalism, liberalism, and communism, of course; but Protestant Bible societies, too, and even the opinion that the church should renounce alliances with a Christian state, or enter into dialogue with the modern sciences. And so on. Then Pius X did the same with the new ideas stirring within the church during his time. The best theologians in the church were then attempting to apply their critical reason to theology and the origins of that church, in order to establish, as far as might be feasible, a harmony between faith and science. Keen spirits descried, in these endeavors, the first faint glimmer of a new day. But Rome smelled mischief, and feared shipwreck. The Holy See spoke of the "pestilence of modernism" and the "mania for the reconciliation of faith and science," and reacted — doggedly, authoritatively, and incompetently.

Concretely, antimodernism was expressed in two documents. In 1907, the Holy Office condemned sixty-five modernist theses, thrown together in an illogical hodgepodge in its decree *Lamentabili*. A few months later, Pope Pius X published his antimodernist encyclical *Pascendi Gregis*.

Neither document seems to have grasped the genuine, justifiable purport of the entire modernist undertaking. Both betray a merely superficial knowledge of the authors and their ideas, and offer for all practical purposes a caricature of modernism. Integralists leapt for joy. Victory was theirs once more. By way of both postoperative therapy and prophylaxis against a recurrence of the cancer, the Oath against Modernism was introduced, and made obligatory in perpetuity. The Commission for the Index was beefed up. And under Monsignor Benigni (1862–1934), a veritable Gestapo network of spies was established: anyone with a new idea could be denounced to Rome and removed from his ecclesiastical post without further ado.

Even the church career of young Angelo Roncalli, later Pope John XXIII, got into trouble in those days. Father Roncalli had been serving as a teacher of church history at the seminary of Bergamo. Highly esteemed by his students and his bishop, he ran afoul of a certain Father Mazzoleni, who (as Roncalli himself observes) "was of the number of those zealots whom no diocese lacked in those days." Mazzoleni took it upon himself to report the young priest's allegedly dangerous notions to Rome, and Roncalli received a warning "that could have made me simply want to give up the fight. But it did not disturb my inner peace." Later, as pope, Angelo Roncalli had his own dossier fetched from the archives of the Holy Office. And there it was, in black and white: "suspected of modernism." What a consolation for the "suspected heretics" of those days and ours! All the antimodernism in the world could never have uprooted the new trend. But the interim goal had been achieved — respite from the problem.

A new conflict broke out under Pius XII. True, this pope did seem to get something moving in the tired old church. In 1951 he restored the Easter Vigil. He allowed converted Protestant ministers to function as priests even though they were married. In 1943 he published his encyclical *Divino Afflante Spiritu*, at last permitting Catholic exegetes to make use of the data of archaeology, ethnology, and linguistics in their own research. Now they might take account of the literary genres of the various books of the Bible, even reconsidering their authorship and the manner of their inspiration. But this same pope, as if suddenly panic-stricken at the breach in the fortress wall that he himself had opened, also published the encyclical

Humani Generis (1950). That document closed the door once more on a so-called false evolutionism and historicism, and reproached theologians with faddishness and insufficient regard for the church magisterium. To show that he meant business, the pope deprived the principal exponents of the *nouvelle théologie,* Henri de Lubac, Jean Daniélou, Yves M.-J. Congar, and M.-D. Chenu, of their teaching office. Now integralists might enjoy another respite — however short-lived, as the censured theologians kept on quietly working, eventually to emerge as the trailblazers of Vatican II. As if by way of occult restitution, in their old age de Lubac and Daniélou were elevated to the cardinalitial dignity.

Secular scholars, of course, had not permitted themselves to be bullied by church authority. But now, with the church overstepping its bounds and attempting to interfere in matters outside its competence, they too fell victim to an ideology of wishful thinking. They conceived the notion that, as religion had been nothing more than the product of a blind, natural evolution, it would now vanish before the face of pure science like bats before the dawn light. Scientists needed courage in those days if they were to remain faithful to their religious beliefs not only privately, but publicly, in plain sight of their colleagues. Some of those who had this courage were botanist Maximilian Westermaier (1852–1903), physicist Max Planck (1858–1947), and ethnologist Wilhelm Schmidt (1868–1954).

After such a prolonged browbeating at the hands of ecclesiastical authority, common sense could come into its own only painfully and gradually. But come into its own it did, and the reconciliation of faith and science was at last under way. If the reader will permit, I shall here present a kind of case study of a series of occurrences that I have personally witnessed in various fields of scholarly endeavor. I was a student at the University of Fribourg, in Switzerland, in the winter semester of the 1944–45 school year, when our pastoral theology professor, Father X. von Hornstein, and our physics professor, Dr. F. Dessauer, offered a joint seminar on the "Pastoral Ministry in an Age of Technology." The course became more and more interesting as it went along. For the first time in our lives, it occurred to us that there had been an unhealthy cleft between the world of the theologians, indeed of religious scholars generally, and the world of technology. Even after the social encyclicals of Leo XIII and Pius XI, one still felt a certain amount of superiority to the "laboring classes," who, when all was said and done, seemed so selfish and unprepossessing. Their mentality was socialistic (antichurch, then), their work was dirty, and they always seemed to be after higher wages. Meanwhile, entirely unnoticed, a mighty class of technologists had sprung up, and were now at work molding the world of tomorrow. Here was a new breed of individuals, and they were now looking on the church and its people with condescension, instead of the other way around. And so there would be an attempt, at this late hour, to build a bridge, in order to afford future pastoral ministers an insight into the spirit and the environment of the technologically oriented society of tomorrow.

No longer could things be done as in the past. No longer could the world seem to be explained sheerly in terms of an "ultimate." The "standpoint of faith," which had seemed so secure, and which had been so strongly urged upon us by the church, must now, in certain questions, come in confrontation with science, and take its humble, dialogical place in the discussion. True, once more a certain "Christian" worldview would come tumbling down, as had the Ptolemaic world of old when Copernicus and Galileo proposed and demonstrated that the earth revolved about the sun rather than vice versa. The Roman church court had pronounced this new-fangled theory both contrary to scripture and without foundation in fact, and had condemned it. Two hundred years later, of course, the church had to change its mind.[2]

Now I had finished my studies, and with a number of years' experience in Africa under my belt, was teaching missiology at the same university. Here I was able to follow the phenomenon of the visible impregnation of theology itself by the new, critical scientific thinking. The latter encountered stubborn opposition once more, however, and when all was said and done, only external pressure made a breakthrough possible. In the case at hand, this breakthrough occurred in the following manner. A certain Dominican professor of ours, who held to a strictly traditional theology, had the habit of citing Rahner, Schillebeeckx, and Küng, now and then, only in order to dismiss their thinking as faddish. In the summer semester of 1960 the students noted down his remarks to this effect, showed them to the dean, and explained that they would be unable to accept this professor the following semester. But the semester began, and the gentleman in question began his lectures once more, for all the world as if nothing were amiss. Then the students threatened to give all their documentation to the press. That worked in a flash. The professor disappeared in no time flat. Later two other professors fell victim to the same sort of "pressure from beneath."

The same sort of thing was happening elsewhere in the world. I was asked, on the occasion of Karl Rahner's seventy-fifth birthday (1979), to write an article for the *Münchener Katholischen Kirchenzeitung*. Rahner had of course done more than anyone else to create a theology that would be readily understandable and useful to today's human being. I was asked to write about his significance in the third world. To complement the information I of course already had, I went over to the Gregorian University in Rome one day and, collaring a random series of third world students between classes, asked them whether the name of Karl Rahner meant anything in their seminaries back home. The response was overwhelmingly affirmative. Rahner was known in all of their theological schools, from the Philippines to India to Africa to Latin America. Some of those interviewed actually reacted almost with anger, offended at my question, as if I were asking whether they were still back in the dark ages. With a time lag of only five or ten years, Rahner's theology had indeed come to the lands of the third world. This had of course occurred mostly on the initiative of teachers who had done their studies in Europe. In some instances, however, it had been the students who had been the first to discover the great theologian, to the embarrassment of their teachers, who had still been forging along with the old manuals — Tanquerey, Parente, and the like. In these instances the teachers could only fall back on the retort that, after all, what was important was not that the students become familiar with this or that theological opinion, but that they learn solid theology. But this line of defense was fast crumbling.

The liturgical renewal, too, was a laborious struggle. At that time, all over the world, the Roman Rite of the Catholic church was employing a four-hundred-year-old liturgy dating from the Council of Trent. No one seemed to wonder whether it was still appropriate for our times. A confrere of mine, Donat Müller, recounted to me how, as a theology student in the mid-1950s, he had gotten into some books by Rahner (*Die vielen Messen und das eine Opfer*), Romano Guardini (*Vom heiligen Zeichen*), and Josef Jungmann (*Missarum Sollemnia*), and how it had occurred to him that things like the Latin liturgy, private masses at many different altars at once, communion before or after Mass but not during Mass, were abuses, and would never stand up to examination in the light of history. But it was a rocky road from this insight to its implementation. As a young priest, he had given his altar server a particle from his own Host at his side-altar Mass so that the server would not have to scamper to the main altar for Holy Communion — an action that merited him a stern reprimand from Father Guardian. Later, as a missionary in Tanzania, he began to sing the Litany of the Saints on Rogation Days in the vernacular instead of in Latin — a practice thereupon promptly forbidden by the local bishop at the following conference of religious superiors.

From my own experience, I can report the dilemma faced by the first World Mission Conference, organized by Father Josef Hofinger, S.J., and held at Nijmegen in 1959. The consensus of the missionaries, including missionary bishops, and various experts in attendance was that it would make good sense to abolish the custom of celebrating Mass facing the wall and in Latin. We ought to be celebrating Mass facing the people and in the vernacular, and with an amplified list of scriptural readings. But then came the dilemma: Should this request actually be made of Rome? Might Rome not simply react by stiffening the rules even further?

Finally, the same thing occurred in the area of religious discipline. It is hard to believe today what people unquestioningly submitted to in those days. When you had to go to see the superior for one reason or another, you knocked, entered the room, kissed the floor, and asked, "Reverend Father, may I speak, for the love of God?" Each week you had to accuse yourself publicly of being "so imperfect and maladroit, so ignorant and incapable," as to have committed such and such a fault.

You had to leave everything about your formation and subsequent assignments to your superiors. You were never asked about your own wishes or inclinations. In the Franciscan order, an absolute monarchy prevailed. Subjects were never asked to think, only to conform. In 1963 (the council was already under way, therefore) I submitted a petition to the Provincial Chapter of the Swiss Capuchins in which I said: Times are changing. Should not all of the members of the province enter into dialogue with a view to adapting our life and mission to the changing times? Each house might hold a chapter, I suggested, discuss questions of our daily order and our ministry, and elect delegates to provincial commissions to consider new approaches to the ministry as well as to our training: people were different now, and so were their problems. These commissions would then make recommendations to superiors. Presiding at that particular provincial chapter was the then minister general, Father Clemens, from Milwaukee. In his response, he claimed right from the start that my petition attacked our constitutions — that we were not a democracy, but a monarchy. My appeals to the Franciscan spirit of brotherliness had been to no avail.

It is simply amazing that such an ossified state of affairs could have been overcome so suddenly, and at the highest level, that of the council. True, there was stubborn resistance, and grudging compromise. Still, thanks to a genuine dialogue between the best of the bishops and theologians present, fine documents emerged. The many postulates of reason that had had to wait so long in the wings were at last objectively discussed, and thereupon accepted as meaningful. At last faith and reason were shaking hands and making friends. The pastoral constitution *Gaudium et Spes* acknowledges the autonomy of the sciences:

> Therefore, if methodical investigation within every branch of learning is carried out in a genuinely scientific manner and in accord with moral norms, it never truly conflicts with faith. For earthly matters and the concerns of faith derive from the same God. . . .
>
> Consequently, we cannot but deplore certain habits of mind, sometimes found too among Christians, which do not sufficiently attend to the rightful independence of science [*Gaudium et Spes,* no. 36].

As if extending the hand of reconciliation to a deplorable past, the document at this point gives a footnote that cites Pio Paschini's two-volume work on Galileo; the work, published in 1964, does justice to that pioneer of modern science.

Since then, Popes Paul VI and John Paul II have taken every opportunity to emphasize the fundamental harmony between faith and science, and to express their regret over the past. Thus, Polish pope and sometime ethics professor Karol Wojtila, in his celebrated allocution to scientists and students in the Cologne cathedral in 1980, spoke of the "burden of the infamous conflicts arising out of the interference of ecclesiastical authorities in the progress of scientific knowledge. The church recalls these [incidents] with regret," Pope John Paul II went on to say, "for we know today of the error and shortcomings of these transgressions. And today we can say that they have been overcome."

At last the church has recognized the God-given importance of common sense. We can go even further and say that "earthly matters and the concerns of faith" do not simply run on two parallel tracks as if they would never meet. A most intimate, personal union obtains between them, a kind of "hypostatic union," so that their roles cannot be divided and assigned now to the Holy Spirit, now to common sense. The Holy Spirit does not operate in a vacuum. The event of revelation occurs only through and with a prophet, in partnership with that prophet, and within the dimensions of that prophet's understanding. The Holy Spirit accommodates itself to each era's framework of thought. It makes no quantum leaps with its revelation that the prophet cannot personally discover and understand. And conversely, wherever common sense is at work—even in the minds of atheists, or of those who regard themselves as such—with its sights set on the true and the good, the signature of an invisible, but incontestably present, Co-author is in evidence: the Holy Spirit, who fills the world and embraces all things (Wis. 1:7), including revelation and science, faith and common sense. Behold the wondrous mystery of the interplay of God and the human being.

In theory, then, there can be no conflict between faith and reason. And on a practical level, for decades now, the pair have maintained a fruitful interdisciplinary conversation.

Another illustration: as a young priest in the mid-1930s, Karl Rahner was sent for his philosophical studies not to one of the great Catholic universities, but to the feet of the existentialist Martin Heidegger. Heidegger's influence on Rahner was decisive. Without it he might never have come to his core concept of the "supernatural existential." By the supernatural existential, Rahner meant that the human being, every human being, antecedently to any sacramental justification, already stands within the compass of the universal salvific will of God, which embraces even sin, both original and personal. Thus every human being is already "redeemed" in the sense of an orientation toward a definitive "supernatural" goal, and is the constant object of God's proffered grace and salvific concern, so that, far from being cast adrift in a meaningless existence, to make our way as we can, whether with cynicism or indignation, we live in an antecedently given climate of the divine benevolence and loving affection. Rahner thus replaced Saint Augustine's gloomy scenario of a *massa damnata* from which individuals can rescue themselves by baptism, with a scenario in which human beings are antecedently embraced by a favor and grace of God from which individuals can exclude themselves only by hardening their hearts. With this new worldview, Rahner founded not just a new theological school, but a new theological age.

The sciences, for their part, have meanwhile made some progress in humility. They are no longer so cocksure. They no longer labor under the illusion of having an absolutely firm grip on things. In the face of the sheer quantitative cognitional explosion, they can no longer keep up even with themselves. Scientific information increases at the rate of roughly 13 percent per year. That is to say, it doubles in quantity approximately every five-and-one-half years. Furthermore, science is terrified at its own power — the power it has acquired through the discovery of nuclear fission and genetic engineering. Finally, in macrocosm and microcosm alike, science encounters qualitative mysteries, mysteries that it finds insoluble in principle, and before which it can only stand in wonder. Honest scientists, then, are inclined once more to listen to the voice of faith, and to let themselves be lifted above the limits of their respective sciences, to surmise, on the heels of all their cold, scientific observation, with sympathy and openness, a veiled reality underlying their scientific data. At last they permit themselves to wonder about the meaning of the universe as a whole, about its origins and ultimate ground, about its ultimate existential meaning. At last they allow themselves to accept the reality of an ordering world-Subject, a world-Ground, an Author of the world, a world-Spirit, a God existing with, over, and in the world.

Believing scientists feel less isolated than before. Now it is easy for them to find fellow believers. The complementarity of faith and understanding, science and religion, is more readily acknowledged by their colleagues. Science alone is lame, religion alone is blind, one hears them say. We no longer have any reason to deny an identification of the principle of the universal order of the natural sciences with the God of religion, they say. Suddenly natural sciences become spiritual sciences. Physics and transcendence extend to one another the hand of fellowship. Albert Einstein went so far as to say that, in our new world of matter, serious scientists are the only profoundly religious people.[3]

Just as it took a number of decades for the antifaith attitude of scientists to overtake the population at large, so also, if we but wait a little, we shall see broad consequences issuing from this new profaith attitude. While so many traditional apologetical arguments for religion have fallen, religion has now begun to find support from science. No need to panic!

Everything seems to be going as it should, then. Of course, there is many a slip between the cup and the lip, and, surely enough, here again we encounter a hiatus between theory and praxis. Despite all the beautiful words, the conflict between faith and reason is once more in high gear. This time the problem is not so much the secular sciences, however. This time it is precisely theology as science. Common sense has never won its rights in the church or in theology. This is not to suggest that theological reason is infallible, or indeed even always within its rights. In its quest for a fuller truth, theology can surely err. But such "false teachings" are ordinarily corrected in intratheological dialogue. Indeed, they are generally propounded merely as working hypotheses to begin with. They should not be forthwith condemned by the highest authority and their authors reduced to silence.

After the conciliar breakthrough, in which the theology of Congar, Rahner, and so on—a theology developed under such suspicion and censure—became official church theology, a new conflict broke out between the vanguard and the rear—between the "new theology," based on faith and science, and certain popular elements determined simply to hold on tight to the "good, old faith." Instead of opening their minds, and going into these matters more deeply, which for various reasons they are unfortunately incapable of doing, integralists simply redoubled their spiteful polemics. One should expect such reactions. Of course, it is worse when the church magisterium itself returns to its appeals to a faith that has been handed down thus and so, and in this way once more "securely, but barrenly" (Rahner) defends the truths of that faith, thereby rendering Catholics of today no service and interfering in theological research too quickly and too directly, as if stubbornly seeking to prolong the painful history that I have described above and failing to learn from it that "heretics" tend to be pioneers of times to come.

Much has been spoken and written about the relationship between the magisterium and theology. Each partner has its proper, specific service to render to the church. Each should acknowledge the other's worth, and, even amidst conflict, strive for honest and better solutions. But if, as is all too often the case, the dialogue that characterized the council is no longer duly maintained in the Vatican, if objective discussion is rendered impossible by the presence of a network of informers and all manner of secret shenanigans, if faith is allowed to run rough-shod over common sense, and authority over competence, if we allow ourselves to be too heavily influenced by a *scandalum pusillanimorum* (the trouble that inhibited souls have with certain religious formulations) and refuse to consider the many Christians who long for a credible, livable faith to be proclaimed to them today—then we shall always have unhappy incidents: a Küng case, a Schillebeeckx case, a Curran case, and now, a Pfürtner case, which not long ago received a monumental, classic presentation at the hands of Father Ludwig Kaufmann, S.J.[4]

Such "cases" are piling up—we need only look at Spain—and spilling over into the third world. The Boff case has been a celebrated case in point. Less well known among us is the case of Father Luis Bermejo, S.J., for twenty-five years a professor at the Pontifical Theological Institute in Poona, India, deprived of his teaching faculties by Rome in 1988. In 1984 he published a book on routes to Christian unity that caused a sensation even in the Western theological world. In the spring of 1987, without any previous discussion, Rome demanded the author publicly retract some of his statements. Instead, Bermejo submitted an explanation of these statements. Whereupon, without further ado, Rome simply deprived him of his teaching office. The rector of the institute, together with the entire theological faculty, expressed to Rome their entire solidarity with Father Bermejo, and their indignation at the manner in which the Vatican had proceeded. They went on to explain that people in the region of the world in question still had a bad colonial aftertaste in their mouths, and were very allergic to anything smacking of paternalism or patronizing guidance from abroad.

More recently, not only are active professors deprived of their teaching faculties, but Rome now vetoes new instructors and professors appointed to a chair of theology by a university or by a local bishop. Rome has always reserved a power of veto in such cases, but is now exercising that power not only when candidates in question are found to have published certain un-Roman ideas, but even when they have simply done some of their studies with a "dangerous" mentor, as it is thought that they might be inclined to transmit that thinker's pernicious notions. It is simply not right and just that, on the right, the Lefebvre group be shown such extreme tolerance, and even be granted doctrinal concessions, while on the left, progressive theologians are simply stacked onto a conveyor belt and beheaded. But time is on the side of the latter. It was ever thus. And Rome will not be able to do a thing about it. In the meantime, of course, common sense will only all too often get short shrift.

The classic case is that of the commission of demographers, economic professionals, physicians, married couples, and theologians appointed in February 1964 by Pope Paul VI to study the birth control question, and of course the then current question of the "pill." Here we had a sincere attempt to let the profane sciences and the *sensus fidelium* have their say. The commission took its assignment very seriously, and over the course of many meetings worked its way through to the insight that use of the pill could be allowed in crucial situations. The twenty theologians of the commission—easily the best thinkers in the church—went on to make a particular point: the commission's conclusion should be understood not as contradicting the teaching of Pius XI and Pius XII, but precisely as extending the implications of that teaching. The consensus was sixteen to four in favor of this position. The minority, which had stiffened in its positivistic approach to revelation from the very outset, and was closed to all considerations of reason, redacted its own report, which climaxed as follows:

> If it were to be explained that contraception is not evil in itself, then, in order to be consistent, one should have to confess that, for half a century, the Holy Spirit had not preserved Pius XI, Pius XII, and a great part of the Catholic hierarchy, from a very serious error. But this would imply that, most unsagaciously, they had forbidden, under pain of eternal punishment, thousands upon thousands of human acts that would now be proclaimed permissible.

By way of a bit of malicious paraphrase, let us put it this way: The official church has been tyrannizing over people for years now, with its narrow, distorted matrimonial morality. Let it continue to do so, then, lest the

., anny of the past be discovered, and the official church be accused of injustice.

We know the sequel. In 1968 the encyclical *Humanae Vitae* was published, in which the pope adopted the minority opinion — that the traditional teaching must continue to be held. And there was a further result. For the first time in history, *Roma locuta, causa finita* (Rome has spoken; the case is closed) failed to hold. Indeed, precisely the opposite occurred: a storm of controversy ensued, and the majority of even "good Catholics" began to be ruled by common sense and conscience in their married life. Now they went their own way. They lived in constant fear of "mortal sin" no longer.[5]

We are not attacking the encyclical as such, with its magnificent portrayal of the Christian matrimonial ideal. We are not attacking "natural birth control" — although peculiarly enough, not to say unnaturally, it "permits" the marriage act only when the female partner, due to the rhythm of her organism, feels the least sex drive or sexual desire. Finally, we are not belittling the question of whether today's "pill" is a healthful solution; but this is a medical question, and science must, science will, make ever superior products available. We are discussing the moral question only — which obviously will be best decided, after all, not by elderly, celibate males, but by good married couples who wish to live in the following of Jesus, who are led by the Holy Spirit, and who best know what it is that serves love and is compatible with the gospel.

Today we call this the moral autonomy of the human being. It is human beings who must observe what is beneficial to the development of their lives. But as human beings are always in the image of God, human autonomy becomes a theonomy, a conformity with God. It is human beings who, in their inalienable responsibility for themselves, must decide the end and aim of the moral life according to the salvific plan of God. Thereby they will recognize that moral doctrines are not stiff, unbending laws, but that they admit of new interpretations in new situations and different cultures. Otherwise we shall be attributing to the Holy Spirit a rigidity proper to human beings, surely, but not to the divinity.

Another illustration: God's mandate to "increase and multiply and cover the earth" (Gen. 1:28) certainly maintained its full import in the beginning of our creation, as also during the hundreds of thousands of years thereafter, when infant mortality and catastrophe performed the role of a brutal birth control. As we know, humankind grew only very slowly at first, until, by the year 1950, there were some 2.5 billion human beings on the earth. But at that point the rate of population growth suddenly went completely wild. By 1987 that figure had doubled. For example, in 1950 there were 330 million people living in India; today there are over 800 million. The population of India increases by some 16 to 20 million every year, an amount equal to the entire population of Australia. The population of Africa doubled from 1950 to 1980; and according to present estimates it will double again within twenty years. And the majority of these persons are born for a life of misery and idleness. In these conditions, was it really necessary that, at the World Eucharistic Congress in Nairobi in 1985, Pope John Paul II intone that verse from Genesis over the continent of Africa, thereby encouraging an even more rapid growth of the African population?

We have seen, then, that for the birth control question a commission was set up, but that the advice of the experts went unheeded. In the following chapter we shall learn that a commission was set up to examine the question whether women are legitimately excluded from the priesthood on biblical grounds, and see once more that the experts' response was ignored. We see the church holding diocesan, regional, and universal synods, but no such convocation has ever been able to shake Rome's position on a question once that position has been taken. All of this betokens narrowness, fear, and incompetence, and not only demonstrates, but realizes anew, Rome's preconciliar, historical, tragic attitude toward church affairs.

The sciences, then, are making unheard-of progress. Consequently, the quantity of theological cognition, too, is increasing at a dizzying rate. Even Karl Rahner could no longer keep abreast of it all, and "suffered from the feeling of a growing dullness of mind." The people of the Club of Rome explain that, when it comes to the threat of the environmental and nuclear catastrophes, everything depends on whether people react quickly enough to present perils and transformations, and engage in a learning process, with all of their creative powers—in an innovative, and not just a traditional way.[6] Today not only future priests, but thousands upon thousands of nuns and lay people are studying modern theology. All of these Christians, on whom the church of the future depends, are educated persons, persons open to the world, and persons who believe that the Holy Spirit sends its signals of inspiration to the antennae of common sense and honest conscience too. Unfortunately, however, there are still too many prelates, in Rome and elsewhere, who claim a monopoly on the Holy Spirit, and think they can play it off against the common sense of the grassroots. In all questions, instead of appealing to the gospel, they appeal to currently prevailing church law. They practice an uncritical, blind obedience to the system, and expect the same from everyone else. They ridicule the "theologians, or so-called theologians"—as I heard them called with my own ears—"who get into pure psychology and sociology, and end up in Marxism. Then their wretched moral state comes to light, and you see that they have only been looking out for their own interests." In all of this, the church is like a mother who has studied child psychology, and can talk about it beautifully, but who in practice is incapable of granting her maturing sons and daughters the freedom to become grown-up men and women instead of big babies tied to their mother's apron strings. Just so, in all its documents, the church loudly proclaims the autonomy of the sciences and the worth of human beings, while in practice never managing to detach itself from its insolent, antiquated attitude. How Jesus behaved with such unteachable persons is exemplified in manifold examples. "He left them standing and went his way." The grassroots church is going its own way. It may be that, amidst the dolorous birth pangs, a new church is coming into being. We shall investigate this possibility further in part 3.

2

You Will Take Yourselves Seriously as People of God

The Laity in the Church

In part 1 we surveyed the amazing story of how the church came to be. Now we shall follow it in the exciting years of its early growth.

It is clear from scripture what God and Jesus had in mind for the church—what Jesus intended the church to be. The church is to have two essential, constitutive elements, and these elements are to be preserved throughout any change or development: unity (*koinōnia, communio*), and service (*diakonia, servitium*).

According to the Fourth Gospel, Jesus prayed for the unity of the church and the world as a matter of utmost urgency. His disciples, especially—but the human beings who are not of his fold, as well—should be one: wrapped in the one love of Father, Son, and all women and men, hence without distinction based on anything like social class. Paul wrote his letters "to the church . . . to the community . . . to the elect, the beloved, the holy," and assured them that their respective charisms were all for the purpose of proclaiming the new doctrine, speaking prophetically, discerning spirits, healing the sick, and leading the community, and that all of these gifts come from the Spirit itself (1 Cor. 12:4–11). Peter all but outdoes himself when he seeks to make Christians aware of their grandeur and worth: "You, however, are 'a chosen race, a royal priesthood, a holy nation, a people he claims for his own to proclaim the glorious works' of the One who has called you from darkness into his marvelous light. Once you were no people, but now you are God's people" (2 Pet. 2:9–10).

To this lofty place in the sight of God corresponded the importance to be attributed to every one of the baptized in the community. It will be instructive to engage in a brief consideration of the model of the first Christian community of Jerusalem, which surely interpreted Jesus' intentions authentically. In a context of the most important event in early church history, the Council of the Apostles, where the courageous leap was made from the Mosaic Law to the freedom of the daughters and sons of God, we read in Acts 15: "The apostles and the presbyters accordingly convened to look into the matter . . ." (v. 6), but then, in two loci: "It was resolved by the apostles and the presbyters in agreement with the whole Jerusalem church . . ." (v. 22), and " 'It is the decision of the Holy Spirit, and ours too . . .' " (v. 28). That was the brotherly and sisterly style of leadership practiced in that church, then, as might be expected of the Spirit of Jesus and the community of Christians. Later, however, a distinction (discrimination!) between two classes, the clergy and the laity, crept in—one that must be characterized as no less fatal than a divorce or a schism, even though everyone continued living under the same ecclesial roof.

Jesus emphasized the hallmark of service with equal emphasis: "Earthly kings lord it over their people. Those who exercise authority over them are called their benefactors. Yet it cannot be that way with you. Let the greater among you be as the junior, the leader as the servant" (Luke 22:25–26). But here too the way was eventually paved for the substitution of human domination for evangelical service. It is disheartening to see the church holding the Marian dogmas, whose biblical foundations are dragged from the text kicking and screaming, in such high esteem, while its precious (antibiblical) "tradition" has allowed the attitudes of unity and service to degenerate.

Thus, after the Constantinian reorientation, the "servants" of the church (the *ministri*) became a social class within the church, with titles, territories, and privileges. Now bishops were nobility, had themselves called Most Reverend Gracious Lords, Excellencies, and Eminences, and built throne rooms and torture chambers in their palaces. Nor did any of this come to an end before the advent of the era of secularization, which the church has decried with such anguish—the victory of the "wicked world."

The mark of unity, too, was betrayed, as now there was a distinction between "clerics"—referred to as having an "interest" in the spiritual office, and as having "drawn the better lot"—and the "laity"—which in Judaism meant "neither priest nor Levite," and in the Hellenistic world meant "the stupid people." The former, also called "hierarchy" (literally, "sacred sovereignty"), now monopolized all offices in the church, and identified themselves with the church, so that the laity were deprived of all authority and worth, henceforward to busy themselves in fear and trembling with their eternal salvation alone, and otherwise to have nothing to say in the church. The only tasks they had left were to "pray, pay, and obey."

Once this church structure rightly came under the fire of the Reformers, office was given all the more central a place in the church of the Counter-Reformation, to be defended in apologetics as the hallmark of the Catholic church. This attitude endured among Catholics until the tidal wave of Vatican Council II, when an earthquake occurred like the one on the first Easter morn, and the Holy Spirit stormed through the church like a new

Pentecost. Now the church went back to its first love and its original view, explaining in *Lumen Gentium* (the Constitution on the Church) that the church was first and foremost the people of God, only subsequently speaking of the hierarchy as standing in the service of that people. In the Decree on the Apostolate of the Laity, all of the faithful were assured of their share in Christ's office of Priest, Prophet, and King, and it was emphasized that they were not simply the lengthened arm of the hierarchy, but possessed the right and duty to exercise the apostolate in virtue of their union with Christ. The laity's new consciousness of their own, proper responsibility in the church was a sign of "the unmistakable operation of the Holy Spirit" (*Apostolicam Actuositatem,* no. 1).

For the 99.9 percent of the church who comprise the laity, then, a new age appeared to have dawned. Once again the laity were included in the life of the church, and the era of council-Catholicism was ushered in. Parish councils were elected to study various questions that might arise; councils of priests were held on the diocesan level; and regional synods were convoked where laity, priests, and bishops, together and in the same Holy Spirit, would wrestle with the problems of updating the church. It was a euphoric time, a moment of the dawning of new ideas, a time of readiness on the part of the laity to take themselves seriously as church.

But just as the golden age of the infant church had vanished so soon, so neither could the soaring conciliar euphoria be long maintained. All too soon the laity had the wind taken out of their sails, as subsequent juridical dispositions dismantled the democratic structures the council had inspired. The numerically weak vertex of the church pyramid reappropriated its pristine power, keeping an eagle eye on the grassroots lest a "parallel clergy" spring up. After all, the laity must remain laity—in other words, they must basically be left out of account.

The reaction was not long in coming: it involved suffering at the sight of what was transpiring in the church, a spirit of resignation, and, in a final phase, a feeling that "I just don't care anymore." Of this situation R. Zerfass writes:

> How many parish councils have given up the fight after one term of office? And who is surprised that suchlike bodies, originally a source of encouragement and locus of solidarity for all manner of grassroots initiatives, have degenerated into institutions in which the main concern is to see to it that "nothing happens"? Parishes will never be places of hope as long as "collaboration" and "consultation" are the only things allowed. These sophisticated, treacherous euphemisms are church leaders' jargon.

I make every effort, in my letters, talks, and articles, to combat this spirit of resignation, which is becoming a threat the world over. I tell my audiences: Humanly speaking, resignation in the church is understandable, of course. But it must not spread. Its very etymology gives it away. The word "resignation" comes from the Latin, *signum*, the standard carried by the Roman legions all over the empire. Re-signation means laying down the *signum*, giving up the flag, handing it over to the enemy. In other words, it means desertion. But desertion is cowardly and immoral, in secular and sacred affairs alike. Further: anyone falling victim to resignation in the church lacks spirituality, lacks faith in the risen Lord, who has overcome death and can overcome all deathlike situations, lacks faith in the Holy Spirit, who is ever capable of astonishing us anew with its creative solutions. Granted, this is easier said than believed, since all human evidence is completely against it.

The 1987 Synod of Bishops dealt with the place of the laity in the church, and at first there seemed to be some hope that apathy and weariness on the part of the laity might be overcome. Many groups and organizations had once more bestirred themselves and submitted their reflections and expectations to Rome to be considered by the synod. The synod itself, according to the testimony of its participants, was a beautiful experience — that of a truly worldwide church. The 232 bishops and 60 lay persons who participated — 32 men and 28 women (30 and 30 would have been even more beautiful!) — expressed their views and recommendations forthrightly. Open-mindedness and an atmosphere of hope prevailed. But when the synod was over, little had come of it. Obviously, little could be done with the lengthy, rich pronouncements of Vatican II on the laity in the church other than abbreviate them. But especially, very little that was new had emerged over the previous twenty-two years. The *Message to the People of God* began very correctly with the concept of ecclesial *communio,* and endorsed Article 1 of the Universal Declaration of Human Rights to the effect that all human beings are of equal worth, without any distinction or discrimination. The document insisted that this was true for the church as well. All believing Christians were of the same worth as priests and religious. But barely twenty lines later we are in for a surprise. Suddenly the text simply contradicts what it has just stated. Certain of the faithful have received the sacrament of orders, "which confers on them a special dignity." It turns out that, at the last moment, a cardinal of the Roman curia had pressured the editorial committee to insert this clause. Evidently he regarded it as beneath his "special dignity" simply to be lumped together with the people of God. And evidently his colleagues felt the same. The German edition substitutes *Stand* (state, estate) for "dignity" in an effort to soften the glaring contradiction somewhat. But *Stand* is just as unfortunate a translation, reminiscent as it is of the medieval "estates": clergy, nobility, middle estate, farmers, serfs, and slaves. The correct expression would have been, "imposes upon them a special service." But that would have no longer reflected the cardinal's intent.

The fifty-four very detailed suggestions formulated at the end of the document had been duly endorsed by vote, and were now available for use in the preparation of the papal document to be published at the close of the synod. These scarcely went beyond the self-evident, however, and seemed mostly for display. They give the impression of rather "dry bones." Each section had won only a minimal consensus, and "actually hid the real problems and tensions rather than honestly permitting them to surface."[1] We shall shortly see, in connection with the question of women in the church, how this meager result is to be explained.

As a matter of fact, based on previous experience, not a whit more should really have been expected. After all, the synod had not been constituted as anything more than a consultative assembly. That is, you could talk to Rome, but you could not help Rome make decisions. That had been stipulated in advance, to ensure that the Roman curia would have no competition when it came to deciding any real questions. Furthermore, important concrete decisions had already been decided by Rome and forced on the synod—for example, the determinations that only the pastor might chair the parish council, that the matter of women's ordination might not be discussed at all in the synod, or that lay theologians might no longer preach during the celebration of the Eucharist.

With respect to this last disposition, you can theologize till you are blue in the face, but pastorally this prohibition is impudent in the extreme, and a heavy burden besides. We need but reflect how many parishes are served by only one priest. In such parishes, the pastor alone, year in, year out, week in, week out, would have to preach at all of the Sunday Masses, while the poor parishioners would now have to sit and listen to the same preacher—and not necessarily a silver-tongued one, at that—Sunday after Sunday, year in, year out. What better means could have been devised to alienate the people from Sunday Mass? By way of a compromise, "so long as no priest or deacon is available," before the liturgy itself some poor pastoral minister may be permitted to give a talk, explaining readings that will be heard only later—sheerly to observe the letter of the law and bow to the superior worth of the priest. One could feel the reluctance in the 1987–88 instruction of the German bishops. The bishops had repeatedly besought Rome to permit a continuation of the successful experiment. The only answer they had received was a blunt "no." And so they had to promulgate the prohibition against their will. Not just poor lay people, then, but poor bishops! The German Bishops Conference, with its theological and financial weight in Rome, ought simply to have informed the curia—not asked, and risked another "no," but informed the curia—that, in view of the prevailing pastoral need, this disposition could not be implemented. Until bishops' conferences begin to deal with Rome in this way, they will only come more and more under the yoke of Roman centralism and juridicism.

There had already been a plethora of complaints stemming from the bishops' synods, especially the one held in the fall of 1985, regarding the Roman curia's centralizing attitude, as well as regarding the procedural clumsiness and inefficiency of the synod itself, regarding the manifold methods of manipulation on the part of the synodal secretariat, and regarding the hostile treatment to which journalists were subjected.

But to no effect. You can talk all you want; they just turn their backs. The synod of bishops, which began in such a climate of hope under Paul VI, has become a frustrating routine. The last thing those in Rome want is a strong synod. Hands off their power! This is also why they downplay the importance of the national and regional bishops' conferences. Roman defensiveness, status-quo-ism, dispositions of church law fixed once and for all, have gotten to be too much even for some bishops. Any secular legislature may adapt laws as the need arises, the better to serve the people. "Eternal Rome" is an inglorious exception.

But this is still no reason for people to drop their hands in helplessness. The bishops' synods have occasioned a great consciousness-raising among the laity, worldwide, and this will not be without effect. No small number of disappointed laity have turned their backs on the church, it is true. But the majority of the laity, and the best of them, remain, taking their own tacks, refusing any longer to be "tame," and in given cases taking the bull by the horns and transforming nonbinding generalia into concrete consequences. Utopia is here!

It is especially in the third world that the council is having its effects. Not that one should idealize the young churches of Latin America, Africa, or Asia. We could sing jeremiads aplenty over the political, economic, even ecclesial shortcomings there. Nevertheless it remains clear that the council has had greater impact there than in Europe and the United States. We might almost say: the Western church, our bishops and theologians, composed the conciliar texts, while the young churches show us how to live up to them. For example, the third world is the scene of a felicitous surge of activity on the part of the laity. The Latin American Bishops Conference, meeting at Medellín in 1968, attempted to apply the council to Latin America concretely, made its celebrated option for the poor, and gave the impulse for the foundation of the base church communities.

Both of the last-named solutions have gone beyond empty words and have transformed the Latin American churches from the ground up. Now the laity gather together — not in the same numbers everywhere, surely, and certainly not the whole people — in thousands of base communities, to analyze the situations in which they are living, to gain light and strength, joy and courage in praying, singing, and reading the holy scriptures, and then to change their daily lives degree by degree. Before, the pastoral ministry was something that "happened" to the laity. It came from above, and was monopolized by the priest, who swooped down on the community twice a year or so, baptized the babies, heard confessions, celebrated Mass, and vanished again like a meteor — and then for the next six months there was no church there. Now "ministry from beneath" is the watchword, church managed by the laity, who are church all year long and who stimulate one another to live according to the gospel. The entire phenomenon has been dubbed a Copernican revolution.

In similar fashion, in Asia, and especially in Africa, outlying parishes have become independent and active. They celebrate a priestless liturgy, and invite their non-Christian relatives and friends along, who often find joy in the experience, enroll as catechumens, and two years later are baptized. One might almost say that the shortage of priests has actually been a blessing from the point of view of the maturation of the people of God. Formerly, the apostolate was in the hands of a hierarchical, monarchical system of bishops, priests, and catechists. Now the model of the primitive Christian living community is once more in place, and operative.

As long as thirty years ago, Father Beyerhaus pointed to the example of certain young churches in Asia, which, due only to persecution and to the expulsion of their missionaries, came to a full awareness of themselves as church and saw a quantum leap in their growth.[2] A more recent example of this kind is that of Guinea, where in 1967 then President Sékou Touré attempted to take the church down a notch and expelled from the country its two bishops and all of its European missionaries. Eight Guinean priests along with Archbishop Tschidimbo, who later was exiled himself, remained to serve fifty thousand Catholics. The first reaction: The parishes will totally collapse! But then a new ecclesial consciousness sprang up: We are church! And parish groups were organized, turning passive, consumer Christians into active, mission-oriented Christians. Christians accounted for 1 percent of the population at the time. Today they make up 6 percent. The new president, a Muslim whose wife is a Catholic, once more permits missionaries in his country. But the parish teams are unwilling to fall back into the old system and relinquish their new responsibilities.

Granted, at the moment these active parishes are not the sole solution. Other developments and changes are needed. If "participation in the Eucharistic sacrifice is the wellspring and consummation of the entire Christian life" (*Lumen Gentium,* no. 11), then Christian access to the Eucharist must not be prevented by stiff, unbending church law. Good, educated parish leaders are available, lay persons often with several years of theological and pastoral training behind them. They *could* easily enough celebrate the Eucharist. But they *may* not do so because they are married. They are not the priestly type. The priestly type is male, single, with five or six years of university education—while the absolute value ought to be the parish and its divine right to the Eucharist. Latin American bishops return to this consideration time and again. Ninety-nine bishops from Asia petitioned for a discussion of this matter by the 1987 Synod of Bishops. But it did not appear on the agenda.

Those setbacks aside, the base communities have been a boon, even in the first world. The base community is where we find active faith in community. It is where we find a church in the freedom of the daughters and sons of God, a church such as one could only wish for. I recently received a letter from Switzerland. "Change and renewal come from the bottom up," wrote my correspondent, "and I'm glad to be able to live and work at the grassroots level." With all due reservations, we must identify such base communities as the locus of the active church, whether they be splinter groups from international movements, or spontaneous communities forming at the parish level.[3] This is where we find Christians eager for renewal, forming, alongside the great, clumsy church, a church according to their wishes and dreams, a church from which impulse, and protest if need be, reach the ears of the great church itself.

Models are more effective than protests and postulates. I was very well acquainted with one Meinrad Hengartner, who died of cancer in 1984. He was a layman and the father of four children. He was head of the male branch of Catholic Youth Groups for many years, the brilliant organizer of the Swiss Catholic Mission Year of 1960–61, founder and director of the Swiss Catholic fast-offering project, and co-founder of many another church project. He seemed to say to us: Stop the palaver! Get moving! Don't just talk about what the laity ought to be in the church, demonstrate what they are. I daresay, Meinrad Hengartner provided more pastoral impulse over the last three decades in the church in Switzerland than did all of the bishops together. I mean no disrespect to the bishops. The bishops simply do not have the task of inventing everything themselves, making all of the decisions and then dropping them down on the heads of the faithful. Theirs is the charism and function of unity in the church. It is not the bishops who should be coming up with the daring ideas and initiatives. They should be creating a climate in which such ideas can grow and mature. They should rejoice at this springtime of the people of God, encourage it, watch over it, and then, at the right time, add their word—give their formal approval, or, in case of a false development, call a halt. In the case just mentioned, that of Meinrad Hengartner, this interplay between laity and hierarchy proceeded in exemplary fashion.

If even male laity are often uncomfortable in a clerical church, female laity are out and out discriminated against by our male church. They have had to content themselves in the church, indeed in the patriarchal cultures of all times, with being more men's helpmates than their partners, more at men's service than enjoying with them a common life of equal rights. The "stronger sex" could attain all things. The "weaker sex" had to exert itself, but without making any demands.

Unfortunately, this contempt for the worth of women has stained through to the fabric of the church itself. The parish community is addressed as "brothers" (even though the Greek word *adelphoi* in Paul's letters meant not brothers, but siblings—brothers and sisters). Women have neither place nor voice in the hierarchy. I received a letter complaining of the "poor old church, that uses women only for cleaning, making coffee, and arranging flowers." Another correspondent remarked, bitingly, but justly: "Women are found in the church wherever they have no right to speak, no vote to cast, and no decisions to make. Where power is exercised, they are missing. Gentlemen think; women pray."[4]

I shall not repeat here what can be found so easily in other books:[5] how Jesus went his own way, and, in contravention of the usages of his time, cultivated most amicable relations with women, precisely making women the first witnesses and messengers of his resurrection; how Paul tore down the walls and declared, "There does not exist among you Jew or Greek, slave or freeman, male or female. All are one in Christ Jesus" (Gal. 3:28); then how Pope John XXIII in the encyclical *Pacem in Terris* championed women's cause for the first time in the history of the official universal church and declared the new efforts in favor of women's rights to be a sign of the times and an expression of the will of God; how Vatican II spoke in the same vein in various connections; and how the present pope repeats these demands, if primarily for secular society—for example, publicly calling on the Australian government in 1986 to concern itself with equal rights for women.

By way of complementing the above, I should like to report how I personally encountered the problem. Since 1976, I had been visiting the United States for talks and seminars, mostly at the behest of CARA, the Center for Applied Research in the Apostolate. CARA already had its own office that focused upon women in the church, and I soon noticed how passionately the religious women in the seminars—all of them in "civilian" clothes, elegant, competent, committed—were devoted to a church abreast of the times and to women's rightful place in that church. On one occasion I met Sister Theresa Kane, who, as president of the Leadership Conference of Women Religious at the time, had publicly asked the pope, during his first visit to the United States, why women were not admitted to the priesthood. His holiness had given the classic answer, "Because women were not present at the Last Supper." Not satisfied, Sister Kane later wrote to the pope asking for an audience, at his convenience, for the purpose of discussing the question more in detail. The answer was that she should do that with the Congregation for Religious. Well aware that she would receive only prefabricated answers there, she once more requested an audience. There was no further response.

In Europe, I have been struck with the currency and urgency of the question only over the last four or five years. After practically every talk I give, I am asked what I think about women in the church. Women turn to me as an advocate. For example, there was Margrit Schöbi, a schoolteacher in Sankt-Gallen. Since 1980, she had been no longer merely asking questions of her bishop and the Swiss Bishops Conference, but making demands of them. She sent me the whole documentation, where I read, among other things, a statement by a mother: "We hope that what we understand as church will sufficiently bear our mark, and that of an *aggiornamento,* that in the year 2000 we shall not have to make excuses to our twenty-six-year-old daughter for having had her baptized into this church."

After having attended a weekend seminar with me in Vienna, Ms. Elisabeth Carlsson gave me no peace, insisting in letter after letter that I make my next book one on woman in the church. I suggested she write such a book herself. Her reply: "Surely I could do that. But it would be just another book. It would not have much of a readership. There would be no reaction. You are well known, Father Bühlmann. And so I entreat you once more. . . ."

Another woman, Irma Büchler of Lucerne, did summon the courage to write such a book. It bore the rebellious title *Ich empöre mich, Herr Bischof! Erfahrungen einer Frau mit der Kirche* (I Am Angry, Your Excellency: A Woman's Experiences with the Church). One of the experiences she relates is that of having communicated her concerns and expectations, together with those of many other women, in a nine-page letter to the president of the Swiss Bishops Conference, only to be put off by an eighteen-line reply that read, in part: "Your questions and requests are too far-reaching to be limited to the framework of a diocese or even of a whole national church. Thus their study will require a great deal of time. . . ."

Disappointed, Frau Büchler considered leaving the church. But then she read my book, *Von der Kirche träumen* (*Dreaming of the Church*), and now admits:

> That's a real plank for me to cling to. People like that give me courage. . . . So I'll stay in this church, to lift my voice as one of its members. My decision to remain is also based on the solid hope that women will do what they must and achieve this great breakthrough. And on that day I want to be standing at their side, and on the road with them once more.

In 1987 a lay theologian of my acquaintance, Mr. Christoph Heldner-Blättler, submitted a thesis to the Theological Faculty of Lucerne entitled, "Der Papst und das Konzil" (The Pope and the Council). In it he investigated the treatment that John Paul II accorded certain subjects — ecumenism, the local church, the laity, and woman in the church — in his addresses on his trip to Switzerland in 1984, and compared this treatment with the corresponding demands of Vatican II. In the area of women in the church, he notes, the pope conceded, in response to a woman's challenge, that "we may well wonder whether woman in today's church and society has now taken the place intended for her by our Creator and Redeemer, and whether her dignity and rights are duly acknowledged. . . ." But the pope never broached the subject again, in the whole course of his trip. And Mr. Heldner-Blättler concludes:

> We observe, then, that the council ascribed greater importance to the problem of equal rights for woman than did the pope in his addresses in Switzerland. . . . Making this subject a nonsubject is eloquent

enough. . . . Scarcely any intraecclesial matter has become as important in the years since the council as this one. . . . The male church,
which John Paul II represents, is masculine for good and all. Only
Mary, a few saints, and nuns are permitted to be feminine. All other
women are warmly welcomed as faithful, surely, but owing to their
"particular nature" are not admitted to offices of service in the church
apart from those that make use precisely of their feminine character-
istics.

I was to speak on the subject of women in the church from a world
perspective over the weekend of November 7–8, 1987, at the Schwarzenberg
Formation Center. My partner for the talks was Dr. Anne-Marie Höchli-
Zen Ruffinen, who holds an honorary doctorate in theology and who for
twelve years was president of the Swiss Catholic Women's League. This
woman communicated to me a great many reflections and pieces of information, and the whole mood of that women's group encouraged me to take
up their demands, along with others, and work for their implementation.

To be sure, one also hears other accents. A woman wrote to me in
reaction to a radio interview in which I had said something about women's
rights:

> As for women: Remember, Eve was created after Adam. Our Lord
> called no woman to the apostolic office. Women, even modern women,
> would have plenty to do in the church without storming the sanctuary
> and even getting themselves ordained priestesses. God help us! I am
> a woman of eighty years, and I know women's soul, their character,
> and their ambition. I have had many experiences in my own life, and
> have a good indirect knowledge of the experiences of others. I know:
> what is lacking today is obedience—that lofty, mighty virtue. Obedi-
> ence is the surest way to humility, and humility is something women
> too often lack. . . .

Of course, it is for the church to decide which kind of woman it will pay
more attention to!

With a prehistory like this, naturally many hopes were pinned on the
1987 Synod of Bishops. Women's cries were reaching a crescendo. Like the
rest of the laity, women's groups and associations in particular, from many
countries, had submitted their petitions. An international colloquium of
leading women had met in Brussels, and had sent Rome its views and
recommendations. But here too, all the real questions had all been decided
by Rome in advance. Where anything of crucial importance was concerned,
the case was closed.

Under Pope Paul VI, toward the end of the year 1976, the Congregation
for the Faith had published a document entitled *Inter Insigniores,* or *Clar-
ifications on the Question of the Admittance of Woman to the Priesthood,*

reinforcing the traditional "no" of the Catholic (and Orthodox) church
when it came to women's ordination. The document climaxed in the following declaration: "In fidelity to its Lord, the church does not regard itself
as authorized to admit women to priestly ordination." In the preparatory
phase of the redaction of this document, the Pontifical Biblical Commission
had been called in to give its opinion on the question from the standpoint
of holy scripture. By a vote of twelve to five, these biblical scholars approved
the proposition that the church could entrust the priesthood to women
without contravening the intention of Jesus. But once more the Congregation for the Faith could not bring itself to part with its dogmatism, and
constructed its own arguments in favor of the opposite conclusion. True,
dogmatic theologians like Karl Rahner or Peter Hünermann give the document a low "dogmatic note," or degree of dogmatic authority. But as far
as Rome is concerned, the question is decided. In fact, according to church
law, a woman's ordination would be not only illicit, but invalid: "Holy
Orders can be validly received only by a baptized man" (Canon 1024). Of
course, one may ask whether in this assertion the term "man" refers only
to males, or whether, admittedly somewhat obliquely, it refers to men and
women, so that the canon would be directly insisting only on the previous
reception of the sacrament of baptism, and not on the sex of the recipient,
as a prerequisite for the validity of holy orders. But this point of question
is scarcely of any consideration in Rome when it comes to determining an
official disciplinary stance.

Alert women, however, no longer accept the familiar argument that
"what Jesus omitted, he intended not be done." There simply could have
been no question of a female priesthood in the patriarchal Judaism of Jesus'
day. Nor do these women accept the rationalization that, since Jesus was
male, a priest must represent him in this quality. Women grant that they
are psychologically and biologically different from men, but to conclude
from this that they are beneath men and unqualified for the priesthood is
reminiscent of other abstruse notions that the church so long taught of
woman, such as her greater inclination to sin, her befouling through the
act of sex, or her penchant for witchcraft. One need only glance at a recent
book by Uta Ranke-Heinemann in order to wish to dissociate oneself from
such a past as rapidly and as radically as possible.[6]

When we say that Jesus did not intend women to be priests, are we not
saddling him with a legalistic mentality that would simply have been foreign
to his thinking? Jesus left the church no code of specific laws. On the
contrary, he bequeathed the church full authority "to bind and to loose"—
to deal with each case in the spirit of his proclamation, and as common
sense might dictate—just as he himself had done. He took bread and wine
as a sign of his special presence because they were substances people in
Palestine customarily took at meals. I for one simply cannot believe that
he thereby intended to determine that the repetition of this act might be
validly confected only with wheaten bread and grape wine, even where these

foodstuffs would have to be imported at great expense and where precisely palm wine and rice or manioc would actually be just the right signs and correspond to the meaning of the liturgical symbol, being the "fruit of the earth and the work of human hands." Nevertheless the new Code of Canon Law imposes this Mediterranean praxis in no uncertain terms on all other continents (Canon 924).

Were we to follow the same line of reasoning with regard to everything Jesus said and did, and especially, did not say or do, we should have to conclude that slavery should be maintained for all time to come. Jesus never spoke against slavery, and Paul actually sent a runaway slave back to his Christian owner, Philemon. But the question of the abolition of slavery had simply never come up. Nearly two millennia later, in 1839, when the question had indeed arisen, Pope Gregory XVI published the bull *In Supremis,* strictly forbidding slavery. (Although in 1866 the Holy Office, in response to a question from Africa, reiterated the traditional teaching: "It is contrary neither to divine nor to natural law to sell or trade slaves. Thus Christians may do so in good conscience.")

Would the time at last be ripe, on the question of women in the church, likewise to depart from the traditional response? The problem of women's ordination culminates in the question of women's priesthood. But it scarcely ends there. As early as 1972, in the papal document *Ministeria Quaedam,* Pope Paul VI reinstated the minor orders of lector and acolyte as terminal offices, but only for "male laity." The new code says the same (Canon 230). Only in case of necessity, by way of exception, may all laity perform these services. True, this "necessity" has become a matter of course in very many churches. But the consciousness that this "isn't the way it should be" has a discouraging effect on women.

Would the 1987 Synod of Bishops now review these various documents in light of the signs of the times, and at last do justice to women in the church? At first things looked hopeful. No less than thirty-two interventions on the part of bishops and laity touched on the matter over the course of the first two weeks. Bishops spoke of a discrimination against women in the church, and demanded the following measures be taken immediately: (1) Admittance of laity, men and women, to all tasks not presupposing the sacrament of orders — therefore to all administrative offices in the diocesan and Roman curias, all decision-making bodies, and the diplomatic corps. (2) The purging of ecclesiastical and liturgical language of all sexist or antifeminist expressions or tone. (3) An experiment with the restoration of the diaconate for women, in conformity with the custom of the early church. (The question of women's priesthood had been decided in advance by "higher authority.")

Even in the second phase of the synod, things seemed to continue to go well. The ideas proposed in the plenary sessions were further examined in the small discussion groups, and formulated as concrete recommendations to the pope. But then, as usual, everything was caught up in the machinery of the synodal secretariat — that is, for all practical purposes, the Roman curia. What was presented to the plenary session in the third phase was not the actual list of suggestions generated in the discussion groups, but only something said to be in "standardized form," in which little survived of what had been concretely recommended. The bishops' protests were to no avail. There would be no debate. Only a vote, yes or no.

The excuse given for this procedure was that it was necessary for the sake of broader consensus. Concrete questions make for division, and the question of women in the church, the synodal fathers were informed, was a current one only in Europe and North America, not on the other continents. Both principles are absurd in their application, of course. If the question of women in the church is not yet felt as a burning issue on the three continents of the third world because other, even more urgent demands displace it, then at least Europe and North America ought not to be prohibited from solving the problem for themselves. Otherwise Rome is like a mother with five children, of whom two, say, eighteen and twenty years old, ask for more freedom, and the mother answers: "The other children have no need of more freedom, so neither do you." You can torpedo anything you please in the name of a "broader consensus." There will always be reactionary groups set to reject any attempt at the renewal of anything, whatever it be. But is this any reason why the rug should be pulled out from under the majority for the sake of a minority, in the church any more than in any other respectable association?

The synod closed with the *Message to the People of God.* Paragraph 9, which is short and spare, speaks of woman. After emphasizing the equal dignity of all of the baptized, it immediately abandons the area of the sacred for that of the secular, inviting the reader to consider the evil of sexual discrimination "in many countries," while greeting with smiles of satisfaction the status quo of "a growing acknowledgment of woman's rights, making it ever more feasible for her to carry out her mission in the church and the world." Among the document's fifty-four recommendations to the pope, toward the very end, amidst the usual generalizations, we find a single, abstract recommendation: that "women be accorded a role in the formulation of conclusions and judgments, without discrimination."

Much had been expected of the synod. It was under a great deal of pressure. Within a framework of the question of the laity in the church, the problem of women in the church had gradually precipitated out as *the* question. It was really the moment to say something substantial. But once more the chance was missed. On the last day of the synod, October 30, the Italian daily *Corriere della Sera* ran a front-page headline: *Il Sinodo cancella la donna* (Synod Drops Woman). Once upon a time — because the signs of the times went unrecognized — the church lost its workers, then its intellectuals, then its youth. Now it is losing its women — and with them, its children! During John Paul II's second visit to Germany, in 1987, Saint Michael's parish in Schweinfurt wrote a number of open letters, each under the salutation "Dear Brother John Paul." One of them was on "Women in the Church," and asked: "Do you [pl.] in Rome think the problem of women in the church will be solved when the last of them has left?"

The "last of them," of course, will never leave. Even apart from the fine, good mothers for whom this problem is not a burning issue—a group whose numbers are dwindling, it is true—there are still the sizable echelons of militant conservative women who will defend Rome's party line through thick and thin. This subjective conviction of theirs should not be made a matter of reproach. The question is only whether, defended by such a militia, the church will make progress, or will degenerate into just one more backward sect with its arsenal of obsolete weaponry.

The third category of women, the glory of their sex, seeks to salvage what is left to be salvaged. These women are determined to exert still more pressure on the future, in hope against hope. For example, on January 11, 1988, the Swiss Catholic Women's League composed a letter to the pope, and later sent it—with 11,500 signatures—to Rome via the apostolic nunciature. The letter reads in part:

> ... For us who love the church, the question of women in that church is a burning one. We rejoice at the progress made in secular society. But this only makes it the more painful for us to see that women are not yet made sufficient account of by our own church leadership. The traditional picture of women as evinced in the documents of the synod does not correspond to reality. It is one-sided. It represents neither us nor our daughters. We are deeply concerned that young women no longer find a home in the church, and leave it. Equal rights are not just for family, society, and state. They should be firmly established in our church, as well, which, after all, is always on the side of justice.... We very much hope that the postsynodal proclamation will demonstrate a readiness for a dialogue that will include women. Ultimately what is at stake is the handing-on, the *traditio,* of the faith—in other words, the future of the church.

The Pope's response to this letter, and to all similar statements regarding the expectations of women, followed in *Mulieris Dignitatem* (Women's Dignity), published in September 1988. The document scarcely caused a commotion, as it contained nothing new. The dignity and worth of woman was clearly developed, true. Unfortunately, however, no practical conclusions were drawn from the fact of this dignity, this worth, this value. In the October 1, 1988, edition of *Neue Zürcher Zeitung,* the religion editor provided a pithy summary of what the document generally conveyed. The first part of the document, he wrote, the lengthier one, "glorified" women, while the second, the shorter part, was tantamount to "mockery," since it drew no consequences from the first part. This *modus procedendi* had been strikingly frequent with the present pontiff. A scant month after his election, he published a document on the use of Latin in the church (November 27, 1978). His phenomenology was very realistic. Latin was no longer what it had been. Today's youth no longer study ancient languages, but modern ones. But when it came to drawing conclusions from the inventory, he returned to his starting point and decreed that Latin would remain the language of the church nonetheless, and that the young must devote themselves to the study of Latin once more. Thus the whole analysis had gone for nothing. The positive thing about the document on women is that it is presented only as a meditation, as the author's personal conviction on the basis of a theological hypothesis strongly influenced by Hans Urs von Balthasar. The majority of women, like the majority of theologians, would scarcely accept its argumentation. To be sure, a sudden decision that women could be admitted to priestly ordination was certainly not to be expected. But the question should have at least been left open for more in-depth study, and this is exactly what the pope categorically precludes. In 1988, the bishops of the United States published their third great pastoral document. Its subject was women in the church. In it they cautiously suggested that "not all of the arguments brought forward" in *Inter Insigniores* (1976) "will be found to be convincing." But they simply omit any discussion of the question of women's ordination. Had they really nothing to say about this, in a country where the question has become so acute? No, the omission was obviously owing to pressure from Rome. The pope had already made it clear to the North American bishops, in the various contacts that they had had with him, that the question had been decided and that therefore nothing remained to be said.

The question is also of great importance for ecumenism. Not only the Catholic church, but the Orthodox churches, as well, are simply adamant on this point. Thus each confession buttresses the other in its position, while most other churches, since the plenary assembly of the World Council of Churches in Nairobi in 1975, have opened the doors. Popes Paul VI and John Paul II formally charged the Anglican church not to depart from tradition in this area, as this would place a "new, grave obstacle" in the way of ecumenism. This did not dissuade the Anglican church from admitting women to the priesthood ten years ago, or even, later, to the episcopate: at the worldwide Lambeth Conference of 1988, with bishops present from 164 countries, the vote on the question of women bishops was 423 in favor, 28 against, with 19 abstentions. Since then a woman has actually been ordained to the episcopate, in the United States. In the Catholic church as well, then, tireless efforts will have to be exerted to make certain not only that old traditions will be preserved, but also that the plenary authority bestowed by Jesus will be exercised to create new traditions; these new traditions must be created to the accompaniment of more profound study and increased pressure and in keeping with the needs of the time and the dictates of sound theology. Until this is accomplished, women must be encouraged, at the local level, not to give up, but to make themselves available everywhere for tasks not bound up with the sacrament of orders, which are many indeed — serving as acolytes, lectors, eucharistic ministers, religion teachers or catechists, pastoral associates, and members of the various councils and commissions. In 1988, the Swiss Bishops Conference named a committee of women to study these and related matters and to determine what ought to be striven for within the limits of the possible; regarding these matters the bishops also asked the committee to function as both mouthpiece and antennae of the conference.

The history of humanity shows us the brutality of our patriarchal culture of men's rights only, spanning the centuries, from the old power struggles and wars to today's exploitation of the poor and our destruction of creation, while a matriarchal system would be characterized by the values of life, love, nurture, feeling, and receptivity — not cold rationality, but warm, interior sensitivity. The Semites and the Romans, however, lived in patriarchal societies, and their frosty inheritance has chilled our church down to our very day. True, Carl Jung has taught us that a man contains something of the feminine (his "anima"), and a woman something of the masculine (her "animus"). In the church, however, the feminine element is very much neglected. Instead, producing, consuming, pushy, domineering masculine types have the field pretty much to themselves.

> In any case, the fact is that woman today is generally more deeply religious than man, more warmly loving, more strongly hoping, more inclined to renunciation, more capable of communication, and with more talent for a new covenant between abstract theology and human existence, between rational insight into the teachings of faith and the entire world of symbol and myth, which is so important for life and essential to all religions [Luise Rinser].

Thus the dramatic growth of women's influence in the church can only be a boon for that church.

Isaiah dreamed that wolf and lamb, lion and calf, would one day browse peacefully together, for the whole earth would be filled with knowledge of the Lord (Isa. 11:6–9). Then surely we can reckon with the possibility that, among women and men with a talent for rationality, the knowledge of the Lord and of the divine plans will establish equal rights for man and woman in family, society, and, most obviously of all, in the church, and that both sexes will share a common concern for the common good. To speed that day, let us dream, let us struggle, and let us pray. Sooner or later, in one way or another, women's consciousness, so dramatically raised over the course of such a short span of years, will attain its goal.

3

You Will Extend Your Hand
to Your Fellow Christians

Ecumenism

In moments of weariness and depression, when we reflect how little progress ecumenism has made, failing as it has to budge an inch from its beautiful dialogue and common prayer—let us remember how things were thirty years ago. Since the days of the Reform and Counter-Reform, people had made no effort to understand one another, let alone be reconciled in the spirit of sisters and brothers. Instead, they had fought tooth and nail. Even saints, like Robert Bellarmine or Lawrence of Brindisi, branded the innovators "apostates," "whoresons," or "devil's spawn." For hundreds of years, Christians not only repudiated certain teachings which they felt to be contrary to their faith, but thundered over the heads of the representatives of these teachings, who were only trying to live according to the gospel, the terrible *Anathema sit*—the wish for their eternal damnation. The efforts launched by the diverse confessions to "convert" their fellow Christians became the target of bitter, bilious "scholarly works" (G. Warneck, J. Schmidlin). The multivolume "histories" penned by Catholics like Henrion, Marshall, and Hahn contain thousands of instances of the "scandal of this division" (*Ad Gentes,* no. 29) and the "injury to the sacred and to the proclamation of the Gospel to every creature" (ibid., no. 6) spoken of by the council.

After three years of missionary work in Africa, I first traversed that continent in 1953. I could see, in the various countries, that the different churches were living in, at best, a spirit of peaceful coexistence. Often enough they would do their best to harry one another to distraction, and with governmental assistance. They stole one another's teachers and pupils, raced for a school location (a school could not be built where another already existed), and in isolated instances actually set fire to one another's little schools. Heroic deeds! The Lord's work! Instead of trying to persuade

Christians to choose Christ, we tried to get them to choose "our" church over "theirs"—often tantamount simply to choosing between the British or French or Belgian or American powers. So far had the Christian missionary effort degenerated.

Indeed, in Nigeria, in 1962, incredible antiecumenical events occurred. Preparations were under way for elections in this newly independent country. The political battle had degenerated into a confessional one, with the Anglicans and Lutherans leaning more toward England and Germany, while the Catholics were more closely bound to France, through the "White Fathers." Catholic Archbishop Joseph Kiwanuka related to me how, for weeks before the elections, Catholics would come to him with bodily wounds, swearing, "The Protestants did this! And they are denouncing us as traitors to our country!" After the election, Kiwanuka wired his congratulations to Milton Obote, the new president. He also paid a visit to Anglican Archbishop Leslie, saying: "My brother, we simply cannot go on living in this way. Our churches must no longer divide our country. We owe it to this nation to unite its people." And Uganda became one of the first countries in the world not merely to foster a dialogue between the Catholic bishops' conference and the Protestant church league, but to establish a council of Christian churches with the Catholic church as a full-fledged member, that all Christians might have a voice with the people and the government, as one Christian church, in important matters. Since that time, common church councils have been created in thirty-five countries in Africa and elsewhere.

In the same year, 1962, in Dar-es-Salaam, I encountered the following situation. The Catholic church, which had long had the New Testament in the vernacular, was now on the point of publishing a vernacular translation of the Old Testament, as well. At the last moment, however, the translation that had been in preparation was found to contain serious errors in certain passages. And so of course the bishops appointed a commission to find a solution. At this point I put in a word, and suggested that the Lutherans and Anglicans be asked whether we might be allowed to adopt their new common Bible. I flew to Nairobi for the express purpose of consulting with the then apostolic delegate, Guido del Mestre, on the matter. His spontaneous reaction was, "Right in line with Pope John XXIII and the coming council!" And so I went as a private individual to the Secretariat for Christian Unity in Rome to find out what its reaction would be, "in case...." The answer: "We would be greatly surprised—and very pleased!" And that is the history of the birth of the first common Bible in all of Africa. Then, once the council had convened, it not only permitted this kind of collaboration, but encouraged it, so that today Africa and Asia each have some eighty or ninety common biblical projects under way.

Times certainly change. After so much human narrowness, what a shift in the direction of the breadth of God! In bygone times we looked at other churches and thought we saw a "ghost." Now we have finally noticed: "It is the Lord" (see Matt. 14:25–33). Five hundred years ago, the "new world" was discovered. Today we have begun to discover the "new church."

It is actually like discovering a new continent — an ecclesial one. We have discovered, often enough to our shame, a deep faith in the hearts of our neighbors. And we have begun to meet with these neighbors, for study days and prayer encounters, in Africa, in Asia, and of course in Europe and America. The reports we read of these encounters have the following tenor: What do we priests who have taken part in this day of dialogue think of these Lutherans? Frankly, they astound us. Now we see how things really are. These people are honest, intelligent, good persons. We feel bound to them now. We know that the cry and the prayer welling up from their hearts are the same as those that rise up from our own hearts, and that they are Christ's own cry, "That they may be one . . . !" These meetings are of incalculable benefit. They clean out a host of prejudices. We come to know one another. And we find convinced, upright, deeply religious Christians. We see how near we are to one another, and how tragic, yet how real, our division is. Until now we knew each other only from a distance. And we find that we have misunderstood each other. This is why the content of our proclamation has so often tended to be the division that distinguished us from each other. Now we are closer, and we are astonished at what we have in common.

True, objective appraisal had begun before the council. In two standard Catholic works — that by H. S. Denifle and that by Hartmann Grisar, both works dating from the early years of this century — the Reformers were still branded as sewers of lust, wrath, pride, ambition, hypocrisy, and psychopathy. But with Schmidlin, Algermissen, Iserlog, and especially Lortz and Jedin, we discovered the actual, objective history of Luther and the Reformation, to the point where, "without having to close our eyes to Luther's shortcomings, we can stand before him with reverence" (J. Lortz).

Then, in John XXIII, the "kindness and love of God our savior appeared" (Tit. 3:4) in a simple human being of our time. Now a Catholic pontiff had found his way into the hearts of Catholics, Protestants, and non-Christians alike. His successor, the humble Paul VI, opened the second session of Vatican Council II with a confession of guilt vis-à-vis the other churches, and this declaration of fault appears in the conciliar document on ecumenism itself: "In humility we beg forgiveness of God and our separated brethren, as we forgive those who trespass against us" (*Unitatis Redintegratio,* no. 7). There are other beautiful statements, as well, in this decree. Catholics "should take the first step" in the direction of those from whom they have been separated (ibid., no. 4). "It is meet and just to recognize the riches of Christ and the deed of the might of the Spirit in the life of those others who have given witness for Christ, at times to the surrender of their lives" (ibid.). "Everything wrought by the grace of the Holy Spirit in the hearts of our separated brethren can contribute to our own edification as well" (ibid.). The document then goes on to encourage concrete steps in the area of ecumenism.

As early as 1960, John XXIII had established the Secretariat for Christian Unity, obviously at the urging of Cardinal Augustine Bea, who was placed in charge, and who, as a scripture scholar by profession, was more open to the inspirations of the Spirit than certain juridically minded curial personnel. An exciting, joyful era ensued, filled with surprises, a time of reciprocal visits between the supreme leaders of the churches, with addresses and common prayer. "Geneva" and "Rome" — the World Council of Churches and the Vatican — gradually began working more closely on questions of society, development, and peace, and even entered into dialogue with non-Christians, holding numerous congresses in Asia with representatives of the great world religions.

But with the end of the first ecumenical decade, the whole undertaking had obviously reached a state of crisis. Headlines asked: "Ecumenical Crisis?" "Is Ecumenism Dead?" "Has Ecumenism Run Out of Steam?" After such openness on both sides, such genuine dialogue and spontaneous demonstration of good will, suddenly things seemed to be at a deadlock. Dialogue is not an end in itself. Of its very nature, interconfessional Christian dialogue must lead to the "reestablishment of Christian unity," to borrow the expression employed by Vatican II in the opening lines of its decree on ecumenism. But when it came to taking concrete steps, the interlocutors suddenly seemed to be smitten with agoraphobia.

Obviously the question of structure had been posed too hastily. Four hundred, or even nine hundred years of division, with all of the differences arising in the interim, all of the hardened suspicion and mistrust, cannot be swept away in a matter of a decade. Further, members of certain Roman circles had a special fear: Catholic theology was already in turmoil, and church authority was in crisis. Protestants were "contaminating" Catholicism, and it was time to close the door a bit. Those within these circles had obviously not sufficiently distanced themselves from the traditional attitude prevailing within the walls of Vatican City, an attitude whose proponents had long been preparing to sabotage ecumenism's timid beginnings. This attitude found its crassest expression in the open letter from Archbishop Marcel Lefebvre to Pope John Paul II, dated November 21, 1983, pillorying all ecumenical overtures:

> This is all in open contradiction with divine revelation, which proscribes "division" and rejects any unification of "righteousness and lawlessness," "light" and "darkness." "What accord is there between Christ and Belial, what common lot between believer and unbeliever? Tell me what agreement there is between the temple of God and idols" (2 Cor. 6:14–16).

The archbishop also charges the pope, "for the sake of the Catholic faith and the salvation of souls, to reiterate the truths that oppose these errors and that have been taught by holy church for twenty centuries." And the poor soul meant this apropos not only of ecumenism, but also of the dignity of the laity, freedom of conscience, and respect for the non-Christian religions. He would maintain at all costs a tradition that today, in the perspective of history, the church rightly regrets as having been untrue to the attitude of Jesus.

A like-minded group had manifested its presence at the council itself, undertaking certain shrewd machinations especially at the moment of the final redaction of any conciliar document, including the Decree on Ecumenism. Otto Pesch has irrefutably demonstrated that, in the assembly hall, a clear, even overwhelming majority was usually in favor of open, self-critical, future-oriented declarations, but that subsequently this influential minority, teaming up with its allies in the Roman curia, made every effort to dilute these statements with ambiguous expressions and compromises. When that failed, negotiations were blocked by parliamentary moves, or even with an appeal to the supreme pontiff. Paul II was unambiguously on the side of the majority of the council fathers as far as his personal views were concerned. But he often allowed himself to become involved in questionable tactics on the part of the minority in order to spare its members anything like a public humiliation, and so pave the way for a broader consensus when it came to the final balloting. Thus, on various occasions, the pope personally ordered alterations in a final draft, thus earning himself the reproach of the press that he had "manipulated the council." Occasionally as well, the council itself would strike a compromise, in the same spirit. The operative principle was: You take my text, and I'll take yours — "a compromise of reciprocal dishonesty" (M. Seckler).

To be sure, the majority hoped — rather naively, really — that what the council actually "meant" would somehow be "apparent" after the council was concluded. Unfortunately, that hope has not been fulfilled. The minority party, with the support of leading curial officials, has subsequently managed, by the route of the concrete machinations of church politics, to have far too much weight ascribed to the conservative modifications they smuggled into the conciliar texts. And so today the "progressives" must appeal to the overall intent of a conciliar text, and say, "This is what the council meant"; while the "conservatives" can point to this or that particular clause and say, "Look at this, though. This is what the council really meant." Thus ecumenism is caught in a deadly "doctrinal pincer movement."[1]

An appreciation of this deliberately constructed situation gives us a better understanding of the grating contradiction between the pope's beautiful words about ecumenism — his "ecumenism of the sworn word" — and the braking function of the Roman curia when it comes to any concrete action. For example, on his visit to Switzerland in 1984, in an address to the World Council of Churches in Geneva that had been expected to mark some manner of genuine breakthrough, Pope John Paul II merely portrayed the requirements of unity in moving words, basically saying nothing that Paul

VI had not said on his visit in 1969. Fifteen years of marking time. In 1982 John Paul had flown to Great Britain, prayed publicly with the primate of the Anglican church in Canterbury cathedral—a sensational event—but had not a single word to say, in the course of his entire visit, about the document that an official commission of Anglican and Catholic theologians had labored over for ten years before redacting a far-reaching consensus that had awakened hope among the faithful of both confessions for a prompt mutual recognition on the part of both churches. Why? Because the Roman Congregation for the Doctrine of the Faith had just rejected the document out of hand as insufficiently consistent with the determinations of the *First* Vatican Council.

Another example: In 1980 the pope had visited the Federal Republic of Germany. By contrast with his usual reticence in the area of ecumenism, understandable in view of his Polish background, he had surprised his auditors in this land of the Reformation with his readiness and his ability to march down the ecumenical road. The Bensheim Institute for Confessional Research of the Evangelical Union had published an analysis of his addresses, observing with satisfaction that his style had become more open, more insistent, and more brotherly than ever before. Now he emphasized not what divided Catholics and Protestants, but what united them—the elements of their common deposit of faith. He employed ecumenical concepts like "organic unity," and "Petrine service." He even cited a passage from Luther's commentary on the Letter to the Romans. Indeed, the high-ranking visitor had personally encouraged a Lutheran-Catholic commission to speed up its consideration of the question of interfaith unity. But then, in 1987, he visited the country again, and had absolutely nothing new to lay on the table as far as ecumenism was concerned. Rather, again according to the Bensheim Institute, he disappointed Protestants with a "hardening of dogmatic positions," and his brusque dismissal of the question of intercommunion. When heads of state go on official visits to other countries, they usually sign new accords worked out in preparatory negotiations. So too, on the pope's many journeys to other lands, something ought to be worked out in advance, in consultation with the bishops, by way of a response to the needs of the local churches, so that, once the pope has arrived, he can have something more to offer than a reiteration of Rome's intransigent positions.

Two of the finest writers in the church, fundamental theologian Heinrich Fries and dogmatic theologian Karl Rahner, had proposed eight theses, eight prerequisites, for a way out of the ecumenical impasse. One of them is that a genuine, theologically responsible union of the churches could occur even in the presence of a multiplicity of ecclesial traditions.[2] But Cardinal Joseph Ratzinger dismissed their book as "theological acrobatics," and the *Osservatore Romano* for February 25, 1985, placed its first page at the disposal of one Daniel Ols, O.P., a complete unknown in ecumenical circles, for the purpose of picking the book apart and dismissing it as "totally unacceptable," full of "serious errors and dangerous illusions, well meant but ill advised, and unsuitable as a contribution to ecumenism." Strangely, and significantly, the specialists of the Vatican Secretariat for Christian Unity had not even been consulted. The assault was simply mounted. When a difficult question arises, Rome has recourse not to experts, but to trusty representatives of the status quo!

A further attempt on the part of specialists to make some modest progress occurred when a commission of fifty Catholic and Protestant theologians addressed the question whether the reciprocal condemnations of the sixteenth century could not and should not be officially revoked. Rome and Constantinople had already done so (1965). But what had been at stake in that other centuries-old division had not been doctrinal content, but the stubborn mentality of church politics. In the case of the Reformation, the mutual condemnations seemed to have been pronounced because of the two sides' apparently diametrically opposing views of justification, "faith alone," certainty of salvation, merit, and so on. Nevertheless, the commission, on the basis of a better understanding of holy scripture, a more profound dogmatic development on the part of both churches down through the centuries, and its own unbiased ecumenical conversation, came to the conclusion that neither church could still be regarded today as committing the errors of teaching and practice of which it had been accused by the other so long ago. Each had been the victim of many misunderstandings on the part of the other. This was not to say that no differences of faith remained. But—and this was the new standpoint taken by the commission—a full convergence in matters of faith was not a prerequisite for corporate reunion. What was needed, then, was not a catalogue of articles of union, not an "ecumenical dogmatics" developed beforehand; what was needed was space for the free interplay of divergences in tension. After all, even among Catholics—we need only think of children and adults, progressives and conservatives—there are remarkable differences in "faith," and yet we all feel ourselves to be members of the one Catholic church. Nor should one require that all of the various churches arrive at exactly the same dogmatic norm—precisely the same point in the development of the one faith—in order to come together again as one church.[3]

But that report has lain on the desks of the German Bishops Conference and the Congregation for the Doctrine of the Faith in Rome since 1986. It could move ecumenism light-years ahead. But it will doubtless suffer the same fate as the Anglican-Catholic study. Rome's reaction to the celebrated document from Lima on baptism, Eucharist, and orders, which likewise was the product of an attempt to achieve maximal convergence, while basically favorable, contained many reservations, simply because that text seemed to fall somewhat short of full, explicit acknowledgment of Roman Catholic doctrine. So neither will Rome be able to stomach the Protestant-Catholic report, with its radically new tenor.

Rome holds firmly to its age-old principle of all or nothing. This attitude has blocked many an opportunity, yesterday as today. Nor does the pope himself omit any opportunity to insist on "full, full, full unity." With that attitude, we shall be waiting for Christian unity throughout the third Christian millennium. Oscar Cullmann holds, instead, that unity must be achieved not in spite of, but because of multiplicity. The one incredibly rich Spirit distributes different charisms, Cullmann goes on to explain, and not only among individual Christians, but among the various churches, as well. "In multiplicity is the wealth of the fullness of the Holy Spirit. Those who refuse to respect this wealth, and seek uniformity, sin against the Holy Spirit."[4] Strong words, but true. It is known that the pope has read Cullmann's book. Apparently, however, he is not willing to be "converted."

By way of one example among many of how Vatican II has been retroactively squelched, let us consider the case of intercommunion. The council fathers sought to encourage the common reception of Holy Communion by Catholics and non-Catholics. The Eucharist is "at once a sign and a cause of the unity of the church" (*Unitatis Redintegratio,* no. 2), they said, and went on to lay down two principles to govern *communicatio in sacris.* First, insofar as the Eucharist is a sign of unity, intercommunion is to be "forbidden in most cases" (not absolutely, then). But insofar as the Eucharist is a mediation of grace, "it is to be recommended in some cases." Further on, we read: "Concrete comportment in this area shall be determined in the prudent judgment of the local episcopal authority, in consideration of all circumstances of time, place, and persons. . . ." And then comes one of those typically squelching additions: ". . . Unless the Bishops' Conference according to its own statutes, or the Holy See, has determined otherwise" (ibid., no. 8). And this addition has had its full effect. Before the bishops or the national synods could come out with anything legally binding, the Roman curia jumped in with "danger of death or another grave need" as the only legitimating circumstances, and besides, permitting intercommunion only when "a minister of one's own community cannot be found" (Canon 844, par. 4). There follows the ominous warning: "Anyone guilty of illicit *communicatio in sacris* is to be appropriately punished" (Canon 1365). Thus both pastoral thrusts on the part of the church of the council have been twisted around to a march to the rear instead of to the front. The intent of the council has been intentionally stunted and crippled, simply trampling underfoot the legitimate needs and desires of couples in mixed marriages. How may one, how dare one refuse one's sisters and brothers in Christ the Bread of Christ? Is this not placing a higher value on membership in a particular church than on membership in Christ? Is the church not making itself an obstacle along the path to Christ?

Now the bishops were under the obligation, "out of loyalty to Rome," to promulgate this solemn threat and to insist on its observance. The Swiss bishops did so in the fall of 1987, with a pronouncement bearing the title, "On Eucharistic Hospitality." A better name would have been, "On Refusing Eucharistic Hospitality." The bishops obviously thought that widespread practices that had come to be taken for granted must nevertheless be taken down a notch. They knew full well how sorely this would afflict the hearts of so many Christians: "We share the pain of these faithful. But we must tell them, in all earnestness, that we shall have a genuine solution for this problem only with the reestablishment of Christian unity. God only knows when this will occur. God alone can grant the gift of oneness." The bishops wanted to be certain that eucharistic hospitality would really be restricted to "emergencies," as the code had formulated it. But then a storm broke over Switzerland. Catholic and Reform circles alike mounted a massive protest. A prospective visit to Rome by the Workers' Association of Christian Churches was cancelled: the desire was simply no longer there, in such a chilly climate. The bishops were driven into a corner. Had they not brought God into play too hastily, in speaking of a unity that would simply fall from heaven one day instead of attempting to motivate us to see to its gradual growth ourselves? Human beings are guilty of the division. Human beings, then, must build reunification, brick by brick.

A great number of women subsequently articulated their discouragement in letters to the bishops. I was shown one signed by Ms. Marlies Fuchs, in which she said:

> Do our bishops really wish to put us on the rack, impose on our clergy still more grave problems of conscience — call our Christian lives even more seriously into question? The women in our parish were on the point of announcing an ecumenical weekday liturgy. We want to live ecumenism, not just talk about it. We want to go to one another, learn from one another, not compete with one another. We are trying to break down prejudices, and encounter one another in openness and love.

With time the dust settled a bit, and a certain balance was struck. No longer was a Sunday Mass or divine service simply announced as an ecumenical service and the faithful practically forced to attend. Rather it is left to each individual's conscience, in view of individual circumstances, whether and when to attend services in a fellow Christian's church and even receive Holy Communion there.

> Within the general order and general regulation of the church, there must be room as well for the personal decision of each Christian's individual conscience, to be made in each individual's personal and distinct concrete situation. This is true for divine services, as well, and especially for Christians in mixed marriages. Each partner should of course foster the Christian unity and communion of his or her own church; but surely no less should both look to Christian unity and communion with their marriage partner. And when that partner feels Sunday worship together to be an essential source of the Christian

union of their marriage and family, then that partner is not only permitted, but obligated, as a Christian, to visit his or her partner's church for Sunday worship [Sigisbert Regli].

The most recent opportunity—not completely squandered, but only half-utilized—presented itself in connection with the World Convocation on Justice, Peace, and the Integrity of Creation. The entire undertaking was projected in three stages. The first took place from August 6 to 12, 1988, when more than five hundred Christians from fourteen European countries, representing the most diverse groups, gathered in Assisi to consider the needs listed in the organization's name. More than 40 percent of those in attendance were Protestants. Protestants and Catholics together, then, sought, in the spirit of the Saint of Assisi, in prayer and Bible study, to prepare the way for the great events of stages two and three: "Not since the Reformation has such a comprehensive, convincing, and mutually respectful testimonial of faith, prayer, and deed been offered by Christians of all denominations to the burning needs of a current time" (Titus Neufeld).

Stage two, of course, surpassed even the remarkable event in Assisi. This was the pan-European meeting held in Basel during Pentecost week, 1989. The official hosts were the Council of European [Catholic] Bishops Conferences and the Evangelical Conference of European Churches. It was a completely ecumenical event, then. At last, a common day of prayer! Finally, in March 1990, the world assembly was held, in Seoul. The idea of calling a world assembly of Christians to consider these urgent questions had been in the wind for a long time. It was finally formally proposed in 1985 during the German Evangelical Day of Prayer in Düsseldorf, on the initiative of nuclear physicist Carl Friedrich von Weizsäcker. The World Council of Churches took up the idea, and officially, urgently begged the Vatican to join the project as cosponsor. Unfortunately, Rome saw fit to reply that, while it would send representatives to the planning sessions, "in view of the essential differences between the Roman Catholic church and the World Council of Churches," it could not act as cohost.

True, the Catholic church is not of the same genus as the World Council, which is not a church, but a work tool of over three hundred churches. True, it would have taken practically an organizational miracle to strike the necessary balance so as not to burden still further the already complex workings of the World Council, which must take account of all its member churches. On the other hand, the churches could have borne a precious witness before the eyes of the world, could they have demonstrated that such diverse institutions could bypass procedural questions sufficiently to map out a common agenda on a matter of common interest. The first great meeting could have been a "council of peace," then, rather than a "council of faith," merely paving the way for the latter, which would be celebrated when at last all Christian churches would have marked out the common foundation on which each would acknowledge the others, in the multiplicity of church traditions, as churches of Christ. But this was not to be. Structural questions were given precedence, instead of being left in the background, left to the future, so that all the churches could begin by putting their hand to the common task of a better world—which, after all, is more important than all structural questions together. Rome's consent would have opened a new phase of ecumenism. Its refusal, however, dealt the project a heavy blow, and the final document issued at Seoul represented not Christianity, but only the World Council of Churches. From this standpoint, the Basel meeting will figure more importantly in history than the Seoul assembly.

Nearly a generation ago, in 1967, when Paul VI published his encyclical *Populorum Progressio,* I said to myself: "Well and good, but what a pity such a document does not bear the signatures of both the pope and the World Council; that would have given it a great deal more impact." Again, in 1986, when John Paul II invited high-ranking representatives of various churches and religions to a Day of Prayer for Peace in Assisi, how much more beautiful and more meaningful it would have been for the participants not merely to pray for peace, but to strike a blow for peace by responding to a common invitation on the part of the pope and the World Council. Was it really necessary to flaunt our division in this manner?

Luckily, the church is far more courageous at the grassroots. From 1920 to 1960 it was the charismatic pioneers who blazed a trail, amidst manifold difficulties. Later, after John XXIII, ecumenism could hold its head high, and—thank God—become the exalted task of the highest levels of church officialdom. Now the hour of the pioneers has apparently struck again. There are Christians among us who, despite all the obstacles, live ecumenically, who are reconciled with one another on the local level of the various confessions, who make openings, who perform, in anticipatory obedience, actions that in all probability will later enjoy the approval of church authority. Is this not how things have usually gone over the course of church history? The grassroots have the right and the duty, then, to be two (or ten) steps ahead of the institution, in hopes that these deeds of theirs, these exceptions to the rule, will one day be seen as having been but legitimate anticipations of official norms soon to be declared.

In a secularized world, confessional boundaries and ancient feuds are simply no longer important. The churches must become far more aware of this, and learn something of Jesus' *kenōsis,* his self-emptying. They must not take themselves as more important than they actually are. Thereby they must allow Christ to increase (see John 3:30), and to become the unifying Center around which all of his followers will gravitate. Many Christians— and they are of the best—protest when others, with their "prudent realism," postpone the union of the churches to the next millennium—or the climax of history. The former would prefer to work, hoping against hope that the great church divisions that mark our millennium—that in 1054 (the rift with the Eastern churches) and that in midcourse in 1517 (the split that followed the Reformation)—will be overcome in this millennium, and not drag on into the third.

In response to an interviewer's question as to what the real obstacle to church union was, Lukas Vischer, a prominent representative of the World Council, said: "Inertia. Coming to terms with the present situation. We don't dare to step into the unknown. Another substantial obstacle is inconsistency. It is easier to dream of church union than to wake up from your dream and come to terms with the realities of your own church." And to a second question—What is ecumenism's driving force?—Vischer answered: "The gospel. It is all but impossible to read the Bible and resign oneself to today's division. The contradiction is too great to keep on living with."

It is a painful thing to see. With the first three "new" commandments of God, which bear primarily on the church, in case after case, the higher instances of the church entrench themselves behind hardened structures, and fail to rouse the courage to face up to the gospel and the signs of the times and force themselves to take new positions. There is a special Vatican congregation, and it is the highest-ranking one—for the preservation of the purity of the faith. But where can you knock on the door of an office whose job it is to discern the "signs of the times," for the good of life, and to make its findings available for implementation in the concrete policies of the church?

4

You Will Take Sides with the Poor

Justice in Latin America

Ever since the Reformation, personal "justice" or justification had been the bone of violent contention. The Catholic church had placed more emphasis on meritorious works, while the theology stemming from Luther stressed faith, and faith alone. Today we understand each other better, and have succeeded in achieving extensive reconciliation on this point.

The void has been filled with the question of justice in this world. So many people wonder: Why should I be so exercised about justification for heaven when there is so much injustice in this world? Let justice be done where the needs of this world, which we meet at every step, demand it! I have no space here to catalogue the thousand faces of need. I shall limit my considerations to the economic need of the countries of the third world.

My own shocking encounter with this particular need occurred during my three-year African assignment, from 1950 to 1953. In the third year I was pastor and superior of the central mission station at Ifakara, in Tanzania. My intention had been to step back a bit at this point, observe, ask questions, and take notes, since by then I had been reassigned to Switzerland for the end of the third year. But in January a famine began, a famine almost beyond imagining. In November we had had rain. Rice and maize were quickly planted. They sprouted. But a stubborn drought followed, and the young shoots dried up and died. Then it did not rain again until February. Again rice and maize were hurriedly sown, but now the harvest would be four months late. And the famine began. I could no longer hole up in my ivory tower, and sent an appeal to the Sodality of Peter Claver, which responded in surprisingly short order with four thousand Swiss francs, which I used to bring two truckloads of cornmeal from Kilosa, a hundred miles away. This sufficed to feed our three hundred families for three months, in exchange for a corresponding amount of work on the part of their breadwinners.

I gained three insights: (1) how the people are at the mercy of the weather; (2) how incredibly patiently they suffer their fate; and (3) how we all, they and we, grow together when we help one another. Whenever I returned to Ifakara, ten years later and even after, I was still remembered as the "bread priest." The unpredictable African climate plays mean tricks, locally, nationally, and continentally. First too much rain, then too little. Now a flood, now a drought. And so it comes about that, for example, in 1978, a normal year, Tanzania exported 484,000 tons of rice and maize; while in 1980, 284,000 tons had to be imported. Again and again, catastrophic famines in Ethiopia or the Sahel provide us who watch from afar with headlines, and those who suffer them with trauma and sorrow. Lurking in the wings is the whole continental threat of "Saharization"—a consequence of soil erosion and deforestation, which no longer stand the ghost of a chance of being halted, since the population increase only requires more and more timber and firewood. And so the vicious circle tightens with each revolution: deforestation harms the climate, and drought harms the forest. Eventually, even where you might be able to find a bit of rice, there might be no wood left to cook it with.

I have already spoken of the population explosion (see chap. 1). The combined effect of the changes in climate and growth in population in Africa is that that continent, which twenty-five years ago could support itself, today can manage only about 80 percent of the task. By the year 2000, according to the experts, the figure will be down to 60 percent. Private institutions, the churches, the state, and multinational corporations have been able to do nothing to halt this trend. Not that their efforts have simply been in vain. Without them, the situation would be even worse.

A further cause lies in urbanization and the flight from the countryside. At one and the same time, farm production is throttled and the misery of the slums increases. I recently received the following shattering account from Christian Brother Leo Egli in Peru:

I happened to hear of his death just the other day. Since then I can't get this three-year-old out of my mind. Some time ago I heard the hollow cry of a child, quite nearby, and went outside to see what the matter was. There he was, with his hollow cry, on all fours, completely naked, in our vegetable garden. "The shepherds found Mary and Joseph, and the Child lying in the manger." There was a little child in our garden! He did not speak, but only crept to the doorstep, where he tried to eat something from the cat's bowl. He lifted his head, and it looked like the head of an old man. He looked at me. Suddenly I realized that he had a horrible case of diarrhea. He was practically drowning in his own excrement. Fearfully, another child now came near. This one was a little older, doubtless his brother. But they paid no attention to each other. What was I to do? "The magi brought forth from their treasures gifts of gold, frankincense, and myrrh." All sorts of good thoughts stormed through my mind. But after a moment their mother came and took them both home. Well, what was I to do? Is this just another little victim of third world misery, or was this the abandoned Jesus today? Now he's dead, this little one I saw. He was the fifth child in that family to die. His parents took some boards, nailed a little casket together, put him in it, and carried him to the cemetery.

I abandoned you in your need, little one. What will you say to me on the Day of Judgment? True, no bond of love had formed between us. Still, it was not just by chance that you crept to my doorstep that day. I have my conscience. . . .

What could and should Brother Leo have done? What good is a drop in the ocean? For an individual, everything! If that child's malnutrition had already caused profound, irreversible damage, then his death was for the best. Otherwise, Brother Leo could have taken him to a children's shelter — if the mother had permitted it, of course — seen him nursed back to health, sent him to school, and given him a chance to live a life worthy of a human being. That would have been wonderful. But then would the little one not perhaps have become one of those parvenu types that never care about anyone else again? That is the tragic thing in poor countries. There is so much selfishness and corruption. One feels almost hopeless. A little bit here and a little bit there does not do the job, we see. What is needed is a change in the system, the structures. And yet the Caritas motto remains true: "A world in which one person suffers less is a better world."

The little boy Brother Leo met is only one of the millions like him in the slums, shantytowns, and *favelas* of the third world, by-products of the rapid urbanization of those lands. After the population explosion, urbanization is the most important demographic trend of our time. Between 1950 and 1986, the number of city dwellers on the face of the earth more than trebled, growing from some 600 million to more than two billion. No government has yet succeeded in bringing the flight from the countryside under control. The people are fleeing from the countryside because they cannot meet their needs there. They dream of a better future, and they fall from the frying pan into the fire. If the present rate holds, by the end of the century half of the world population will be living in large cities. In Latin America, 65 percent of the population already live in overcrowded city slums. There we find some of the largest cities in the world, like Mexico City with its 18 million, or São Paulo with 14 million inhabitants — the expression of a heaven-storming hope, but of an experience, as far as the majority are concerned, of bottomless degradation. At present, it is estimated that over a billion human beings are without minimally decent lodging. Of this number, 100 million live literally without a roof over their heads. Nearly three million of Lima's six million inhabitants sleep on the street. Throughout Latin America, more than twenty million human beings sleep on the streets. The Vatican document of February 1988 is correct: we are faced with a "scandalous, alarming housing shortage." And then we can only imagine the filthiness of the air of cities like these, where bumper-to-bumper traffic, dirty industries, and unregulated sewerage poison the atmosphere day and night, year in, year out. The authorities should condemn these areas. No one should live there. But the authorities do not always have the initiative and the means to remodel their cities, as has been done, for example, in Tokyo.

The tropics girdle the earth with a belt of climatic catastrophe. Many bacilli, bacteria, and viruses that devastate human health are most at home in these climes. While the biologist stands in awe of the life of these tiniest of living creatures, their victim must deplore their pernicious contagion. The Anopheles mosquito transmits malaria, with its intractable fevers. Twenty years ago, we thought we had all but eliminated this insect with DDT. But it has become resistant, and is on the move again. Then there is hookworm, one of the most widespread of all epidemics, afflicting more than 100 million persons, causing anemia and, not infrequently, death. Amoebic dysentery, with its chronic digestive disturbances and depression, is another example. And the list could go on and on, as any physician in the tropics will attest. We can only be astounded at the sunny dispositions maintained by the survivors.

We of the northern climes simply have no idea how privileged we are. Nor therefore do we appreciate our obligation to enter into solidarity with the underprivileged and help them emerge from these desperate straits. It is not enough to thank God that we are not like the rest of humankind — that we have a good climate and good hospitals and adequate sanitation and so on. Otherwise we shall be like the Pharisee in the temple, who, Jesus points out, does not go home justified (Luke 18:9–14).

A further, and most unhappy, cause of third world need resides in the individual and collective selfishness of human beings themselves. The gulf between rich and poor stretches not only between the Northern and Southern hemispheres, but also between the poor masses and the new rich, the parvenu class, in the poor countries themselves. Those who manage to fight their way to the top, not infrequently thanks to the mission schools, often promptly forget their fellow human beings in need, and even exploit them.

On one of my trips to India, Indian Capuchins gave me an account of the devastating corruption in their society. To get a good grade in school, to get a good shot from the medic, to have things go smoothly on a construction project, you have to pay bribes. I responded that I had never given a bribe in my life, and still always got what I wanted. The fathers were incredulous. And their situation prevails not only in India, but practically everywhere in the third world — and of course in Europe, too, if perhaps in subtler forms.

On his first trip to Africa, in 1980, at a liturgy in Kinshasa, in Zaire, Pope John Paul II exclaimed to the bishops, in the presence of President

Joseph Mobutu: "One of your tasks is to do all you can to contribute to the formation of the citizens that the country needs—enemies of the bribe, the lie, and injustice!" He was interrupted by prolonged applause—a sign that his listeners agreed with him, of course, but an expression, as well, of the suffering of an exploited people. Kwame Nkrumah's "golden bed" once was widely mentioned in the world press. Then it was Mobutu's luxury resort, Gbadolite, built out in the bush for the personal enjoyment of his hangers-on, his villas in European countries, and his personal fortune of $5 billion. Or the Marcoses' millions in various banks in various countries. You no longer hear about ex-Emperor Haile Selassie's millions as they are the well-kept secret of Swiss banks.

But these are a few names only—just the tip of the iceberg. The Institute for International Economic Relations in Washington, after investigation, has determined that, in countries like Mexico, one-third of the monies coming in from other countries leaves the country again, in private hands; that, in the five most debt-ridden countries in the world, at least $86 billion was invested abroad between 1976 and 1984; that, in 1984, Switzerland had on deposit 230 billion francs in foreign monies. One can only conclude that there is an immense and unjust imbalance here, one that is at the very heart of the debt crisis. Where could we possibly begin to dismantle such structures of injustice?

Of course there are those who have taken up this challenge. In his *A Theology of Liberation,* Gustavo Gutiérrez writes that the first generation of genuine Christians is presently growing up in Latin America. That is, after hundreds of years, Christians are finally abandoning their unworldly, pie-in-the-sky "faith" and beginning to realize that being a Christian has to do with honesty and justice in economics and politics, too. There used to be only nonpolitical Christians, content with processions and the rosary, and un-Christian politicians, who, while baptized, flouted the principles of their religion at every turn. Now, says Gutiérrez, a generation of Christian politicians is about to make its appearance.

President Julius Nyerere of Tanzania, whom I met personally for the first time in 1952, belonged to this hope-inspiring vanguard. With his "African socialism" he sought to construct a socioeconomic model midway between capitalism, which operates for the advantage of the talented and the shrewd, and communism, which deprives people of their freedom and forces them under the yoke of ideology. Instead of quick progress for the elite, Nyerere strove for the slow development of the entire people. I followed his experiment for ten years with great hope. Sad to say, that experiment failed. One more hope to be written off.

Those responsible for the church have obviously taken insufficient account of their opportunity to render their faith incarnate in earthly realities. The Christian social strata who owe their success precisely to the mission schools have demonstrated their lack of willingness to turn their own head start to the advantage of those left behind. Today we see that neither capitalism nor socialism is a good system in itself. Both can be too easily abused. They both need constant *aggiornamento*. Perhaps we shall strike a happy balance one day—an economic system that will make the most of economic realities and natural resources alike.

The refusal of the citizens of the third world to cooperate is no excuse for the final, and principal, cause of world need: the current system of world commerce maintained by the industrialized nations. Through this mechanism, the price of finished goods that we export constantly rises, while the price of the raw materials supplied by the third world constantly shrinks. In the last decade it has fallen to the purchasing power of 1938. By way of a concrete example, in Tanzania in 1960, a tractor could be imported for the export price of 5.5 tons of sisal hemp; by 1980 the price had risen to thirty-one tons. For decades, the third world proposal that the price of raw materials be stabilized has been rejected in the various world trade conferences as incompatible with the principle of free trade. In economics too, then, might makes right. And so the poorer countries find no way out of their need, and their debt steadily increases. Between 1980 and 1987 it grew from $650 billion to $1.08 trillion.

The rich countries grow richer and the poor ones grow poorer. For example my own country, Switzerland, is the wealthiest country per capita in the world. A mere tenth on the world list of per capita imports from developing countries, it is far and away number one in per capita exports. One hundred thousand jobs are maintained thanks to our trade with third world countries. Our exports come to about 8 billion francs; our public and private assistance to developing countries amounts to only 599 million. Our per capita income from our dealings with third world countries is 1,245 francs; our per capita contribution to their development is only 87 francs. Switzerland boasted that its public contribution to development abroad in 1985 rose from 0.30 percent of the gross national product to 0.31 percent, and insisted that it hoped to arrive at a figure of 0.34 percent by 1990. But the Western industrialized nations decided on a full 1 percent some time ago (with only Norway fulfilling its pledge so far). Another blow: from 1980 to 1984 the large Swiss banks increased their credit to South Africa from some 800 million francs to 3.68 billion, thus practically nullifying the international boycott against the land of apartheid. Business is business.

One might say, the first United Nations Development Decade (1960–70) began euphorically and ended depressingly; the second (1970–80) was a tragedy; and the third (1980–90) ended in out-and-out catastrophe. The future of the North-South dialogue, or rather, conflict, looks bleak. One official report after another makes this clear. But no one pays any attention.

In 1969, L. B. Pearson and other specialists published a report portraying the first Development Decade in somewhat more optimistic tones. Ten years later, one of the studies commissioned by President Carter, *Global 2000*, made a far gloomier economic forecast, and prescribed as follows: "Courageous, determined new initiatives must be undertaken worldwide.

And there must be a readiness to implement them. The necessary changes far outstrip the capacities of any individual nation. It is time for an era of global cooperation unexampled in history." The Reagan administration shelved the study and refused to undertake any of the initiatives it indicated.

In the Carter years, West German chancellor Willi Brandt was president of the North-South Commission, founded in 1977. He too had published a very depressing analysis. In 1985 he asked himself what had come of it. "I have tried to give an honest answer," he said, "and honestly speaking, things do not look well." He referred to the relationship between the absurdity of the arms race and the unspeakable conditions of world hunger, dubbing it "organized insanity," these "swelling stockpiles of engines of destruction, that kill even before they are used, by gobbling up money that could have rescued people from death by starvation." Still today, some 13 to 18 million persons starve to death yearly—a daily catastrophe, then, of 3,500 victims. A billion human beings—one-fifth of humanity—are chronically and acutely malnourished. At the same time, the world spends a trillion dollars annually—a thousand billion dollars—on weaponry. Resignedly, Brandt cited the words of Albert Einstein: "The atomic bomb has changed everything except the way people think."[1]

As Chancellor Brandt examined the effects of the North-South report, L. R. Brown has done the same with President Carter's *Global 2000:* "No generation in history has faced such a complexity of problems. These problems brook no postponement. Earlier generations were always concerned about the future, but we are the first to have to decide whether the earth that our children inherit will still be habitable."[2]

So many studies, so many documents, so many calls to action, but so little action! If wishes were horses, beggars could ride. And so von Weizsäcker says:

> Never have so many lived in prosperity as today—a material prosperity that outstrips that of all previous times. Never have so many lived in misery and hunger as they do today. The number of people who die as a result of hunger is greater than that of those killed in all of the wars of our century. Never has there been such widespread awareness of injustice in the distribution of goods as there is today. What are we to do?[3]

And in order to compel us to do something, von Weizsäcker proposed the idea of the World Convocation on Justice, Peace, and the Integrity of Creation—since, as he so rightly observed, these questions are so intimately bound up with what it means to be a Christian.

Too long had we preached a piety that was individualistic (you and your Jesus), spiritualistic (save your soul!), and supernaturalistic (make no account of the goods of this world; strive rather for those of eternity). Then we rediscovered the fact that the God of the Bible gets very involved in politics, takes sides with the poor, hears the cry of the beloved people, and leads them out of the Egypt of their political and economic misery. God can do very well, thank you, without incense and animal sacrifices. God wants a commitment to the poor, and the prophets said so in no uncertain terms.

> This, rather, is the fasting that I wish:
> releasing those bound unjustly,
> untying the thongs of the yoke;
> Setting free the oppressed,
> breaking every yoke;
> Sharing your bread with the hungry,
> sheltering the oppressed and the homeless. . . .
> Then your light shall break forth like the dawn,
> and your wound shall quickly be healed;
> Your vindication shall go before you,
> and the glory of the Lord shall be your rear guard
> [Isa. 58:6–8].

Jesus, too, wrought signs of God's power and love for all women and men, especially the poor, the sick, the starving, and sinners.

And so we Christians have come to know once more that it is not enough to cry, "Lord, Lord!" It is not enough to sing our beautiful liturgical alleluias and recite our professions of faith. One of Marxism's distortions of the Christian message is that while Marxists fight for this world, Christians hope for the next. No Christian may ever neglect earth for the sake of heaven. "Christian hope is not in something yet altogether lacking. Christians hope in something already here, later to appear in even more obvious and visible form."[4] Today we know what "sin of the world" is so horrible, and cries to heaven: world armament, which results in the brutal exploitation of the poor and the wholesale destruction of creation. Just as ecumenical openness, or the dynamics of mission, are not just scholia to be inserted somewhere in the major theological tractates, but essential to any genuine Christian theology and spirituality, so is Christianity's social dimension. To sit on the sidelines, uninvolved, instead of fighting for change, would be to betray Christianity.

It is most striking that certain important third world authors—for example, Leonardo Boff, Jean-Marc Éla, or Aloysius Pieris—are deeply concerned with the inappropriateness of celebration of the Eucharist by Christians indifferent to the injustice prevailing in the world. Such a Eucharist cannot be pleasing to God, these authors say. Indeed, in such conditions, the celebration of the Eucharist is actually sinful. The Eucharist is not Christian when those who celebrate it leave the millions of suffering men and women on the other half of the earth to their fate. It is meaningless to commemorate the bygone sufferings of Christ if we have no sympathy for the suffering Christ of today's world, Christ in need in our sisters and brothers.

No technological contribution is expected of the church. This is the responsibility of the economic and financial community. The task of the church is to raise people's consciousness, to motivate them to break out of the vicious circle of nationalistic selfishness. Without new and higher motives, they will never do so. The church must incessantly remind us of the discrepancies that prevail on our little earth. Let the church issue a prophetic warning: You are not permitted to delight in your prosperity while your neighbor starves to death.

There is surely no dearth of church documents proclaiming this message. In 1961, in his encyclical *Mater et Magistra,* Pope John XXIII insisted that the right of private ownership is always conditioned by the interests of the "entire people." Vatican II emended that expression to read: "all peoples" (*Gaudium et Spes,* no. 69). Paul VI confirmed this in *Populorum Progressio* (1967) — an unprecedentedly dramatic appeal, and as urgent today as when it was first issued. Then the synod of bishops taught the same thing (1971): commitment for justice and development is an integral, constitutive part of evangelism itself, and not just a means to an end, a "pre-evangelization" calculated to render the heathen more willing to be baptized. We read in Pope John Paul II's first encyclical (1979):

> This pattern . . . and the contrast referred to . . . represent, as it were, the gigantic development of the parable in the Bible of the rich banqueter and the poor man Lazarus. . . . These structures unceasingly make the areas of misery spread, accompanied by anguish, frustration, and bitterness.
>
> We have before us here a great drama that can leave nobody indifferent. . . .
>
> This difficult road of the indispensable transformation of the structures of economic life is one on which it will not be easy to go forward without the intervention of a true conversion of mind, will, and heart [*Redemptor Hominis,* no. 16].

Many bishops and bishops' conferences, especially in the third world, have issued a call to the faithful not only to assist at the Eucharist, but to make a commitment for justice and peace, to protest corruption and all manner of exploitation. Especially remarkable is the letter of the bishops of the United States on the subject of the economic system, in which the authors address the conscience of the world's most capitalistic nation. Throughout the economy, say the U.S. bishops, absolute priority belongs not to investors, but to the poor, in one's own country and the world over.[5] Urgent appeals resound in the documents of the Pontifical Justice and

Peace Commission—a call for disarmament (1977), reflections on the international debt crisis (1987), solemn warnings concerning the housing problem (1988). In his social encyclical *Sollicitudo Rei Socialis,* of February 1988, Pope John Paul II speaks a language scarcely calculated to rejoice the hearts of the Western world. The reason the situation in the third world is not improving, writes the pontiff, is that it is not third world interests, but those of the Eastern and Western blocs that determine the way that situation is regarded and handled. Each in its own way, these blocs, laissez-faire capitalism as well as Marxist collectivism, foster a tendency to imperialism; and like the laws of world trade, or the dictatorial regimes of so many national states, each system is a sinful structure. At long last, the pope goes on, we must have worldwide solidarity, for the good of all. Will this encyclical bring a change for the better? *Populorum Progressio* failed to do so. Once again, the chances would be considerably greater if it had been not just the pope, but the World Council of Churches, as well, who had signed the document. After all, the world economy is preponderantly in Protestant hands.

Forthrightness in word, then, is scarcely wanting. And yet, in all local and regional churches, we encounter groups of people who will not hear of this "politicization of the faith," and wish with all their hearts to be left in peace about these matters, at least when they go to church. On occasion they actually rise from their places and ostentatiously march out of church when a "liberal" priest "starts in on justice" and political freedom for East, West, or South. They even mount campaigns to counter any economic movements that may appear at the behest of the church, since such movements attack not only the symptoms of world poverty, but their causes, which, overwhelmingly, reside in the area of world trade. We really have to ask ourselves whether it is worth the trouble to try to involve the faith in problems like these, if the majority of church-goers will only be antagonized. But then, of course, a second question arises. Are church leaders willing to entrust the future of the church to these "good Catholics"? Would it not actually be better to join hands with the influential groups that are actually building the world of tomorrow? Whether it is the people or the hierarchy, then, who reproach certain elements in the church with the "reduction" of the faith to sociopolitical commitment, must not the corresponding question also be asked?—namely, is it not just as un-Christian a reduction of the faith, and an even more pernicious one, for Christians to be concerned only with the forgiveness of sins and life everlasting?

Problem number one is the problem of justice, on all three third world continents. But the problem has crystallized in a special way in Latin America. There we encounter the first of three third world "continental churches" once dismissed as a negligible quantity and referred to as the "missions." We have since become aware that these churches constitute the main component of the church, and this not merely quantitatively, but in promise and influence as well. To be sure, we can intone our jeremiads.

The third world continental churches live in economic misery, and often under political dictatorships. Nor is everything ideal even in the church itself in these lands. Far from it. Nevertheless, the state of affairs there shows us that Christians in Latin America have obviously implemented Vatican Council II with more courage and enthusiasm than we in our Western church, with all these rigid historical structures of ours. We really must say: the Western church held the council—composed and published its documents—and the Southern church shows us how to live up to it. I repeat this for emphasis. The Latin American people are astonishing. After all these centuries of oppression, in the successive phases of the *Conquista,* feudalism, and finally, the national security regimes, they refuse to give up hope. On the contrary, they stand today as the people of the continent of hope par excellence. The church can scarcely glory in its past there. It was part of the system. True, it called for mercy, now and then. The poor Indians and campesinos could be the object of ecclesial pity. But otherwise the church tolerated the system, and was rewarded for its complicity with cathedrals that shimmered with gold and bishops' palaces bursting with ostentation.

How times change! In 1968, the Latin American Bishops Conference, meeting at Medellín, in Colombia, attempted to apply the council to the problems of Latin America in a concrete way. In an honest examination of conscience, the bishops came to the conclusion that this heretofore utterly hierarchical church must rely much more on the people of God—the laity— and by way of implementing this decision, endorsed the base church communities. They further concluded that this heretofore decidedly wealthy church must address itself a great deal more to the poor, and the second application emerged: the option for the poor. The council itself had paved the way. During the first session, in the autumn of 1962, Cardinal Lercaro of Bologna, at the urging, it is said, of John XXIII, delivered a most remarkable intervention. He suggested that Jesus was specially present in the church in a twofold way: in the Eucharist and in the poor. Jesus, the cardinal went on, had not only entered into solidarity with the poor, but had totally identified with them. And yet the cardinal lamented that he had searched in vain for any mention of the poor in the prepared schemas of all of the proposed documents. The poor must figure in every document, he concluded. And it happened. In nearly every document—in twenty-three places, to be exact—we find some mention of the relationship of the church to the poor. The movement known as the "church of the poor" dates back to the days of the council, then, with Cardinals Lercaro, Montini, and Suenens, along with Archbishop Hélder Câmara, in the vanguard.

Medellín's option for the poor meant that, henceforward, the church would understand and implement its ministry from a point of departure in the interests of the poor—and no longer do things "for" the poor, but do them *with* the poor: be on their side, take their part. The church was not taking sides against the rich; only, now the rich must see themselves in function of the poor. Without the cooperation of the rich, of course, the problems of the poor cannot be solved. Thus the church has executed a total about-face. Leonardo Boff has repeatedly used the illustration of Saint Francis of Assisi.[6] Francis had been the social lion of the youth of his city, and had squandered much of his father's wealth in riotous living. Then it suddenly occurred to him that he was not really getting very far with this kind of life. So he looked for a new direction. First he began merely to distribute money and clothing to the poor. But then he hit on a more radical solution: abandoning his father's palatial mansion, and the wealthy, ostentatious part of town, he went to live in the slums, among the poor, in order to live for the poor, with the poor, as the poor—and as a pauper himself.

No one imagines that Medellín has transformed the Latin American church from steeple to stylobate in the twinkling of an eye. But happily, a great deal has occurred. In most Latin American countries the church has now taken a critical distance from the system, and has become the "voice of the voiceless." Not only retired Archbishop Hélder Câmara has become "converted" to the poor—that had happened to him before the council[7]—but many bishops have done so with him.

Theologians, as well, especially in the religious orders, have been converted to the poor, and have developed a new style of theology, called the theology of liberation. Liberation theology is intended not to contradict, but to complement classic theology, as a theology of the whole gospel from the standpoint of the poor. Indeed, it is conceived not for its own sake—not for the teaching of the faith as an end in itself—but as a tool for "doing" the faith. Our Western theology has always been so ponderous, so intellectual. It has been written out by professors at their writing stands, brought to light in university lecture rooms, shielded from the problems of the world, and faithfully recited by students in examinations, but it has changed life little. Now, in Latin America, simple folk gather in groups, undertake a concrete analysis of their life situation, and seek to draw from the gospel the light and strength to change this situation, in small stages. Liberation theology is conceived as a subsequent reflection on this "liberative praxis."

In the act of performing these liberating deeds, the Latin American faithful experience salvation history today. They believe in the name of Yahweh: "I am here, I am with you, ever to deliver my people." They believe Jesus' promise to be with his church, with us now, all days, even to the consummation of the world.

Faith in action! And a second peculiarity: a powerful emphasis on integral salvation. Too long had the poor been consoled with the promise of heaven. Today, without dismissing hope of heaven, Latin American Christians complement that hope with the other dimension of salvation. In actuality, God wills to bestow on human beings a full, integral salvation, a salvation on two levels. God wills to save us both in heaven and on earth, in the hereafter as in the here and now, in the resurrection of the dead, but also in the resurrection of the living and suffering, the one dimension maintaining its center of gravity in the resurrection of Jesus, the other in the Exodus, the liberation from Egypt, the one dimension endowed with absolute finality, the other with more immediate urgency.

A third peculiarity of the Latin American church is its development of a theology of dependency. The poverty of the poor is not simply a coincidence of fate, these Latin American Christians insist. It is the by-product of a particular economic system, a system having the interests of the wealthy, the powerful, investors, and multinational corporations particularly in view. The challenge, therefore, is to win independence from this system, to stand on one's own two feet, to follow the inspiration of a sound social analysis, not to wait until the quasi-organism of human society heals itself, as conservative folk have in mind; nor, again, simply to hope that increased investment will do the trick, as moderate reformers would have it; but to effectuate a radical reconstruction, by means of as strong a popular participation as possible.

Naturally this "conscientization," and the consequent "uprising" of a people so long oppressed, little pleased the mighty. They saw subversive elements, and communism, lurking in the background. Rome itself was alerted to the perceived danger, by certain "princes of the church," and reacted accordingly in the document of the autumn of 1984, in which liberation theologians were warned that they were playing into the hands of Marxism. The greatest fear on the part of certain elements of a laissez-faire world economics, as also in the church, is the specter of "communism." These elements would prefer to support national security regimes, which trample justice underfoot, provided only they be anticommunist, instead of making a radical commitment to the elimination of injustice and thereby obviating the need for the radical communist therapy.

The absurdity to which this attitude can lead has been demonstrated by the behavior of the Argentinian bishops. The majority of them, during the military dictatorship of 1976–83, while mothers screamed for their disappeared children and husbands, excused the murders being committed by government forces, parroting the propaganda of the generals: this was the only way to save Argentina from communism. Now these bishops are calling on the people to forgive and forget. But injustice, once committed, is not that easily forgotten, even in the presence of Christian motives.[8]

A major event in the history of theology is the publication in Latin America of a new theological project of encyclopedic dimensions: the Theology and Liberation Series, projected for 53 volumes, with three or four volumes appearing annually.[9] It is the first comprehensive, Christian theological series ever to be generated outside the sphere of influence of Euro-North American culture. Now that 42 percent of all Catholics live in Latin America (with only 33 percent in Europe and 8 percent in the United States), it is high time for the continental church of Latin America to do something besides consume European theology. Rather, it is creating its own theology—and not only for its own sake, but for the enrichment of the universal church itself. We have only to read Leonardo Boff's book on the Trinity,[10] or José Comblin's on the Holy Spirit,[11] to realize that, while these theologians are perfectly well acquainted with classic theology, they integrate it with the existential questions of daily life. This is a genuine breakthrough. The Trinity is not simply a "celestial" event. Neither is the Holy Spirit. Through these theologians, the Trinity and the Spirit become events of our daily lives, for they bestow on us the strength we need to work toward an integral liberation.

But let us return to the world situation. Here an atmosphere of helplessness prevails. The three United Nations Development Decades have failed to lead the third world out of the vicious circle of subhuman poverty. In its 1986 report, the Club of Rome observed that too many grand industrial projects on the Western pattern failed to correspond to the needs of the people; that too much of the money invested benefitted only the privileged few; and that a policy of development was being practiced that collided head-on with local and regional structures and cultures and triggered a defense-reaction on the part of the population. The result is that our own economies are in crisis, and the thrust of the 1960s is lost.

What is to be done now?

In the third world, the way seems to be being paved for a shift in direction. Less and less is salvation awaited from the West. Instead, one relies on one's own efforts. The new, dynamic element is self-reliance. Third world peoples now turn their eyes to their own living space, and strive for an independent economy and a development guided from within, with a hefty dose of regional and local subsidiarity and the full participation of the people.[12] Even world organizations — UNESCO, the World Health Organization, the UN's Food and Agriculture Organization — have formulated their goals more modestly. From global plans, and mammoth studies that led nowhere, strategy first shifted to "country projects," which allowed each national government to plan its own projects, and then underpinned these projects with experts and financing. But this did not work satisfactorily either. So now it is "grassroots projects" that are being mounted. Latin America, Africa, and Asia are the scene of an ever-increasing number of agricultural and village associations, which operate on the principle of self-defense, and take the initiative for development themselves. Their survival depends on it, these people see. Their movement has been called the "barefoot revolution." Here we note the importance of small, nongovernmental organizations, which, out of ethical, humanitarian, or religious motives, cooperate on miniprojects, providing incentive and encouragement for these new grassroots initiatives.

In some circles, still more radical alternatives are proposed. The third world should make a clean break with the Western economy, we hear. These continents once provided for themselves. They had their own economies. Could not those economies be reproduced today? But the wheel of history can scarcely be thrown into reverse that readily.

What is needed now, in the area of the world economy, are genuine prophets—persons and groups inspired by the Spirit of God, but possessed of professional knowledge as well. These prophets will be able to build utopias right in this world of ours, by getting the global economy back on track. They must convince the Western world that its economy can be healed only if it fuses with the economy of the third world on a basis of equality, in a spirit of genuine solidarity; that the insane weapons industry, which produces nothing in terms of consumer goods, must be converted, on a world basis, to the manufacture of products and the furtherance of projects that serve justice and foster peace. The new prophets will spur the bold advances needed to render the "new economic order"—so much spoken of for so many years—a reality.[13]

On January 26, 1988, the European Parliament officially launched a publicity campaign calculated to awaken Europeans to the need for North-South interdependence and solidarity. Everyone must come to see that no people can any longer solve the problems of our time on its own. Nationalism, which has always sought to fulfill its dreams by "going it alone," if not indeed at the expense of others, is no longer viable. All peoples together must seize control of humanity's past, present, and future. We seem to behold the faint glimmer of a new day. Hope stirs.

We of the North shall surrender primary responsibility, then, to the third world countries themselves. But on the basis of the principle of solidarity, we cannot excuse the Western economy from the efforts required of it in this area. The prophets we wish for will have to issue a call for a kind of "third world Marshall Plan." At the close of World War II, the European economy lay in smithereens. Thereupon the United States, through the Marshall Plan, provided $11 billion for the rebuilding of Europe, from 1948 to 1951. The effect was all but miraculous. Europe recovered from the war with astonishing rapidity. True, that continent had a strong force of skilled workers at its disposal after World War II, and this contributed to its economic recovery. And this is precisely lacking in so many parts of the third world. Further, certain observers saw the Marshall Plan as a tool of U.S. imperialism in the postwar period. These are two important cautions, then. Still, it should be possible, after appropriate negotiations with the interested nations, and in tandem with their own efforts, to implement certain projects calculated to further third world development, projects that the nations in question are not in a position to carry out alone—in areas like reforestation, irrigation, transportation, energy, health, and nutrition.

Just such a project, "Transaqua," is being developed for Africa by a group of Italian technologists. The aim is to divert 5 percent of the water of the Zaire, the greatest river in the world after the Amazon, into a 1500-mile canal flowing northward to Lake Chad. The latter, once a mighty inland lake, is evaporating, and threatens to dry up altogether, which would mean a quantum leap for the Saharization of Africa. The projected canal would generate an excellent region for both crops and livestock, and thereby support millions of human beings presently able to survive only with help from outside. The new waterway would be used for both irrigation and transportation, and the regional economy would soar. The technologists charged with this task have said they would make a firm proposal to the interested governments by 1990, and begin work by 1995. "We have the technological means; now all we need is money." Only international cooperation can make this canal a reality. Dare we believe in this kind of utopian cooperation? Dare we hope that, in token of a new era of world politics and world economics, East and West together could work to realize this kind of project? Can large-scale human solidarity actually work? The canal would surely be a more worthwhile undertaking than a joint U.S.-U.S.S.R. Mars probe!

A last question remains. Is the option for the poor valid only for Latin America and the rest of the third world? Or would it be appropriate for our Northern countries as well? Behind the scenes, in our society of prosperity and affluence, lurks a poverty that we must ferret out and eliminate. Were we to delve beneath the surface, we should find working poor, dischargees from mental institutions, physically and/or mentally handicapped persons, unemployed youths, the lonely, alcoholics and other drug addicts, former convicts, and so on, on our own streets. They must not be left to their fate. It is estimated that eight to ten million persons in Western Europe live below the poverty line, excluded from the advantages of societal life, eking out their anonymous existences after their flight from the villages to the cities. In the United States the number of persons living below the poverty line has been estimated at 32.5 million. We must not simply leave them to Caritas or Catholic Charities, happy as we are to see these organizations functioning. All of us, as Christians, must see to it that the signs of Jesus' love are present in our own neighborhoods.

The fact of poverty, among us and the world over, challenges us no longer to give "something," but to give ourselves—our intelligence, our energy, our prophetic words and deeds, in order to change structures and uproot poverty. We are being asked to adopt a "world culture of asceticism" (C. F. von Weizsäcker). No one can justify misery. But if we are silent about it, we might just as well be attempting to justify it, and are guilty of complicity. The luxury of some amidst the misery of others constitutes a scandal. A contented poverty, a modest lifestyle on the part of each and all, could help strike a balance, and lead to the birth of a new humanity.

5

You Will Wonder at the Breadth
of the Creator

Inculturation in Africa

In an earlier book, *The Church of the Future,* I devoted a chapter to each of the three third world continental churches — those of Latin America, Africa, and Asia. I shall not rehearse that material here, but merely complement it, and therefore not attempt to exhaust the subject. I shall only point to certain new elements that have emerged, portray my personal view of the problems involved, and attempt to indicate approaches that we ourselves might take in an effort to aid in finding solutions to these problems.

Anyone who has traveled in Africa will surely have taken a liking to it. Much is not going as well as it used to: the economic situation in most places has become more oppressive, and in the area of health and medicine, AIDS, the modern epidemic, has joined the classic tropical diseases as the bane of the continent. Still, Africa remains the land of nature's enchanting wonders, a paradise of wild beasts, and above all, the continent of cheerful people — people far more spontaneous, affable, and effervescent than the Amerindians, for example, or even the Asians.

Africa has had three chances to become Christian. The first lasted six centuries, was limited to northern Africa, and produced a flourishing church, but fell victim to internal struggles and the invasion by Islam. The second began with the circumnavigation of Africa by the Portuguese mariners, and lasted from the sixteenth to the nineteenth centuries, with short-lived mission foundations here and there, and in the Congo, a church with solid roots. But, once more, little has remained of this opportunity. Then, just over a hundred years ago, a third opportunity arose, and this one was made the most of, thanks to the heroic sacrifices of the missionaries of that time. D. Barrett calculates that, by the year 2000, Black Africa will be 57 percent Christian.

We can speak of a geographical catholicity of the church in Africa, then.

Christianity is now solidly established in Africa, and is there to stay. One often hears anxious reports to the effect that Islam is making more progress in Africa than all of the Christian churches together. This is by and large an optical illusion. Thanks to financing from oil-rich nations, Islam has been able to build new mosques and social centers in many cities. This has led some to draw the false conclusion that Islam is mightily on the march. But have not the Christian missions done the same for decades—raised mighty churches and cathedrals, schools and hospitals, in the city and on the countryside? One must grant Islam the same right to develop. The right to religious freedom is not a monopoly of the Christian churches. It is a human right, one that belongs to everyone. We should not be panic-stricken, then, or fall on our neighbors with our polemics, but should attempt to defuse the situation, in a genuine spirit of obligingness and readiness to strike a dialogue. In terms of percentages, by the way, things are not nearly as "bad" as they seem. True, the Muslim population in Africa is growing slightly faster than the Christian population. But this is owing mainly to the population explosion in northern Africa. Islamic growth in terms of adult conversions is only 6 percent per annum, alongside 32 percent for Christians.

This geographical catholicity is not there to be abused. It must not be used to strengthen the church's position of power. It should be used to serve a cultural catholicity. A church *in* Africa is only the prerequisite for a church *of* Africa—a church with the scent of the African soil, a church with an African character. Too long, unfortunately, in our high and mighty European presumption, we have mistaken, condemned, and humiliated the Africans. The refrain has resounded down the centuries: "The blacks are absolutely ignorant of God. They live to eat, like cattle. We must civilize them!" In my book *The Missions on Trial,* I listed the transgressions of our African missions. We have labeled African premarital practices and Africans' polygamy as mortal sin; we have ridiculed the whole African philosophy of life, we have brought Africans the *Summa Theologiae* instead of the Bible; we have made Africans into mini-Europeans instead of mystics.

True, we have also defended their human rights, and that is the brighter side of our missionary endeavor. Thanks to that, there is a Christian Africa today.

But there is no excusing our missionary history. The missions have done African culture and religion a great injustice. We did the same thing to the Indians of both Americas, and even to the peoples of the ancient cultures of India, China, and Japan. Today we are ashamed and humiliated to have looked down in contempt upon those peoples for so long. But Africa has suffered more than have the other continents from our tactlessness and insensitivity. All the more, then, over the last thirty years, we have sought to make amends. A newly awakened African national consciousness, in the various lands, and the sudden decolonization of the continent, have not been without their effect on the church. One almost instant result has been a veritable springtime of African Christian hymnody. Previously only European hymns had been sung in church—French, Italian, or German ones, depending on the nationality of the missionaries on the spot—with the original text simply translated into the local vernacular. But now school-teachers, priests, and even uneducated persons will, for example, begin to sing a psalm, altogether spontaneously, in an African rhythm and melody, and the people will repeat the rhythmic refrain. On my journey to Africa in 1962, and then again in 1966, in so many countries, I had the happiness of hearing this new African church music.

I recalled my own first attempt to do something in this direction. I was working as a missionary in Tanzania. In 1951, before Christmas, I asked some other missionaries whether Christmas carols might be composed on the basis of African lullabies. "There are no African lullabies," the mis-sionaries replied. Unconvinced, I paid a visit to a schoolteacher who knew something about music and even about musical notation. I asked him to listen to his wife singing their baby to sleep and then to write down the melody to fit the text of a carol I had brought along. He had a scruple: "You couldn't sing that kind of thing in church." I explained that our European carols were often based on lullabies, and that that was why they were so appealing. After all, Mary had been a mother too, just like most other women. That did it. "Then I won't just listen to my wife, I'll go next door—the woman there can sing a lot better!" (Aha! So there was such a thing as an African lullaby.) After a few days he came around with a carol. But he was right, it would have been simply unthinkable to sing it in church in those days. First there had to be an awakening of national and ecclesial consciousness.

Now came a whole stack of documents on the subject of inculturation, with an eye especially to Africa. In 1967 Paul VI published *Africae Terrarum*, calling for a mighty ecclesial endeavor that for the first time would be not just centripetal, in terms of an increased emphasis on the African mission itself, but directed without, as well, in the hope of generating a respect for African culture. Two years later this pope made his surprise flight to Uganda, to tell the African church that its hour had come, that it had come of age, and was now a fully responsible, adult church, enjoying equal rights with the rest of the church. "We have no other desire than to strengthen you in what you already are: Christians and Africans. Thus may our pres-ence among you be a token of our acknowledgment of your having reached the age of majority. . . ." In 1974, the synod of bishops met to consider the problems of evangelization in today's world. The African representatives energetically called for an authentic, cultural African church. Paul VI then fully endorsed these aspirations in the final document of the synod, *Evan-gelii Nuntiandi:* inculturation not only may, but ought to occur, and this in the areas of liturgy, theology, and secondary church structures. The wealth of the various cultures demands this, wrote the pope, the peoples expect it, and the church will be the richer for it.

After the end of the synod, the African bishops in attendance published their own particular view. The time of mere accommodation, or adaptation, when only external things like hymns, vestments, and church art were to be adapted to the local or regional culture, was over and gone, they said. The age of the full incarnation of the gospel in African culture was at hand. In 1975, the African Bishops Conference held its meeting, by way of exception, in Rome. The topic was "religio-ecclesial inculturation in Africa." In the same year, an international mission congress was held in Rome, at the Pontifical Urban University, on evangelization and culture, and the addresses delivered there fill three thick volumes. Finally, John Paul II, on his repeated journeys to Africa, has encouraged Africans again and again to appreciate their cultural values, and to build an African church.

What we have in all of these pronouncements is not just concessions or tactics, but a new sense of the breadth of the *Creator Spiritus,* the Spirit of Creation, who "in the beginning" hovered over the waters, converted chaos to cosmos, and caused a plenitude of forms, colors, and species of unimaginable variety. Everywhere we look, if only we stop to look closely, in the world of orchids, butterflies, or seashells, in the macrocosm or the microcosm, we are simply astonished. This same Spirit presided over the birth of the church, allowing itself to be grasped in all tongues, and bestowing upon the apostles the courage to go to the ends of the earth, and to preach the good news to every creature (Mark 16:15). The signature of this creative Spirit is to be read on the good, the true, and the beautiful, wherever these are to be found. How, then, shall we dare to say that it is this Spirit's will that its church, formed of creative men and women, should come off an assembly line in little replicas of itself? How shall we dare insist that the ecclesial form that happened to arise in Roman and Western history is the only valid way of being church today?

A great deal has occurred in Latin America over the last twenty years in the area of the option for the poor. A new age is dawning in Asia—just first light, but real light—in the area of dialogue with the Eastern religions (see the next chapter). So too, after this avalanche of documents and theories on inculturation, especially in Africa, surely it was to be expected that something should happen. A plethora of inculturated forms of being Christian ought to have appeared, in which the Holy Spirit and we could now have our joy.

But we are disappointed. The church of Africa can point to a positive balance on many points: a dynamic growth; powerful, captivating liturgies in the city, in the countryside, and even in the many priestless parishes; the courage to persevere in the midst of the current politico-economic turmoil. But in matters of ecclesial inculturation, we look in vain for a genuine breakthrough. Once more the principle holds: talk is cheap, deeds are dear. There are various reasons for this. First of all, the politico-economic situation has taken the wind out of the sails of all other endeavors. *Primum vivere, deinde philosophari* (First you have to live, then you can philosophize), as ancient Roman wisdom would have it. Or again, *Inter bella silent musae* (In time of war, the Muses are still). Better, headier, more inspiring times must be awaited.

Secondly, Africa comprises at least fifty nations. Within these individual states, tribalism and a clan mentality make a national consciousness difficult to come by. Rarely is a national language spoken; some European language must generally provide the common bond. Major cultural units which might help bring forth an "African" culture are as yet not in place. Modest attempts on the local level fall through, and, much to the dislike of church strategists, each country and clan decides its own "inculturation."

We must cite a third factor. All too many African priests behave like typical yuppies. They attribute enormous importance to their European schooling and living standard, and have no wish to "fall back into the old primitive culture." Of course, genuine inculturation seeks not simply to rescue at all cost folkloristic elements of doubtful value. Genuine inculturation seeks to make of the church of Africa today and tomorrow a genuine "domestic" church, where believers can feel genuinely at home.

As once upon a time a Greco-Romano-Germanic culture plus Christianity yielded the Middle Ages, so in Africa today, Western Christianity and Western technology, plus African culture, must be called upon to produce a new form of religion for the coming Age of Africa. Even a fair number of African bishops seem to love going about in their red robes, being greeted as Excellencies, and living in their fine residences built with contributions from Rome. Theologically they are rather conservative, not yet having experienced a theology of liberation in the company of their people as have many of the bishops of Latin America.

The real obstacle to a concrete liberation, however, comes precisely from Rome. Rome falls all over itself producing documents in favor of inculturation. But the moment it comes down to brass tacks—concrete consequences—it forbids this inculturation. Let a bishop attempt to undertake something for the enhancement of the laity as church, for ecumenism, for the Africanization of the sacraments, and he forthwith receives an admonition through the papal legate. If that has no effect, Rome reduces its financial contribution. And if even that tactic fails, an auxiliary bishop is sent into the breach, someone absolutely loyal to the party line, to see that nothing further goes amiss. This reinforces Rome's identification of unity with uniformity, and cuts all concrete forms of inculturation off at the knees. Nor is it apostolic nuncios alone who keep watch over the maintenance of Roman doctrine and discipline. For some time now, in Abidjan, Kinshasa, and Nairobi, where theological institutions of higher learning are in full operation, and have long been working to develop an African theology, Opus Dei centers have been established, like guard towers in a prison yard.

The inculturation of the African church, then, is transpiring in a climate not of encouragement, but of anxiety. Rome concedes that the questions involved should be investigated and studied. But this is purely a delaying tactic. Woe to the theologian, or even bishop, who decides on anything that is not in complete conformity with universal canon law!

The bishops seem to be bending to Roman pressure. In the 1970s a pastoral dynamic and openness still prevailed, in all of Africa, especially in the region of the East African Bishops Conferences. There was a will to reopen many questions of evangelization, even in the area of African marriage conventions. But at the ninth plenary assembly of the East African Bishops Conferences, held in April 1986, in Moshi, little of this dynamic attitude seemed to remain. It was decided simply to abide by a strict adherence to canonical provisions, as if this would solve the pastoral problems. The committee responsible for the apostolate to the nomads felt this handicap, and, in 1988, submitted an inquiry to scholars and other professionals in Europe whether the polygamous form of marriage practiced among these nomads must really be, for the first generation, an impediment to their baptism.

In October 1985, Father J. Henschel, editor-in-chief of the German mission periodical *Kontinente,* accompanied a camera team from German Television Two to Tanzania to film "Christ was a Massai." One must really keep a sharp eye out in order to catch a glimpse of such occasional strokes of good fortune in the area of inculturation — like the films of Hans Schotte (for example, *How Abraham Lived*), as well. They show how inculturation is actually managed only in secret, at the hands of occasional courageous missionaries and African priests. Father Henschel comments:

> There, missionaries take entirely new approaches to the Christian kerygma — not out of a spirit of frivolity, but out of love and respect for the men and women of another culture, and for love of the good news of Jesus Christ. There, in exemplary fashion, it becomes clear that our good news from God is capable of transcending cultures. In these lands we stand today before a problem like the one that faced the infant church at the apostolic Council of Jerusalem. But our experience today is that no sooner does inculturation reach the limits of simple external adaptation than it is blocked once more, in favor of universality and uniformity. . . .

I have already indicated, in my reflections on the laity and ecumenism, the contrast between theory and praxis. Lovely dissertations are in abundance, but concrete steps are vetoed. The same occurs with inculturation. Are we to acquiesce in such discrepancies, simply out of "loyalty to the church"? To be sure, there are instances in which it would be criminal to apply certain legitimate theoretical research in practice. Von Weizsäcker spoke to this effect as early as 1954, apropos of the atomic bomb:

> [There are cases] in which scientists must actually renounce not only the practical application of their research in certain areas, but the

research itself, in view of the consequences they know would eventually follow upon their discoveries. The nexus between theory and praxis is growing ever closer, ever more inevitable.[1]

But von Weizsäcker is speaking of nuclear physics. His justifiable reluctance to see theory applied to practice has no place in the area of inculturation. On the contrary, African Catholics should be encouraged to create openings, make daring experiments, come up with models of inculturation, even for the sake of the other continental churches, even for the sake of the Protestant churches. As long as the official Catholic church keeps harping on uniformity as the be-all and end-all, there is scant likelihood that Rome will ever accept an ecumenical model of greater breadth of tolerance for other churches. Besides, after all, any narrowness, anything like a spirit of uniformity, is an attempt to narrow the breadth of the *Creator Spiritus*. Narrowness is a sign of human pettiness, and of a lack of faith in divine providence — and yes, of a covert will to power.

Jesus bequeathed to his church very different teachings as to how to conduct its pilgrimage. With the parable of the seed that grew of itself (Mark 4:26–29), Jesus sought to deliver our church from a will to compulsion and constraint, from all "bossiness," from all overestimation of our own importance and corresponding underestimation of the freely developing powers of others. With the parable of the wheat and the weeds (Matt. 13:24–30), he sought to free it as well from a puritanical, and ultimately destructive, fixation on formal purity, and order for the sake of order. "Why have you so little trust?"[2] If Jesus' remonstrance be valid for authority as exercised in local churches — if it serves so aptly as a warning and recommendation to bishops — how much more ought it to be taken to heart by an authority that thinks itself obliged to supervise and regulate everything at a distance of over six thousand miles!

If we are unwilling to be instructed by the gospel, then at least let us learn a lesson from history. M. Hay has convincingly demonstrated how Rome's ill-advised decision against the Chinese rites put an abrupt end to the friendly relations with China that had been built up by the Jesuits at the close of the sixteenth century. The collapse of the mission of the Far East is to be laid to the account, then, not of the bad old world out there, but of the bad old world in here — in the church. That is, it was due to the fact that the Roman curia, with its incompetence, and its false notion of unity, failed to recognize the signs of the times. And so, with an appeal to the Holy Spirit — today we should have to say, with a blasphemous appeal to the Holy Spirit — the curia condemned the methods of the Jesuits. Why? "That God may be glorified in perfect unity of thought and speech."[3] But it is precisely this Roman style of "perfect unity" that was, and is, unworthy of the Holy Spirit. Thank God, in Africa, at the grassroots, in perfect silence, without any shouting from the rooftops, much more is occurring than one might think. Many a remote mission station celebrates one- or two-hour Sunday liturgies without a priest. Many a base community gathers to read holy scripture, pray over it and discuss it, and especially, apply it to life. A great deal happens there that is not always according to Roman rules. People live "under a different sky" out there, and create their own rubrics — rubrics dictated by common sense, approved by God, and in the service of life. It would be interesting to make a systematic tour of parishes like these, and be able to peek at a popular ministry and a popular theology in the making — to see how a twentieth-century Acts of the Apostles and "Fifth Gospel" look.[4] Even the four canonical Gospels express Jesus' single proclamation differently from one another. They were written for different milieus and from different theological positions. Such an "evangeliogenesis" must occur in our time, as well.

Many an African — or European — priest solves his concrete "cases" according to the "rules" of common sense, and with the genuine interest of the persons involved as the prime consideration. He has no wish to go looking for exceptional cases that show the church's rules or law to be unworkable — he takes no pleasure in a tactic of taking advantage of loopholes of the law. He would like to have many of the rules themselves reconsidered, so that solutions could one day be more open and aboveboard. Practically speaking, this could be achieved only in an "African council," in which new formulations would be sought for African premarital regulation, the "matter" of the Eucharist, the function of married parish leaders, and so on.

Given its present mentality, Rome will not be eager to permit an African council. In anticipation of, and preparation for, such a council, then, African theologians might do very well to publish their theological theses in some kind of ordered collection, a *Mysterium Incarnationis* (Mystery of Incarnation), in meaningful sequel to the European cyclopedia *Mysterium Salutis* (Mystery of Salvation) and the comprehensive Latin American *Mysterium Liberationis* (Mystery of Liberation). The African contribution would center on the core Christian mystery of the Incarnation of the Second Person of the Blessed Trinity in Jesus of Nazareth, and draw the appropriate radical conclusions for a genuinely incarnate, inculturated church in Africa.

In the meantime, as we wait with anticipation for a genuinely African council, the only open door will be that of "anticipatory obedience." One does things not currently permitted by human law, but meaningful in themselves, and surely destined for acknowledgment by the legislator when the time is ripe. What else has occurred all through the course of ecclesiastical and secular history? Life is urgent, and blazes its own trails. Law, of its very nature, is static, and adopts life's rules only when it recognizes them through the lens of its own status quo. We have seen examples of this in modern times. In the 1930s, Romano Guardini was already celebrating a new, meaningful German liturgy with his student groups at Rothenfels Castle. A generation later, Vatican II not only permitted this sort of liturgical activity, but established it as the prevailing norm. By way of an even more respectable case of "anticipatory obedience," we might cite that of the future Pope St. Pius X, who, in his younger days, as a pastor in Salzano, found the practice of admitting children to the Eucharist only at the age of twelve to be inconsistent with his conception of Jesus' love for children. And thereupon, on his own responsibility, he began to permit children to receive their first Holy Communion at the age of seven. As providence would have it, Giuseppe Sarto eventually had the opportunity to communicate his successful experiment to the whole church as sovereign pontiff.

I wonder—with great hesitation, but I wonder—whether, at some time, somewhere in Africa (or Latin America) a bishops' conference (if an individual bishop tried this he would at once be removed from office) ought to begin, out of theological conviction and pastoral necessity, to ordain married men to the priesthood, in order no longer to deny parishes their divine right to the Eucharist simply out of consideration for the ecclesiastical law of celibacy. Were I to be asked for my own recommendation in the matter, I should have to respond that no outside instance is in a position to say whether bishops ought to adopt such a practice or not. It is for these bishops alone, were they to reach a two-thirds majority, to make such a decision, on their own responsibility. (If I were present and voting, I should say yes!) And then of course they would have to take all the risks that such a decision might entail. But let Rome take notice that these bishops would only be taking cognizance of their proper responsibility. Whatever the Roman reaction were to be, then, these bishops would be positing a sign, a token of the future, and later times would be grateful to them. If this "trifling" pastoral decision were to entail a schism in its wake, that would be a pity, but the blame would lie with Rome. God forbid there should be any more schisms; but if schisms there must be, then at least let Rome no longer be partly to blame, as it was in the divisions of 1054 and 1517.

The church in India seems recently to have taken an important step in the area of inculturation—concretely, in the direction of a settlement of a recent rites dispute. Since the inauguration of the modern Western mission in India in the sixteenth century, the "Thomas Christians," whose history dates from earliest Christian times, and who worship according to a Syrian rite, were subjected to a despotic Roman tutelage, and had been forced to Latinize their rite. But then, Pope John Paul II, in a letter dated May 28, 1987, acknowledged the equal status of all three rites used in the area: the Latin, the Syro-Malabar, and the Syro-Malenkar. Not that the pope's letter worked any miracles. It established not an objective, normative reform, but merely a jurisdictional, regulatory one, with the great danger that energies will be unduly concentrated in intraecclesial disputes instead of on an inculturation for today and tomorrow in the Indian context and in a spirit of openness to the activity of a Holy Spirit who reaches out beyond the confines of the church. This leads us to a consideration of a further stage of inculturation: not merely external accommodation, and not even merely an incarnation of the church as church in the culture of a given land, but an interpretation of reality outside the church itself, with the church interpreting all questions of world religions, world poverty, world peace, world environment, and so on, as areas of the development of God's salvific plan for the world—interpreting all of this "secular" material as the Reign of God at hand, that Reign of which the church is to be the fertile, mighty seed and credible sign. (I shall have more to say about this in the next chapter).

The Ecumenical Association of Third World Theologians (EATWOT) has understood this. It is very much committed to the interpretation and transformation of earthly realities. If indeed the church is to be a "sign and warranty of salvation for all humankind," then its witness will have to include everything human—everything that should form a world worthy of human beings and of God. From this perspective, "sacristy problems" like communion in the hand, preaching by the laity, clerical attire, or the licitness of spontaneous liturgies, and so on, are not merely ridiculous, but exasperating.

Finally, once more: Is inculturation such an urgent matter only for Africa? Or will it be important in our own lands, as well—in the North? True, our church once became inculturated into the Greco-Romano-Germanic cultural world. So it can be done. But we must all surely admit that it is as yet anything but adequately inculturated into the Western European cultural world of the close of the first millennium. Hence our discomfiture in the presence of so many official church positions and declarations that are simply incompatible with the times.

Old Pope John XXIII, of the youthful spirit, bequeathed the church the charge of an *aggiornamento*. Let the church become current. Let it heed the "signs of the times." Not that it ought blindly to adapt to the world. Its function as cultural critic continues to be incumbent upon it. But neither must it entrench itself in its old positions. In this regard I would like to make some urgent recommendations as a close to this chapter:

1. Our discussion with our secularized world must undergo a complete renovation. Christians alone will be the losers if we fail (see chap. 7, below).

2. On the problem of women in the church, surely we all realize that the attitude of the church, far from being "current," has remained stagnated and medieval, if not indeed ancient (see chap. 1, above).

3. In these times of nuclear and ecological threat, we should adopt new, unconditional ethical priorities. In addition to the traditional Ten Commandments of God, we should declare everything that promotes peace and disarmament, justice and the third world, the environment and an alternative lifestyle, to be eminently Christian behavior. Both dimensions must be taken seriously, of course: the world to come, with its absolute ultimacy, and the temporal world of the present, with its immediate urgency. If the ideal were out of the question, however, and I had to choose, I confess I should prefer those Christians who are powerfully committed to the current

agenda—even if, incidentally, for reasons of their own, they no longer went to church. I had rather cast my lot with them than with those who are faithful to their Sunday obligation but who, for the rest, let the world go its way. Let this not be called horizontalism. In Jesus, God has been revealed as a God concerned for human beings, and Jesus himself will one day bring it to light that what has been done for human beings has been done for himself. The triple agenda cited above—that is, the agenda that furthers peace, justice, and the preservation of the environment—is still promoted largely by persons outside the churches. Thereupon people of the churches hastily dub them "reds" (or "greenies"). The danger is that nineteenth-century history may repeat itself. The condition of the working classes was then largely of concern to those who flew red banners, and the last the churches saw of the labor movement was its rear, scooting ahead to the future. The "conciliar process for justice, peace, and the preservation of creation" offers us one last chance to introduce this agenda in the church.

This necessary process of inculturation should be broached in every parish. Let the church of the hierarchy and the church of the grassroots, the older generation—those partisans of the "good old days"—and the younger, enter into dialogue. Let them attend to this process. Let them get a sense of its existential meaning today. Let the hierarchy and older generation take note that, to the young, with some justification, many Christian traditions have an old-fashioned ring. Let the hierarchy and the grassroots, the old and the young understand that inculturation may well be an inspiration toward a new way of being Christian, an essentially more humane way. Mutual empathy of this sort would be of profit to both "sides." In this way they could draw nearer one another, however gradually, move forward together, and gradually draw a blueprint of church that would still be usable in the third millennium.

6

You Will Acknowledge That the "I Am Here" Is Present among All Peoples

Dialogue with the Religions of Asia

Vatican II opened the church to the laity, to our fellow Christians, to the world, and to non-Christians. It is with the last of these overtures that, quantitatively speaking, we experience the most broadening. Here we are linked with the mass of humanity. In terms of content, it is here that we have the most radical of the council's four conversions to the breadth of God. Almost exactly two-thirds of the human race belong to other religions. They live preponderantly in Asia. In 1985 this colossus of a continent had a population of 2.874 billion human beings. Catholics numbered only 72 million, or 2.5 percent. Were it not for the 46 million Catholics of the Philippines, that number would be only 26 million, or 0.9 percent. Adding in the 24 million non-Catholic Christians of Asia, the figure is still only 1.74 percent.

We dare not ignore such a mighty column of human beings on the march along the highways of history. If we take the human race to be a million years old, then we must say that for 998,000 years women and men wandered over our earth without knowing anything of Christ. It is high time for the church, which has only been an institution, to become an interpretation, and to pronounce a prophetic word of salvation upon this mass of humanity. Besides, our own self-concept is at stake. We can understand ourselves as Christians, and understand Jesus Christ, rightly and wholly only in relation to the whole of humanity.

Unfortunately, we have sought to cast that humanity in very narrow molds. We have styled the Indians of both Americas, the blacks of Africa, and even the peoples of the ancient Asian cultures as heathens, idolaters, and unbelievers, the whole kit and caboodle. Today we have adequate grounds for characterizing them as "believers of other religions."[1] Likewise we have too long thought of ourselves as the chosen people, to the exclusion of other peoples, and our God as the only god. After all, "all the gods of the heathen are nothing" (Ps. 96:5)!

More recently, however, thanks to more thoroughgoing study, we have been struck by the universality of this ethnocentrism of ours. All peoples believe that their land is the center of the earth, and that "their" God, with whom they have struck a special relationship, is mightier than the deities of other tribes and peoples. The notion of "belonging," being a chosen people, then, is not peculiar to the Israelites of old. In other words, our church, like ancient Israel, is guilty of having distorted a theology of election into an ideology of election. Christians can correct this today, by regarding themselves no longer as monopolists, but as models, of election. Our task is to render authentically credible, and historically visible, how much God loves this people that we are. But God, precisely in order to be God, must love all peoples in the same way.[2] Unfortunately, due to our technological superiority, our narrow, European Christian ethnocentrism has had a most oppressive — indeed, downright brutal — effect among other peoples.

Where have we gotten to with the catholicity of our church? Having achieved geographical and cultural catholicity (see chap. 5, above), we have now reached the threshold of a catholicity of salvation history. Now we may joyfully acknowledge that Yahweh, the "I Am Here" whose solemn self-attestation came to the ears of the people of Israel at the foot of Mount Sinai, was also "here" as the first human beings appeared on the face of the earth, and has guided the "chosen" men and women of all religions throughout all of the ensuing hundreds of thousands of years, hence from their first beginnings until today, bestowing on them the gift of the divine favor and love, raising prophets and mystics among them, and granting them the Holy Spirit and inspiration.

This suddenly creates an altogether new relationship with "believers of other religions." Twenty years ago I spoke with missionaries in India who were discouraged that, after such long years of missionary activity, so many Indian men and women were "not yet" in the church. Today we feel blessed in the belief that all men and women are *already* living in the Reign of God, in the favor and love of God. In no other area has theological reflection come as far as it has here. The difference is as day and night. In no other material has postconciliar theology, with the impetus it has received from the council, proceeded as boldly as here. Once more we are shown that we must not simply stop where the council itself left off, but march ahead in the direction the council indicated, attending to the signs of the times and the dictates of common sense.

At this point I should like to examine somewhat more closely the problem of how we are to understand the all-embracing salvific activity of God, indeed of God in Trinity. To this purpose, I shall make no attempt to distinguish among the various non-Christian religions, which, after all, are only historically distinct forms of the human being's basic religious orientation. (Let us only mention in passing that we ought not to let our fascination with the so-called high religions—Hinduism, Buddhism, Islam, and so on—cause us to overlook the more humble, but more ancient, primal religions. On April 27, 1988, the Vatican Secretariat for Non-Christians addressed a letter to the bishops of Africa encouraging them to appoint capable persons, and establish institutes in their schools of theology, to study these primitive religions, from which Christians still tend to show such aversion, and to offer the women and men of these religions both an opportunity for dialogue and a pastoral accompaniment.) Now I should like to make some remarks about our Christian notion of God with reference to the non-Christian religions.

In the area of pneumatology (the doctrine of the Holy Spirit): It is impossible to "overdo" the Holy Spirit. Any narrowness or exclusivity, any fanaticism or condemnation, is not from the Spirit, but from some crimped, crippled human mind. It was the Spirit who wafted over the waters of creation (Gen. 1:2), transforming chaos into cosmos. It came, in countless visitations, to the mighty figures of the Old Testament—judges, generals, prophets, kings—filled them, led them, spoke through them. It "drove" Jesus into the wilderness (Mark 1:12), and Jesus, "filled with the power of the Spirit," returned once more to Galilee (Luke 1:14), inaugurated his mission in the synagogue of Capernaum with an appeal to the great messianic text from Isaiah, "The Spirit of the Lord is upon me" (Luke 4:18), drove out demons "in the Spirit of God" (Matt. 12:28), and was filled with the joy of the Holy Spirit at the revelation of the mysteries of the Reign of God to the humble (Luke 10:21). To his disciples, the men and women who followed him, he promised that the Holy Spirit would speak through them (Matt. 10:20) and lead them to the fullness of truth (John 16:13). On the day of Pentecost, this same Holy Spirit came in fire and storm upon the little band of apostles gathered in the cenacle with Mary, and was "poured out upon all flesh, on sons and daughters, on infants and graybeards" (see Acts 2:1—4:17). It was the Spirit who stood behind the magnanimous decision of the Council of the Apostles to extend the Christian mission to the gentiles: "It has seemed good to the Holy Spirit and to us to lay upon you no further burden . . ." (Acts 15:28). And on almost every page of the Acts of the Apostles the Spirit's mighty works appear. Can we say as well: on almost every page of church history? That is not so clear. On the contrary, solid evidence against such a proposition would seem to abound. At the same time, perhaps we can say that without the governance of the Holy Spirit, the church would long since have disappeared from the pages of history, at the hands of its all too human leadership.

At all events, the new, surprising thing is that we are given to see the work of the Holy Spirit even beyond the confines of the church. This is the teaching not just of a few would-be avant-garde theologians, but of Pope John Paul II himself, who, in two places in his first encyclical, *Redemptor Hominis,* insists that non-Christian religions, too, are the deed of the Holy

Spirit; for the Spirit blows where it will. And he added a further clarification during his trip to Japan in 1981, when he declared to representatives of the Japanese religions:

> I find in the virtues of friendliness and kindness, delicacy, and valor, which are so recommended in your religious traditions, the fruits of that divine Spirit who, according to our faith, is the "kindly Spirit" who "fills the world" and who is "all-embracing" (Wis. 1:6–7). Especially, this same Spirit, in all men, and in all religions, creates that openness to transcendence, that tireless search for God, which can only be interpreted as a response to God's search for man.

Further, in two documents from the Secretariat for Non-Christians—one in 1984 on dialogue and mission and the other in 1989 on dialogue and proclamation—we find long, beautiful texts on the Holy Spirit in the non-Christian religions.

From here it is only a short, logical step to the conclusion that revelation and inspiration are to be found in the holy books of these religions, as well—"only analogously," to be sure, as the theologians would say—not in the same sense in which we find revelation and inspiration in the Old and New Testaments—but they will nonetheless be there. As early as 1974, at a congress in Bangalore, India, theologians developed a convincing presentation of this concept, and suggested in consequence that—after a suitable preparation of the people—some of the most beautiful passages of these non-Christian texts could be used in the liturgy, not in order to replace the Old Testament, but in order to complement it: to make Indian Christians aware that the Spirit of God has loved their people, too, from ancient times, and had been leading them to Christ. The Roman authorities have not been able to bring themselves to accept this view. But the Holy Spirit will defend its "other" scriptures, too, when the time comes!

With regard to christology: The mystery of Christ is simply unmanageable in human categories. If we start with a "low" christology, a christology "from beneath," we are simply dumbfounded that this Jesus of Nazareth, with all his benignity and friendliness, all his consoling teaching about a caring Father in heaven, should have aroused so little response in his auditors. Even his disciples failed to understand, and Jesus sighed, "How long must I be with you? How long shall I have to put up with you?" (Mark 9:21). The religious authorities repeatedly sought to lay hands on him, even attempting to cast him from a cliff, and had no rest until they had him on the cross. This is simply mind-boggling.

But if we make our approach to this Jesus in terms of a "high" christology, a christology "from above," then how are we to conceptualize what John and Paul declare of his preexistence, his condition as Son of God, his universal causality? "In the beginning was the Word; the Word was in God's presence, and the Word was God" (John 1:1). "The real light which gives light to every man was coming into the world..." (John 1:9). "In him everything in heaven and on earth was created.... Through him we have redemption, the forgiveness of our sins" (Col. 1:16, 14). This is simply incomprehensible. We can only stand in awe and believe, surrender to the mystery, and suddenly descry that the mystery of Christ has to do with ourselves — that our "attitude must be that of Christ":

> He humbled himself,
>> obediently accepting even death....
> Because of this,
>> God highly exalted him....
> So that at Jesus' name
>> every knee must bend
>> in the heavens, on the earth,...
>> and every tongue proclaim,...
>> JESUS CHRIST IS LORD! [Phil. 2:8–11].

These propositions, these approaches to what today are called the cosmic dimensions of the mystery of Christ, were later "cut down to size." The Reign of God was confined within the frontiers of the Holy Roman Empire of the German nation, and the *operatio Christi* was limited to the sacraments of the Catholic church: "Outside the church there is no salvation." Instead of a sign of salvation raised over all peoples, the church became the ark of salvation for the redeemed few. Instead of being the visible, privileged, authentic model of God's all-embracing salvific activity, the sacraments became exclusive channels of grace. We had shortened the mighty arm of God. We believed that not even God was capable of saving a dying heathen over whom no human hand had spilled the waters of baptism.

It was high time we subjected all of this narrow-mindedness to an honest, thoroughgoing examination. Karl Rahner and others began to see structures of salvation even in the non-Christian religions, it is true. But they never changed their minds about it being the salvation, the grace, of Christ which had preceded all the missionaries and was present and effective always and everywhere. No one winced, then, at Peter's cry, "There is no salvation in anyone else, for there is no other name in the whole world given to men by which we are to be saved" (Acts 4:12).

More recently, however, even this mainstay of the whole Christian tradition seems to be weakening. It is not only in the Western world that a wave of demythologization has assaulted the erstwhile "essentials of the faith" — Jesus' miracles, his virgin birth, his expiatory death, his bodily resurrection, his divinity, and so on. In Asia, his uniqueness, and consequently his universal significance for salvation, are more and more called in question. At a congress of theologians held in Nagpur, India, in 1974, there was a great deal of insistence that the religions of the East could not be kidnapped in the name of Christ. God has willed these religions for their own sake, and not just "in view of Christ." Western theologians were reproached with seeking to do their theologizing "in blissful ignorance of other religious traditions," and with failing to pay serious enough attention to the rise of the new theological pluralism. Traveling in India in 1980, holding seminars and giving talks from Kashmir to Kerala, I heard, in three different theological institutes of higher learning, from Catholic professors, in the presence of their students, that my talk on the various religions was fine when I stuck to my subject, but that my christology was still strictly traditional, strictly Western, strictly provincial. In a word, I was not sufficiently catholic.

Those who speak in this way recognize the uniqueness of the Logos, the eternal Word of God, the Son of God, *in sese.* But the moment this Logos submits to the conditions of the world and historicity in an avatar, an incarnation, they think the Word can no longer be universal. Now the Logos has been restricted to a particular group in space and time, the objection goes. And so the conclusion is drawn that Christianity, in its historical expression, must no longer contain the only full truth.

In essence, these Indians were advocating a re-envisioning of christological doctrine. Jesus, they would argue, can be understood as the Logos of God incarnate, but the possibility that the Logos had been manifested also in the Buddha, in Krishna, in Zoroaster, and Mohammad should not be rejected on an apriori basis.[3]

Here the question arises: Do such interpretations represent a grand and glorious broadening of our faith in Christ? Or are they only its radical dilution? Are they an epoch-making step in the development of dogma, or the beginning of the end of dogma? We should proceed very cautiously here, and not be swept away by our first reaction. We must not instantly launch into apologetics, defending our old positions like the Western know-it-alls we have so often been seen to be. First we should listen. Then we should engage our interlocutors in a discussion at once both sympathetic and critical. Nor should I wish to give the impression that this is the "new Asian christology." It represents only a series of groping attempts at a new approach to christology. But it is spreading from country to country. Finally, we must not overlook the fact that the Fourth Gospel itself contains certain possible indications of this sort of amplification of the Jesus-event: all who receive the word of God "are gods," have the "power to become the children of God" (John 10:34–35; 1:12).

What we are basically witnessing is something analogous to recent developments in the Christian theology of the inspiration of scripture, to which I have alluded above. We are not concerned to deny that the Old and New Testaments have been inspired by the Holy Spirit (however we may seek to explain the "mechanics" of that inspiration). It is just that we conceive something similar for the sacred books of other religions. So it is in the present case. The point is not to deny Jesus' divinity. The point these Indians make us ask is whether the Logos may well have taken flesh in other religious figures as well.

Might we be able to say, purely in the abstract: this would imply no intrinsic contradiction, were God to have willed it thus? Or must we say that the concept of person, as verified in the Logos, has to do with a being whose very reality is so unique and exclusive that its multiple incarnation would be a metaphysical contradiction? Jesus' unicity, his uniqueness, is not emphasized in the dogmas to the same extent as his condition as Son of God. Is this simply because, in those days, no dialogue with the "pagan" religions existed, so that the question simply never came up? However that may be, today it is a question that can no longer be evaded.

We may follow this development with a certain amount of anxiety, then. Nevertheless, we should encourage Asian theologians and bishops to search for the right path, in common prayer and dialogue. Without painful tensions, the answer will not be forthcoming. By virtue of their office, bishops are more conservative, more cautious, and more responsible, than theologians must be. Also, they are often simply not up-to-date in theology. Hence their frequent mistrust of the "new theology," and their appeals to their own authority when confronted with theological problems. Theologians, on the other hand, likewise by virtue of their calling, go in quest of new responses to the new discoveries of science and to the new questions that arise in human minds. In December 1987 a meeting of forty bishops and theologians was held in Bangalore, India, in order to discuss inculturation of the church in socioeconomic and religio-cultural conditions. At that meeting—which was set up not only to produce documents about inculturation but also to explore implementing inculturation in deed and truth—it was suggested that bishops delegate some of their administrative duties so as to be able to give more time and attention to theological questions. With a view to a better cooperation between bishops and theologians, it was likewise recommended that the two groups continue to hold meetings, annually on a regional basis, and every three years on a national level.

Then, with time, just as an African council might meet to deal with questions of ministry and church discipline, so it would be appropriate to convoke an Asian council to deal with the christological question. The dogmas of the ancient councils, with their Greek philosophy, must be reformulated for Asian reality, and an expression must be found that will safeguard what is essential (Jesus and his Spirit will see to that!) while at the same time echoing God's salvific plan for all humanity.

The mystery of God in Christ cannot be "proved." One can say only that scripture and the church "teach" thus and so. But so far, this is just cold "doctrine." I must dare to make the leap of faith. Whatever direction the development of christology in Asia may take, then, for myself and my faith it is crucial that I not rely on dogmatic formulas to refute my adversaries, but that I profess my faith in such a way that all genuine disciples of Jesus, the women and men who follow him, may make their own free, joyful decision for this discipleship, steep themselves in Jesus' proclamation, and see in him the all but incredible ideal of everything God has willed to bestow on humankind—including God's very self—and all that that humanity can bring forth in the way of goodness, magnanimity, and generosity.

The religions of humankind can be approached in either of two ways. Seen from without—considered from the point of view of religious science—there are various "true religions," and the scholarly observer portrays them, admires them, and studies them, one after another, as equals, even if that observer be inclined as a Christian to grant that Christianity stands as historically the strongest and (prescinding from its distortions, and attending to its sources, Jesus and the gospel) most ideal of them all. (Of course, a Muslim will doubtless come to different conclusions.) But in an observer's role, one does not reach the innermost core of religion, any more than an outside observer might do justice to the protestations and experiences of two lovers. Of its very essence, religion is a matter not of objectivity, or of science, but of faith, of astonishment, of total identification.

"From the inside," then, for me as a Christian, with my existential orientation to Jesus and his gospel, there is only one true religion, and I live and profess that religion. No one can know any religion in its inmost depth without having affirmed it, said "yes" to it, from within, with ultimate existential passion.

> Only when a religion has become *my* religion does a conversation about its truth acquire a depth of passion. When I speak of "truth," then, I am speaking of my faith, just as for a Jew or a Muslim Judaism or Islam, for a Hindu or a Buddhist Hinduism or Buddhism, is that person's religion, that person's faith, and thereby indeed the "truth." What is at stake in my religion, or anyone else's religion, is not general truth, but an existential truth [Hans Küng].

With this attitude, Christians and representatives of other religions can meet together and maintain a dialogue—that is, respect one another's personal conviction, profess and report their own faith experiences, pray and live with one another, complement and enrich one another, and, especially, deal with one another for the good of all human beings.[4]

Then what are we Christians to do? The answer might be formulated in three words:

Evangelize: Proclaim throughout the world the "good news" of the all-embracing love of God for all human beings, as Jesus has taught us that love.

"Shalomize": Not just speak of God's love, but render it empirical, by reaching out to believers of other religions for the sake of a better world.

Christianize: Whether and to what extent we are to undertake this third element—making Christians of people by baptism—is a question whose answer will depend on God alone. We need not agonize about it, then. But the "thirst for souls" that once drove missionaries to the ends of the earth (otherwise those souls would be lost!) is no longer justifiable, however evangelicals may continue to strive to keep their baptismal statistics abreast of the population explosion. On the other hand, the right to change religions is guaranteed by the right of religious freedom, and the church continues to enjoy the right to attract disciples, for love of Jesus, for love of human beings, and thus for the enhanced performance of its task in the world.

While we European and North American Christians are enmeshed in an intra-ecclesial dispute over intercommunion, the corresponding question that has arisen in Asia is the urgent one of extending eucharistic hospitality to non-Christians. In India, for example, many Hindus read the Gospels, love Jesus, and are convinced disciples of Jesus in practice. A recent survey in Madras revealed that 60 percent of the Hindus living there believe in the resurrection of Jesus, but for socio-historical reasons are unable to surrender their ties to Hinduism and join the "Western" church. Would it be unthinkable to admit these persons to the Eucharist? In January 1988 a seminar was held in Bangalore on the self-image of the church in the religious pluralism of India. According to the eight-hundred-page report published by that seminar, the vast majority of those participating believed that the doors to the Upper Room must stand open for these persons.[5] Such intercommunion, it was observed, is actually practiced, occasionally and surreptitiously. Of course, the participants knew that neither the Catholic Bishops Conference of India, nor, surely, Rome, would accept their recommendation. Still, it is useful to toss such bold ideas into the wind, since situations like these compel us to re-think the relationship of Jesus to the church and to the whole human race. Must the church really be a practically insurmountable hurdle to Jesus, one which the majority of human beings are simply unable to leap? Or should the church simply open the way to that Jesus?

In the area of theology: finally—in just the opposite order from the one usually followed in the theology of the Trinity—we arrive at a consideration of God as Father. We ought to call such a consideration, "patrology." But this term has been preempted by the theology of the Fathers of the church, and so we cannot use it for the theology of God the Father. And so I shall dub the latter simply theology—theology in the stricter sense, the doctrine of God.

Christ, the Logos, entered into Jesus of Nazareth and his church in a limited historical space. Subsequently, however, this horizon extended beyond the furthest reaches of the universe, to plunge into that unbounded, uncreated, unfathomable mystery we call God. As Christians, we profess this deity not only in its timeless divine essence, but also as "maker of heaven and earth," and especially, of humankind. Even today, we do not know the precise manner of the genesis of the human being upon earth. But whenever and wherever it happened that certain sentient beings became women and men—came to self-awareness, and thus to questions of whence, wherefore, and whither, with a surmise as to an ultimate mystery wafting over and permeating their lives—in any event God was already there from the first, as the "I Am Here" of Exodus 3:14, accepting these women and men. And they took this God as their God. This so-called covenant of creation was never abrogated. The subsequent covenants, with Abraham, Moses, and Jesus, only ratified, clarified, and fulfilled it. It is still in effect today.

Geographical and linguistic distances resulted in human beings' naming and revering their "own" respective gods: practical polytheism. Today, then, we may posit this theological interpretation and proposition: Whenever and wherever men and women have prayed to "their" God, the one and only existing God has heard and accepted their prayer. There can be only one Transcendence. Under the thousand names of God, then—Mungu, Nzambi, or Lesa in Africa, Allah, Brahman, or Kame in Asia—we may understand one and the same God. I have sought to convey this in my book *All Have the Same God.*

Of course, the representations of God cultivated by different peoples will not be carbon copies of one another. Theology is always accompanied by a hefty admixture of the temporal and the historical. No individual, nor any people, has ever fully grasped and comprehensively defined God. There is always the stammering and the patchwork. Today we observe that, due to Christian influence, even in the Asian religions, in which God and the All have always tended to be identified, the concept of God is gradually coming to include that of Person and Parent.[6] How wonderful it would be were this process to continue, so that not only the representation of a Father, but that of Jesus' *Abba,* "Papa, Daddy," would become part and parcel of the religions of Asia. Joachim Jeremias has written of Jesus' word *Abba* that it launched the historical revolution called Christianity. Might that revolution ever spread to the point of becoming worldwide?

With this overview of the God and Father of all human beings, we come once more to the first eleven chapters of Genesis, in which the word *Adam,* "human being," occurs 539 times in the collective sense of the whole of humanity. Throughout those hundreds of thousands of years, God has been "making history," divine history, with the whole of humanity. Today we acknowledge this all-encompassing love of God for all persons and peoples. We Christians, as God's "chosen people," as the model of what a people of God ought to be, must then have the task of fostering the concept of the unity of all peoples by every means. It would be our task to attempt to carry this concept to its ultimate consequences. Today, for weal or woe, the human race is destined for unity. One way or another, we shall strike a universal fellowship of brothers and sisters, unless we simply wish to go up in nuclear smoke together. We are condemned to unity. But what is more, we are called to unity, by the saving plan of one and the same God and Father.

How fine a thing it would be, then, were the theologians of Asia to publish a *Mysterium Revelationis* (The Mystery of Revelation) — a series of studies developing the cosmic dimension of the entire revelation-event, and setting in perspective the meaning of the non-Christian religions vis-à-vis Christianity. Such a universal overview could then function as the basis for an official Christian recognition of the "larger ecumenical phenomenon." Then, just as all of the Christian churches should gather around Jesus Christ in a Second Council of Jerusalem, to acknowledge one another as the one church of Christ in the multiplicity of ecclesial traditions, so also should the various religions of the world gather in a First Council of Hebron, at the graveside of Abraham, the "father of all believers" (Rom. 4:16), to acknowledge one another, gathered around the mystery of God, as together constituting the one world religion in a multiplicity of religious traditions. Then the "Cosmic Grail" of the Austrian architect Clemens Holzmeister could at last be erected somewhere — eight circular chapels, each representing one of the great world religions, ringing a central sanctuary accessible from each of the chapels and thus available for common prayer as occasion might suggest.

How utopian! What music of the spheres for the third millennium! Actually, of course, even the preliminary step of an ecumenical day of prayer for peace in Assisi in 1986 was scored as an outrage, a scandal, indeed a betrayal of the faith, by Archbishop Lefebvre and other fundamentalists. Yet Christians had not prayed together there, but only met together. After separate gatherings in the morning, all came together in the afternoon and each prayed in succession. However, if we suspect that representatives of the other religions, too, might hesitate at common prayer, let us remind ourselves that, as early as March 1970, at the first meeting between the World Council of Churches and representatives of other religions, in Ajaaltoun, near Beirut, on the evening of the first day none other than a Muslim from India asked why the participants should only discuss their religions, and not pray together as well. Thereupon it became clear that the Muslims had the least hesitation at implementing such a suggestion. Then the Hindus and Buddhists joined in. Some Christians at first doubted whether they might permit themselves this latitude, but others agreed, and on the last day of the conference, in the presentation of the summaries, the participants unanimously agreed that it had been in this common act of prayer, regardless of who might have been leading it, that they had most clearly felt their human bonds and their common situation before and in God. Since then, at so many meetings like this one, including more modest ones, believers have lived, eaten, spoken of their holy books — and prayed — together.

Why not another Peace Day, then, at Assisi, at which the actual leaders of the world religions, with one mind and heart, would pray together: for example, the Christian Our Father, the Jewish Twenty-Third Psalm ("The Lord is my shepherd, nothing shall I want . . . "), the first Sura of the Koran ("Praise to God, the Lord of humankind throughout the earth, the merciful, the good . . . "), and something from the Vedas ("From the unreal lead me to the Real, from darkness to Light, from death to Immortality . . . ")?

Surely Jesus would be there too, rejoicing to see so many children of his Father gathered in praise, thanksgiving, and supplication. What a great leap forward in salvation history! The "I Am Here" would now be acknowledged as the God of all peoples. Now God would deliver the "chosen people," become the whole of humanity, from servitude and lead them to a land flowing with milk and honey, to rule over them in justice and peace (see Exod. 3:8). Such occasions would have a ripple effect, like pebbles dropped into a pond, to create ever-widening circles of the good news of God's universal favor and love, even to the ends of the earth.

The heart of many a Christian will leap high at such a thought. But others, in dismay, will ask: "Where have we come to? Have we any identity left? We have opened ourselves to non-Christians; well and good. But in so doing, have we not simply surrendered everything we had?" Such questions must be taken seriously. At least it was easy, however un-Christian, to portray our fellow believers as our enemies, wall ourselves off from them, exalt ourselves, and damn the rest. And it remains an important task, even in community with all the other churches and religions, to restate our own identity. The two above-mentioned documents from the Roman Secretariat for Non-Christians, of 1984 and 1989, will be of help to us in doing so.

First and foremost we must think through the relationship between the church and the Reign of God, and be ready to accept all of the consequences. Too long had the church absolutized itself. It was exaggeratedly ecclesiocentric. It would have liked to see the whole of history converge on the aggrandizement of the church. We may catch a glimpse of this mentality even, for example, in the architecture and appointments of our baroque churches. In the new theology, the accent visibly shifts from ecclesiology to christology, to pneumatology, and "patrology." Now humanity, split and shattered in the ecclesiocentric worldview, can find its way to unity, in a theocentric worldview. Now the church exists no longer for itself, but for the world. Now the church is a "sign and promise of salvation to all men" (*Lumen Gentium,* no. 5), or, in other words—again the words of the council—the "germ and commencement of the Reign of God" (ibid., no. 9). Jesus speaks of the Reign of God in forty-two places in the New Testament, but of the church only twice. The church is the historical precursor, founded by Jesus but molded by human beings, of the eschatological Reign of God. The Reign is definitive, eschatological, and the pure gift of a bountiful God to beloved human creatures. In the consummation of all—beginning with each individual's death—God will astound us with the Reign. But God wills that the divine love be effective beforehand, even now—not by way of awesome divine interventions, but by way of awe-inspiring contributions on the part of women and men surprised by love. Now the church— the church that is ourselves!—must enter the service of the Reign of God, see its identity in a context of that Reign, and for Jesus' sake take over the function of vanguard, of special escort, of inspiration, in this endless caravan of humanity on its journey through history.

This sign, this seed, of the salvation that is the Reign will have a twofold task: (1) to awaken faith in the definitive promise, to strengthen hope in the goal; and (2) to make the journey itself, this sojourn on earth, a lovelier thing for all—to practice better politics, then, better economics, to be a pioneer of the demands of justice, peace, and the preservation of creation, and to this purpose to take bolder initiatives and carry them through with more perseverance and confidence. This "new identity" is fascinating. It will demand very much—so much that we shall never "have" it, but only be able to seek it, continuously, and seek to improve it. In the fall of 1987 the (Catholic) Association of Bishops Conferences and the (Protestant) Christian Conference of Asia held a joint conference in Singapore which they called "Living and Working with Sisters and Brothers of Other Religions." The participants were aware that the churches in Asia must meet the challenge of the other religions together, and that this must transpire no longer simply on a theoretical, other-worldly, theological level, but in the concrete defeat of the problems of that continent—poverty and exploitation, war and oppression, overpopulation and ecological destruction. A response to this great question was found in the principle that all religions have their place in God's salvific plan, and that all should work together as equal partners on their pilgrimage to the future Reign of God, to the emolument of all human beings. Here again is a shift from old struggles for positions and prestige to a new behavior on behalf of justice and progress, from orthodoxy at any price to orthopraxis at any price, not suppressing orthodoxy, but only pressing it forward to credibility.[7] Meetings like this one reveal that something is happening in the church. Someone has caught a glimpse of the signs of the times. A new day of interchurch and interreligious ecumenism is dawning. We are on our way to a catholicity of salvation history. We are drawing nearer to the breadth of God.

This brings us to the important question: Will this new salvific optimism in Asia bring anything to light for Europe and North America? Europe is on the point of becoming a mission continent once more. Are we simply to stand by and watch this happen? Or are we still in a position to rise to the occasion, and be a missionary church all the more energetically, scattering the good news of salvation to every corner of this unsaved world? It will be worthwhile to examine this question. We shall see an answer, and gain an impulse, in the following pages. Shall we manage a resurrection from our hopelessness?

7

You Will Accompany Religious Nomads

Secularization in Euramerica

It is difficult to say anything about the situation of Euramerica (Europe and North America) that will be valid across the board. This is precisely what is typical about that situation: it no longer represents the closed, sealed "Christian West" of history. Developments in the Soviet Union and Central Europe make us aware that the problem of spiritual emptiness is acute also there. But the loosening of antireligious barriers against the churches' free operation do not seem to lead people automatically to seek their spiritual nurture in the churches. The chance that secularization and a relegation of the church to minority status will proceed much as it has in Western Europe cannot be discounted.

As Delumeau has taught us, we must not idealize the Middle Ages with their religious ignorance, fears, and superstition, while we wring our hands over the religious situation of today. God was not as near in those days, he says, nor as far from us today, as we often think. There is no denying a religious crisis. Church attendance, vocations to the priesthood and religious life, and the influence of the churches on societal events are on the decline. From 1959 until his death, Karl Rahner never tired of reminding us Christians that we are on the threshold of a worldwide diaspora. There are no Christian countries left today, he said. Sociologically, the churches are more and more like a sect, a little remnant. "We have not yet gotten over the dream of a homogeneous Christian West." But we must awaken from this dream, and come to realize that we can no longer count on a guaranteed growth for Christianity. By contrast, an elective Christianity offers a new pastoral opportunity.[1]

Over the years, we have managed neither to reverse this trend, nor adequately to exploit the opportunities it offers. Analysts confirm this on all sides. In 1987, the Franciscan mission headquarters in Bonn held a meeting of confreres from far and wide, at which, on the subject of the regional churches of Europe, the following conclusion was reached:

The *Volkskirche* [the hereditary, cultural church] is on the point of collapse — even, more recently, in the countryside. No account is taken of this in pastoral structures. . . . Many no longer trust the church very far where human or social questions are concerned. A mistrust "from above" has generated a mistrust "from below." The church has all sorts of prefabricated answers at the ready, but has largely lost its competency in the area of the questions. Questions that are uppermost in people's minds either are not addressed at all, or are addressed inappropriately, for example in the domain of sexuality. Traditional parishes and church officials are an obstacle here. This brings up the question of training. Should training for the ministry not be completely revised? Ministerial formation is still too priesthood-oriented. . . . [2]

How many parents — and not just Sunday Christians, either, but good Christians, good human beings — complain that, once their sons and daughters reach their teen years, they refuse to go to church. Not the least of the reasons the youngsters give for this is peer pressure. They are unwilling to be ridiculed for being the only ones "still going." Former bishop of Strasbourg L. A. Elchinger, pondering a number of phenomena of this nature, wondered aloud whether perhaps the problem we face here might be analogous to that of environmental pollution. Perhaps the air and the soil that ought to be nourishing faith are poisoned. Could the church be sowing its seed on concrete?[3]

The situation of the church has changed basically over the last twenty years. The phenomenon is a worldwide one. The world can no longer be divided into the traditional categories of "church" over here and "missions" over there. What we have today is a church on six continents (our erstwhile missions have become independent, full-fledged churches) and a mission on six continents (on every continent, even in Europe, the church finds itself in a missionary condition once more). Indeed, Europe has become the most difficult of all the mission lands.

But is this not precisely an opportunity of sorts? Minority status is not necessarily such a bad starting position for Christian life. On the contrary, perhaps more strength can be mobilized in this kind of situation than in the old, massive church, where people grew fat and inert from Christian satiation. There is a lesson to be learned from the early church, where the little Christian communities survived all obstacles and spread nonetheless. We learn it from today's young churches, too, "our former missions," which have generally constituted the most dynamic part of the church in the past and still do today, so that we borrow from them more and more for appropriate pastoral initiatives in our ecclesial perplexity. Not that we should idealize either the early church or today's young churches. All history communicates to us the sober insight that the church is ever the people of God *in via,* covered with sweat and dust and sin. But faith reveals to us, behind or within this human misery and wretchedness, the mystery of church, and gives us the courage, even in a situation of minority status, not to fall victim to a minority complex, but only to become all the more active.

Now let us examine the phenomenon of secularization in Euramerica a bit more closely. It is occurring in three stages. Let us note in passing that in the United States, that most progressive country in the world, religion has been more tenacious than in Europe, and currently seems to be on the threshold of a lively development, however little liking we might have for some of the proselytizing methods employed. At all events, according to a Gallup poll, one-third of Americans claim to have experienced a personal religious renewal over the past few years.

Here it will be important to attend very closely to what we might call the "Christian substance." We hear so much today of vitamins. These chemicals occur only in small quantities, provide no nourishment, furnish no energy, and yet are necessary for the smooth functioning of the living organism. Similarly, with persons whom we so often "write off" ecclesially just because they make no palpable contribution to the institutional church, there is usually more in the way of hidden Christian substance than we might think.

Again ecclesially speaking, we can divide people roughly into two classes: churchgoers and nonchurchgoers—those committed to a church in some way, and those who have nothing to do with church. In the United States, the latter are called the "unchurched"—persons who belong to no church, and have no wish to belong to one.

As regards the Catholic church in particular, the first category could be subdivided in turn into three groups. The members of the first subgroup might be called the conservatives. These churchgoers accept the council's new overtures only with reservations, perhaps even regarding them as unhealthy. Their allegiance is to the official church and to the pope, and they will promptly denounce to Rome or to the local bishop any priest or lay person who does not behave strictly in accordance with canon law. These Catholics are to be respected. They are acting in accordance with their conscience. They think they have to do what they do, in order to rescue the church from shipwreck. Of course, they represent a model of church accepted only by Christians who have as narrow a vision as themselves.

A second group of churchgoers is made up of average Catholics, still faithful to their Sunday obligation and making some effort to lead a Christian life during the week. These are the silent majority. They suffer in silence as they watch the foundations of their church crumbling away and their young people thinking and living entirely differently from themselves. These Catholics are to be encouraged in their fidelity to the church and their trust in God.

A third group of churchgoers consists of those active Christians who sit on the parish councils, serve on the various committees, and belong to the various associations. They bring life to the parish, or, in some cases, to a base community. They are signs of hope. The more we suffer at the hands of church structures, the more we can rejoice at such glimmers of new, genuine religiousness at the base; in the midst of a winter of the church, we can reflect upon these glimmers of hope and then with Eugen Biser speak of a "faith-swerve"; under the snow-covered fields and frozen lakes we feel the stirring of strong, new life. In all three groups, then, we can find a corresponding measure of Christian substance—never chemically pure, of course, and always mixed with humanness and fragility.

So it is with the second category, as well, the "unchurched," secularized men and women who, depending on where we live, make up 50 percent, 70 percent, or 90 percent of our neighbors. Even here we may still encounter Christian substance. The unchurched say they are unwilling to have anything more to do with the church, which they generally identify with its structures. They believe they can live just as well, or better, without the church. I like to call such persons religious nomads. They have abandoned the sedentary church, but have certainly not become "godless." They find it fascinating to "go it alone" now along the pathways of their religious life. They prefer the life of the pioneer. We must not write them off. We must accompany them on their journey, and discover in them the hidden buds of Christian substance. The church is also, and mainly, for them, if it means indeed to be a "sign and promise of salvation for all."

Here again, among the unchurched, we find three subgroups in relation to the Catholic church. The first consists of those who have had unpleasant experiences with a pastor, who are annoyed with certain "pious" folk, or who have been alienated by Roman decrees and attitudes. They have turned their backs on the church, in some instances even formally and explicitly. "Jesus yes, church no," they say. They may read the Gospels, meet with like-minded Christian persons, and basically seek to be good persons. It is they, and their growing numbers, especially among the young, who inspire B. Stähelin to say: "The most religious, and the most unconfessional, of ages is under way." We must take account of this corps of religious persons, take seriously their reasons for leaving the church, see them as a challenge that leads to our own examination of conscience, and not condemn them. Otherwise we should be like the disciples who told Jesus: " 'Teacher, we saw a man using your name to expel demons and we tried to stop him because he is not of our company.' Jesus said in reply: 'Do not try to stop him. . . . Anyone who is not against us is with us' " (Mark 9:38–40).

We might designate a second subgroup of the unchurched by the chameleon word "esoteric." The word could refer to a perfectly legitimate introduction, reserved to a select few, into the mystery of God. The esoteric way is accessible only to the initiate, only to an inner circle of adepts. There is no reason to reject this understanding out of hand—Jesus remains the Way, the Way into the mystery of God: "No one comes to the Father but by me" (John 14:6). However, that is not the sense of the word that I am intending here. Rather, I am using the word in its more modern sense: today the word has come to denote a whole spectrum of practices calculated to impart a secret religious or quasi-religious knowledge—which is of course reserved only to a kind of elite—instead of a knowledge grounded ultimately in the free love of God for all human beings. The "esoteric" today is concretized in names and concepts like Transcendental Meditation, reincarnation, spiritism, astrology, New Age, age of Aquarius, and so on. It is also called the new religiousness, and these religious or quasi-religious movements astonish us, appearing everywhere around us with their promises of a secret meaning in reality, in life. It would take a whole library to present all their aspects. A plethora of books, periodicals, and public events is available for our instruction. Evidently these movements respond to powerful, unslaked longings in human beings of today. We cannot simply condemn them out of hand. At the same time, we can scarcely simply approve them. Here is a mighty challenge to Christians. We are challenged to practice a discernment of spirits, to enter into dialogue, to be willing to learn, and especially, to demonstrate, with credibility, the Christian alternative. If we demonstrate the viability and attractiveness of life in the "New Covenant," perhaps seekers will no longer feel the need to fly, in ennui or panic, to the "New Age."[4]

The third subgroup of the unchurched, whom we call "atheists," seem entirely bereft of Christian substance, that relic of prescientific times. We find the classic atheists in the Communist states of the Eastern bloc. But they circulate in the Western world, as well, and in droves. Here, they present themselves as agnostics, and practical atheists. Christianity has regarded them as its black sheep—they personify the incomprehensible. How can anyone be so myopic, so blind, so limited, as to fail to descry the mystery of God in creation, or in Christian history? What must such persons be looking for, when they dare to rise up against their God? And we can only think of Lucifer's cry, his company, and his fate. "I will not serve!"

Today we begin to feel a kind of sympathy even with these atheists. First of all we must surely say that there simply are no "textbook atheists"—atheists in the sense in which we used to find them in our lists of theological "adversaries"—just as there were no "heathen" in the sense in which they were defined in the old lexicons: "those who know nothing of God." Surely we shall find no atheists who, if they are honest, will deny wondering now and then about the ultimate meaning of human seeking and sighing, loving and living. If it is understandable that we Christians should feel doubts of faith within us from time to time, the thinking atheist, too, will occasionally doubt his or her position.

We can no longer condemn such persons for failing in religious practice. We must judge them on the basis of their conscience. Or rather, we must leave that judgment to God. But God will take them seriously as human beings. God will judge them on the basis of their ultimate conscientious decision. Despite all, they belong to the human race, to the "race and family of Jesus." Not infrequently, they lead exemplary lives. Today we must admit, not invidiously, but joyfully, that holiness is as ubiquitous as sin, within church structures as without. To be sure, secularization effects the decay of many a Christian value. But it also creates and fosters new values and forms — those of a profound, lived, implicit Christianity — like love, trust, hope, responsibility, generosity, solidarity, and commitment to justice, peace, and the environment. Anyone acquainted with such people knows that many of them are full of religious questions, and people who know these atheists cannot understand why priests spend all their time talking to nice, affable Christians, instead of engaging those others, as well, in religious discussions: "What if there's no God? What if there's a God?"[5]

The conciliar document *Gaudium et Spes* (The Pastoral Constitution on the Church in the Modern World) has brought forth such marvelous fruit in Latin America. *Unitatis Redintegratio,* the document on ecumenism, has done the same in Africa, as has *Nostra Aetate* in the area of the relationship between the church and the non-Christian religions. So too in Europe, I believe, the council's final decree, *Dignitatis Humanae,* on freedom of religion and conscience, will yet produce far-reaching results. That decree declares human beings' proper worth to consist in this: that they are not the simple executors of orders of other instances, but "possess their own judgment and a responsible freedom in their actions, and should make use of these." Thus "no one can legitimately be compelled to act against his conscience, or prevented from acting in accordance with the same," especially in religious matters (*Dignitatis Humanae,* nos. 1–3). In his proclamation on the occasion of the World Peace Day proclaimed by the Catholic church for January 1, 1988, Pope John Paul II insisted that the right to religious freedom is a right invested in all religions, as well as in atheism itself. We used to say that only truth had rights. Thus it was observed, with satisfaction, that, in this proclamation, the pope had made the transition from an objective to a personalist ethics.

For a theological reflection in depth on the question of the right of conscience, we may once more consult Karl Rahner. There is no such thing, Rahner explains, as a human being of good will who would be bereft of all experience of God. Wherever any human being freely accomplishes an ultimate, radical self-fulfillment, making a selfless commitment to any person or cause, we may take it that this has occurred in the Holy Spirit and in grace, in the kiss of a mystical rapture, however unaware the person in question may be that this is the case. Rahner writes of an "everyday mysticism," then, and concludes that "the one we call God, as infinite offer, as silent love, as absolute future, is already present, indeed already accepted, wherever any human being, in response to the call of conscience, bursts the prison walls of his or her selfishness."[6]

Thus, even among atheists, we find a surprising quantity of Christian substance, and this gives us the right to hope that sooner or later they will come to a better knowledge of themselves. The critique of religion lodged by Feuerbach, Marx, and Hegel is no longer valid. It is refuted on the inner, psychological level, and so Heinrich Lübbe can posit his thesis: "The illusion has proved to be not religion, but the theory of religion that regarded it as such."[7] Even the outward, sociological aspects of religion would teach Marx better today. In his day, Marx indeed knew a religion that was simply the ratification of "order" — the reinforcement of antidemocratic monarchies and exploitative capitalism. Even the Eastern-bloc ministries of worship have gradually come to the realization, first of all, that it has been impossible to uproot religion "on schedule," and second, that consequently, religious citizens should be shown tolerance, so long as they collaborate loyally with the socialist state.

The Gorbachev era has brought this budding insight into full bloom, though developments, it must be confessed, are ambiguous as we head into the 1990s. The Russian Orthodox church, for instance, is experiencing rebirth. But it appears increasingly true that ultraconservative, antisemitic elements seek to hijack the resurgence of religion for their own ends. The year 1988 clearly marked a turning point, and matters have only accelerated since then. For example, in 1988 Soviet television broadcast the Orthodox Easter liturgy for the first time, and with a sympathetic commentary. Again, to mark the one-thousandth anniversary of the Christianization of *Rus'*, old Russia, the Soviet party chief received Russian Orthodox patriarch Pimen, taking the occasion, according to the papers, to express his regret over earlier persecutions of the church and referring to them, verbatim, as "tragic events." Since then the Soviet leader has gone on to insist, on repeated occasions, on the equality of atheists and believers and on the importance of according believers full civil rights. Raissa Gorbachev, wife of the chairman, joined high-ranking politicians at the millenary celebration. The Western world, especially, noted with interest that the party chief and head of the Soviet state received Vatican secretary of state Cardinal Agostino Casaroli for quite a lengthy conversation.

The good news may continue. According to reports, Raissa Gorbachev is going to publish a book on Russian spirituality. In 1988 and in subsequent years the pope's traditional Christmas message has been carried on Soviet television. Then in December 1989 Mikhail Gorbachev made his historic visit to the Vatican, where he met with Pope John Paul II. And so on.

And we can go on and cite other examples: In September 1988, Konstantin Kharchev, president of the Religious Affairs Council of the U.S.S.R., paid a visit to the World Council of Churches in Geneva and reported the establishment of four hundred new parishes in the Soviet Union since the turn of the year. A new religious code was in preparation, he stated, and would provide for juridical recognition of the various churches. Soviet television regularly carries discussions of religious and church questions, in which one hears things like, "We shouldn't have fought the churches. They're part of our cultural heritage." A state exhibition in Leningrad commemorating the destruction of churches in the Soviet Union was called: "Our Sorrow and Shame." And the list goes on.

China had had a change of heart even sooner even if events from June 1989 through Spring 1990 show exactly how precarious such gains may be and how easily they can be reversed. The new Constitution of 1982 recognizes the five great religions of China: Islam, Buddhism, Taoism, Protestantism, and Catholicism. Each of these is declared to represent a particular pedagogical doctrine and lofty morality, and thereby to be of utility to society. The number of Christians in China is increasing at a rate twice that of the general population.[8]

This is all wonderful news. Ultimately it expresses a new attitude on the part of the Communist powers concerned — an attitude of good common sense, which has thus managed to carry the day over the narrow-mindedness of prevailing ideologies. But surely we may also be allowed to see here the fruit of so many prayers for the conversion of Russia. Nor must we forget the prayers of Gorbachev's mother, who, according to reliable reports, is a believer, attends church every Sunday, and sells votive lamps there, to be placed before the icons of Our Lord and the saints. Each year her son travels the nine hundred miles to Stavropol to visit her on her birthday. The individual is helpless before the ossified structures of the world and the church. But there is One mightier than the individual — the Holy Spirit, who has power to conquer the hearts of those we regard as powerful, and thus to change the very structures of power.

Secularization, we see, has lost some of its horror. Even in secularized persons we discover a considerable measure of humanity, or on a deeper level, of Christian substance — buried, but not altogether crushed. It will be well worth the effort to uncover it, to heal it, and to make its vessels, along with ourselves, more aware of it.

Then where are we with the Christian hope of salvation? We Christians, at any rate we who are loyal to the church, are obviously becoming a minority. Two-thirds of humanity is non-Christian, and at least two-thirds of baptized Christians no longer attend church. Must we continue to rend our garments at the sight of these latter, label them rebels, threaten them with God's judgment?

In the preceding chapter, we came to the realization that we need no longer regard the "heathen" as idolaters and unbelievers — that they, too, live in the favor and love of God. Now, may we not dare to regard this liberating overture of salvation, this light dawning over the erstwhile "heathen," as beaming upon our secularized fellow-mortals as well — not only see the traditional "heathen," then, but these "neoheathen," as well, from a new viewpoint? Before we plan any pastoral activity in their regard, let us find a new theological, prophetic interpretation of them. Otherwise our attempts to approach them will be without interior sympathy, and will backfire. Obviously we must not burst through their door with the question of their eternal salvation on our lips. Before we speak of that, we should first, very earnestly, and perhaps at length, converse with them over worldly salvation, that of themselves and of all humanity. But the moment will come when we must not gloss over the other question, either. Then let us not hesitate or fall silent. Otherwise we shall be guilty of unfaithfulness toward these very persons. For we shall have betrayed their deepest hopes and expectations.

I should really like to regard, then, the secularized, of every hue, as enfolded in the all-embracing, anticipating, incomprehensible, utterly effective love of God. After all, the concept of God's mercy belongs to the core teaching of the Old and New Testaments. Again and again we read, in the Psalms: "The earth is full of the mercy of God. . . . The mercy of God abides forever. . . . As far as the sun moves and the clouds go, so far does God's mercy extend. . . . " And then let us think of the parables of the lost sheep or the prodigal child, and the stubborn insistence that Jesus' blood was "shed for all" (Matt. 26:28); that "God our savior . . . wants all persons to be saved. . . . Christ Jesus . . . gave himself as a ransom for all" (1 Tim. 2:4, 6). And: "All persons have sinned and are deprived of the glory of God. All are now undeservedly justified by the gift of God, through the redemption wrought in Christ Jesus" (Rom. 3:23–24). May we not take such texts at their word? We hear them again and again in the liturgy. Will God, too, be guilty of that fatal gap between documents and praxis?

On the basis of biblical statements like these, I make bold to propose the following theses. Those who call themselves godless are not thereby rid of God. Nor are even they who "give up on God" thereby given up on by God. No one can fall so low as to fall from God's love. Thus I should credit God with the capacity for the ways and means, somehow, to gather up and lead home all human creatures. Mothers worthy of the name understand this attitude. Neither do they give up on their children, even when the latter have "gone wrong." They seek to understand them, excuse them, give them a new chance. If human beings are capable of this unshakable love, will God not be capable of this and even more?

We *need* not accept this hope of universal salvation, but we *may* accept it, and we have good biblical grounds for doing so, so long as we do not take out of context biblical assertions to the contrary but hold to the core of the biblical teaching. Not that we can ever have a certainty of salvation, a guarantee of salvation, or, surely, a claim on salvation. Our ultimate destiny is as yet undecided. We are still under the judgment of God. And so the threatening passages in the Bible, too, are valid. They are for our instruction. They are there as salutary warnings. Nevertheless we may, and should, hope and pray that the God who wishes to save all human beings will actually do so. In this hope of ours we posit an act of a Christian virtue, precisely the virtue of hope.[9]

Thus we may confidently defend and proclaim this salvific hope—which is not the same as a naive salvific optimism—not as an encouragement to sin, of course, but rather as an encouragement to myself, to all women and men, to atheists themselves, to remain confident despite sin, which, after all, we do not wish to commit, but which nevertheless we do commit (see Rom. 7:16). We have always spoken of God's universal salvific will. Henceforth let us also confidently think of God's universal salvific deed.

There are a number of steps in the Christian osmosis. Let us be honest enough to call the latter by its name—proclamation, kerygma—and ask: Are we permitted to rest content with "still" going to church and saving our souls, and leaving our secularized fellow human beings by the wayside? But have we not just come to the consoling realization that we may leave them to the mercy of God? Or instead, are we challenged not just to keep sitting in a sedentary church, but to wander forth with these "religious nomads," accompany them on their way, be for them, even in this life, signs of the all-encompassing grace and love of God? How might this be done? The Symposium of the European Bishops Conference, meeting in Rome, on two occasions, once in 1982 and again in 1985, dealt with "Europe as a mission land," but did not actually do anything about that situation concretely. Not that we ought to plan a frontal assault on these "godless," or somehow imagine that we might "get them back to church" in droves. Rather we ought to make them offers, send signals, create a climate of fellowship in humanity and thereby of God's love for humankind, and, throughout, make these persons aware of the ultimate questions, the questions that bear on the meaning of life, and help them answer them. In a word, we should stop being passive, consumer Christians, as we were brought up to be, and start being active, mission Christians, as Vatican II asked all in the church to be.

The actual problem, then, lies not with the masses of "unchurched," but with ourselves, the minority loyal to the church. We must ask ourselves whether we shall manage, through our presence and behavior, to be for these others both question marks and exclamation points, whether we shall develop a proecology, prohuman pastoral ministry. A church that gives prefabricated answers to questions that have become nonquestions, but knows or dares no satisfactory answers to the questions of today, will have no success. A church authority that does nothing but repeat its condemnations of divorce, abortion, the "pill," homosexuality, and trial marriages will have been of no help whatever to the many who find themselves facing these issues and situations. In Dortmund, two Franciscans, together with a group of laity, lead a "Catholic Forum for Questioners and Seekers." The forum is a meeting place for people in search of something, who would like to have a new orientation, who no longer feel at home in the church, who want to experience faith more in depth. The members of the audience are intentionally not referred to as having "left the church." Who has "left" whom? Perhaps it is the church that has "left" the seekers. Various formats are offered, for example, a Friday forum with a tape, a talk on some current subject with a discussion, or a thought-provoking slide show. The four hundred to six hundred participants attend two evening sessions as the high point of their introductory week, and then select their method of continuation. There should be something like this in every city.

The decisive thing in Christian outreach has always been a testimony in love and life on the part of Christians, parishes, small groups, and individual families. Are these individuals and groups really stamped by a commandment by which they may be recognized? A new commandment I give to you, that you love one another; even as I have loved you, that you also love one another. By this all will know that you are my disciples, if you have love for one another" (John 13:34–35). Does Christian outreach really bear the mark of the parable of the good Samaritan, who, unlike the priest and the Levite, who continued on their way, stopped to care for the poor, wounded victim lying by the side of the road and even spent his money on him (Luke 10:30–37)? Let Christians be genuinely marked with the example of Jesus himself, who washed his disciples' feet and then said: "Do you know what I have done to you? . . . If I then, your Lord and Teacher, have washed your feet, you also ought to wash one another's feet" (John 13:12–14). Jesus is not simply "suggesting" this single commandment of love—simply offering an "evangelical counsel." He is enjoining it upon us as a strict imperative. The Greek word *opheilete* has only one meaning: "You ought, you must, you are obliged." For disciples of Jesus, then, there is no shilly-shallying, no alibi! Were Christians actually to perform this service of the washing of the feet more credibly—in appropriate service in their dealings with one another, with other churches, with other continents—doubtless many "religious nomads" would feel something like a nostalgia for a church like that.

True, people who live a life this radically evangelical are not the rule, but the exception. This is as true today as it was in the days of the infant church. Further, they are likely to be misunderstood and ridiculed in certain circles. The people crowded around Jesus because of his message and his cures, but his reputation among his relatives was something else again. They came and tried to take him home "by force, saying to one another: 'He's out of his mind! He's crazy!' " (see Mark 3:20). Francis of Assisi's nickname was "Il Pazzo," the "Crazy One." And yet Jesus and Francis have been the model and inspiration of so many, that, today, the best Christians actually function as a kind of "contrast society" (G. Lohfink), and show many others a way of escape from the absurdity and meaninglessness of their daily round.

Certain occasions are particularly appropriate for sending signals, for broadcasting waves of the Christian proclamation, simply in hopes that they will be received by someone's antenna somewhere. There are funerals, for example, which for many people are the only time they come to church. There is Christmas, when, despite the commercial bustle, so many things—the lighted streets, the Christmas trees in the squares, the carols on the radio, the people on their way to midnight Mass—create a certain mood, and stir memories and longings. And so on.

Even the various kinds of base communities should not close themselves off. They should become more and more a place for the unchurched. In the "neocatechumenal groups" in Rome, for example, I have heard that, on the average, one-third of those involved had not gone to church for years, until a friend invited them to visit one of the groups and they discovered fellowship and joy—in a church such as they had never known.

Again, religious bookstores, Catholic and Protestant alike, attract the unchurched in astonishing numbers. A survey taken in Germany revealed that, of 3 million regular clients, 800,000 were without church affiliation; of 3.7 million occasional clients, 1.5 million were not affiliated with a church. The personnel in these establishments would do well to be aware of this opportunity, so that they can stand at these persons' side with both professional competence and Christian understanding.

8

You Will Swell the Ranks of the Peacemakers

Justice and Peace

"Blessed are the peacemakers; they shall be called children of God" (Matt. 5:9). Like any of the rest of us, Jesus knew from experience that human beings, narrow-minded, stubborn creatures that they are, are constantly ensnared in hostilities, strife, and war. And he discerned by intuition that to live in peace, to establish peace, can be the gift only of God. Those who succeed in this, then, show themselves as the daughters and sons of God. And Jesus regarded it as one of his disciples' most important tasks to bring peace to a world without peace. "When you enter a house, first say: 'Peace be to this house' " (Luke 10:5). Today, of course, it is no longer enough simply to communicate a cheerful, serene atmosphere by our presence, in an idyllic visit to a family. We must carry this peace into the hard, brutal structures of the world, and not merely passively, by refraining from disturbing peace, but actively, by establishing peace, by creating peace, not just as meteorologists forecast probable developments, but actually by causing peace, "making" peace.

Peace, well-being, *shalom* in the biblical sense of the word, embrace all that human beings most deeply long for: health, prosperity, joy, and fulfillment, now and hereafter. In today's atmosphere of the constant threat of war, peace especially means the absence of war, and concretely a defusing of the East-West conflict with its baneful influence on the world politics of the postwar decades.

No sooner had the fires of World War II been quenched and the rubble of bombed-out cities cleared away, than the erstwhile partners against the common enemy, whose marriage of convenience had suddenly become a struggle for politico-economic world hegemony, began stockpiling weapons for a possible World War III. World War III, of course, would in all probability be the last, since the peoples of East and West alike would be so shattered and crushed that survivors would have basically lost both the desire and the strength for any more wars. Despite their peoples' humble standard of living, the nations of the Eastern bloc threw themselves into the weapons race with such wholehearted fervor that they surpassed the conventional land, sea, and air forces of the NATO countries. Events occuring in winter and spring 1990 make the days of that cold war seem distant, indeed. Nevertheless, the upsurge of ethnic hostilities and regional conflicts throughout a formerly quiescent "Eastbloc" reminds one daily of the sort of rivalries that have led to a host of wars since 1517, especially since 1914. The demonstrated willingness of nations to use chemical weapons in the Iran-Iraq war shows, too, that the downturn in East-West conflict may not portend a less dangerous world.

No one can guarantee that a nuclear strike will not occur. Anything human beings can do, they might. It could actually happen that what the Americans call "overkill"—letting fly with several times the fire power needed to annihilate an enemy—will become sheer reality. After all, with their fifty thousand nuclear warheads—packing *in toto* a million times the power of the bomb that destroyed Hiroshima—the Soviet Union and the United States could destroy each other thirty times over. As if once were not more than enough!

Realism is a plus when it comes to ethics. Pope Pius XII in his celebrated Christmas address of 1941, and then John XXIII in *Pacem in Terris,* as well as Vatican II in *Gaudium et Spes* (nos. 79–82), and finally, Popes Paul VI and John Paul II in their addresses, especially to the United Nations, have condemned war in no uncertain terms, summoning the world to negotiations based on trust, treaties, and mutual verification. In view of the monstrous commitment of countries large and small, rich and poor, north and south to conventional weaponry, and the even more monstrous potential for annihilation residing in biological, chemical, and nuclear weapons, the traditional "just war" doctrine has become questionable in the extreme. As for the use of nuclear weapons, this is clearly impermissible in itself. But does not the rumored proliferation of nuclear weapons to nations such as Israel, South Africa, Iraq, India, Pakistan, and Brazil lead to completely incalculable threats of war? Everything possible must be undertaken to dismantle this apocalyptic situation as quickly as possible. Those who cannot accept this compromise formula should make courageous use of their right to freedom of conscience and oppose the armament machinery more radically, by all responsible means, as the U.S. bishops recommend in their pastoral letter *The Challenge of Peace.*

While there may still be some hope that humanity will not be so foolish as to start World War III, the deadly flurry of small wars continues unabated. The International Institute for Peace Research in Stockholm has calculated that, in 1986, thirty states were directly involved in wars or armed conflicts, and that the cost of these wars in human lives was some three to five million human beings. With the exception of Northern Ireland, all of these states were beyond the borders of Europe, this is true. But the first and third worlds are responsible for them as long as we grow rich and fat on the filthy business of arms exports, without which these "little wars" would quickly run out of steam. Also, the majority of these conflicts are so-called wars by proxy and "low intensity" conflicts to wear down nations such as Nicaragua where the superpowers test their weapons and stake out their spheres of influence at the expense of the small powers that actually do the fighting and dying.

Here too, we must finally have disarmament instead of armed conflict, bilateral negotiations instead of bilateral shooting, and not just a moratorium on stockpiling but a disarmament contest. The Roman maxim *Si vis pacem, para bellum* (If you will have peace, prepare for war) has been given the lie a hundred times over. Might it not be worth it to try out the other possibility: prepare for peace? Again, Lorenz von Stein's motto, "A people unwilling to maintain its own armed forces will be constrained to maintain those of the enemy," collapses in the face of an ever-growing peace movement. Governments today are faced with their peoples' declared will for peace. An organized earthquake of public opinion must now shake the world. A little over a hundred years ago, slavery was finally recognized as incompatible with human dignity, and abolished. So today, the time is rapidly approaching when the people themselves will no longer accept military "solutions," and will boycott the armament industry. The principle of non-violence and the spirit of the Sermon on the Mount are on the point of becoming incontrovertible postulates of practical politics.

Stop being so "idealistic," we are told. The arms industry provides employment and income. In the spring of 1988, the Federal Republic of Germany decided to invest $22 billion in two hundred European jet fighters for the 1990s, and justified its decision by pointing to the 25,000 jobs this would create. When will prophets arise who will persuade our peoples to convert the military-industrial complex from the manufacture of the weapons of death to the production of the necessities of life, at a decent profit for themselves and the incalculable good of the third world? Then the vicious circle of armament will have burst, that $22 billion in public investment will still be making money, and all the lovely words about world solidarity will have been translated into deeds.

Christians, precisely, on the basis of the gospel, should be cooperating in all efforts to build peace, and should be assuming a dynamic leadership role in the peace movements. But here we come up against the paradox of the so-called right-wing Catholics, who mount such energetic campaigns against abortion, but have no problem with a ballooning military budget, while those on the left hold their protest marches against the arms race, while generously tolerating abortion. Neither position is logical. If you are for life and against violence, you should be consistently for life and against violence. Until now, all revolutions have been violent revolutions. When will we have a nonviolent revolution, a revolution of love? The time is right.

This is the message of the Sermon on the Mount in the nuclear age.[1]

The conflict between East and West was waged not only in the form of military standoffs, but in the area of human rights as well. The East was accused of violating human rights, and was surely guilty, from the gulags of yesterday to more recent forms of persecution of dissidents, which, we may be thankful, seems to be currently abating. But are the West's hands so very clean? In 1988, the fortieth anniversary of the Universal Declaration of Human Rights, Amnesty International reported that, in eighty to ninety states in East, West, and South, men and women who express their convictions openly are not only arrested, but tortured. In many countries, "undesirable citizens" are kidnapped and killed, with the death squads that commit these murders often acting in collaboration with government troops.

It is a matter of human rights to refuse military service for reasons of conscience. Vatican Council II tells us that, in concrete political questions, it is often possible, on perfectly reasonable grounds, to come to any of a number of different conclusions (*Gaudium et Spes,* no. 43). Thus, those who serve in the military for the defense of their country are not necessarily poor Christians; nor is someone who refuses to serve in the military on grounds of conscience necessarily a poor citizen. Fourteen European states still imprison those who refuse military service, including Switzerland, the "model state." In a 1984 referendum, the Swiss government proposed a bill that would have offered conscientious objectors alternative civil service. All three state churches urged the adoption of the measure. It was precisely the Catholic cantons that rejected it, and they rejected it massively. Apparently if you are brought up with a particular concrete attitude on a moral question, you cannot allow others to abide by their conscience, even if your church tells you that you should.

Every citizen, and every Christian, is permitted to express his or her conscientious objection in deed and not merely in word. We may not only teach the healing power of nonviolence, but live it, as well.[2] The Roman Congregation for the Doctrine of the Faith has announced that it is preparing a document to address this question. Generally speaking, it ought to be left to Christians and their individual conscience to give their altogether concrete answers to altogether concrete questions. Let us honestly admit that in our church, too, human rights, or in this case let us say Christian rights, have not been adequately respected. Leonardo Boff has clearly demonstrated this in his *Church: Charism and Power.* It is also abundantly shown in my *Dreaming of the Church.* Just as I have often pointed to a gap between documents and deeds, so Boff speaks of the tension between "proclamation" and "realization" in the area of justice. It is not a matter simply of the shortcomings of individuals, he explains. It is a state of affairs stemming from the system itself, from the image of the church that has been passed on to us, from the authoritarianism of feudal times. The Roman curia is like the headquarters of a giant multinational corporation, he goes on, and the dioceses are like branch offices that merely implement the decisions of the main office, all of the officers practicing obsequious obedience in the hope of furthering their careers.

In the 1971 synod, which convened to address the problems of justice in the world, the bishops had the courage to broaden the question to include that of justice in the church. They observed that a great deal was left to be desired in this area: inadequate wages and salaries for lay employees, especially women; unfair procedures in ecclesiastical courts; an inadequate opportunity on the part of the church at large to participate in church decisions. Concretely, the synod recommended the appointment of a mixed commission to study the question of justice in the church. Many years have elapsed since this proposal was made. That study has not yet been commissioned. The system is not going to slit its own throat. The Symposium of the African Bishops Conferences, in a seminar held in Rome in 1988 on justice and peace, with an eye as well to Rome as to the dioceses, rightly formulated the desideratum as follows: the church must "be not only an agent of justice, but also be seen to be just." In other words, the church should not simply demand justice of others, but, above all, demonstrate its own justice.

To return to the East-West conflict: The rather ambiguous diagnosis I gave above took a sudden turn for the better with the spring 1985 election of Mikhail Gorbachev to the post of First Secretary of the Communist Party of the Soviet Union. For years this intelligent, bold, and clear-sighted theoretician and tactician had been acting as the mouthpiece of a new guard, gradually filling so many influential positions with his own people that eventually his election to the top Soviet post was a foregone conclusion. In March 1990, he succeeded in changing the Soviet Constitution to wrest control of the Soviet state from the Communist Party. While that could only be cheered, its ambiguity was revealed in the lack of ultimate accountability of the new presidency to voters, parliament, and independent courts of law.

Gorbachev set forth his ready analyses from the first party meeting onward, castigating the crusty apparatus that had done such harm to domestic democracy and economic prosperity at home by refusing to tolerate any new blood in the higher echelons, a repressive administrative system plagued with all manner of dogmatism and bureaucracy.[3]

No one, surely, is in a position to say what further developments the coming years will bring in Soviet affairs. If Western press reports are to be believed, Gorbachev's strategy is coming under increasing criticism, and obstructionism is becoming an ever greater danger. Still, the Soviet Union's many peace initiatives must be appreciated. We need only mention the sensational address of December 7, 1988, in which Gorbachev announced his readiness to reduce the Red Army by 500,000 persons, convert two weapons plants to civilian manufacture, and grant third world countries a prolonged respite on their debt.

In the area of international security, he expressed his proposals even more promptly, publishing a remarkable paper on the occasion of the meeting of the U.N. General Assembly in 1987.[4] The world has come to an absurd impasse, he writes. The only way out of it will be to cease to regard power and prestige as nonnegotiable commodities, and give the norms of common sense the status of political principles. Present efforts to scrap nuclear weapons have just begun, he goes on. Nuclear weaponry must be reduced not to 50 percent of the current levels, or to 5 percent, but to 0 percent. And then, in this qualitatively new situation of stability, it will be possible to secure the peace, "through measures based on trust and international cooperation in all areas." He declared himself prepared to dismantle the Soviet advantage in conventional weaponry, and to use the monies saved for the development of poor countries, together with long-term expenditures for environmental protection. He urged the establishment of a world council, under the auspices of the United Nations, to be composed of the world's intellectual elite—scientists, politicians, cultural figures, and church dignitaries—who would reflect on the future of humanity.

> We can talk all we want about the need for ending the arms race, eliminating militarism, and initiating an era of international cooperation—but unless we begin to act, nothing will change.... The solution to this political and moral problem will be found only in a new atmosphere of mutual trust among states and peoples, and in respect for international agreements and institutions.... This notion of a comprehensive security system will be the first draft of a possible new way of life in our common house, earth—a test printing of our passport to the future.

And ever since, on frequent occasions and in even clearer terms, he has reiterated all of these same ideas.

Gorbachev has doggedly sought to communicate these ideas to the West as well. After the two meetings with President Reagan, in Geneva in 1985 and in Reykjavík in 1986, pressure was put on the stalled SALT talks, and agreement in principle was quickly reached on the elimination of medium-range missiles, to be signed in Washington on December 8, 1987. To be sure, only 3 percent of the total nuclear arsenal was involved. But it was a beginning. It was disarming instead of arming further. And the six thousand journalists covering the story trumpeted to the world: "Washington Miracle ... Historic Milestone ..." World consciousness heaved a sign of relief over this partial agreement. Would wiser heads at last prevail? The fourth summit conference, in Moscow in 1988, added nothing in terms of concrete progress, but it did create a favorable climate for further negotiations. Speaking within the very walls of the Kremlin, Reagan in 1988 declared that he no longer regarded the Soviet Union as the "Evil Empire." And in his farewell response to Gorbachev's address he said: "We think of you as friends. We feel a great friendship for you and your people." In December 1989 this climate of dialogue yielded the Malta "minisummit" between Gorbachev and President Bush. At the end of the meetings President Bush proclaimed: "We stand at the threshold of a whole new era of U.S.-Soviet relations."

In this new climate, even the regional trouble spots of the world—the "wars by proxy"—one after another, have quieted down, although a full solution will require a great deal of patience and continued goodwill on all sides. In the spirit of enlightened self-interest, the parties concerned have finally come to see that shifting the cold war into the third world is simply unprofitable. It costs more than it brings in. And so, in 1988, things happened that no one would have thought possible: a troop withdrawal from Afghanistan, a cease-fire in the Gulf war, positive negotiations in Angola and Namibia, in Mozambique, in Nicaragua, in Kampuchea, and so on. And these trends have only accelerated in the years since 1988.

It has long been feared that Mikhail Gorbachev would be unable to maintain his position and get his reforms through. So many Soviet reforms have already seen shipwreck on the shoals of the Soviet establishment—the some 400,000 elite who occupy the top posts in the party, the government, the military, the administration, and science, and who connive with one another to maintain all privileges intact. Will these echelons now simply let *perestroika* ride over them roughshod?

During the meeting of the central committee in February 1990, Gorbachev's reforms—particularly those that helped bring about the momentous changes in the Eastern bloc and those that would allow a multiparty system in the Soviet Union—once again came under fire. And yet, again, Gorbachev was able to maintain his power and initiate new reforms. Now the problem is with the intermediate cadres—the 18 million privileged citizens who will not just lie down and die with the opening onslaughts, and may yet boycott many elements of the projected renewal. This explains why Gorbachev's first priority, economic recovery, has not yet made itself felt, and why the people are gradually becoming disillusioned with *perestroika.* Let us hope that time will be on Gorbachev's side.

And the reaction of the West, or at least of typical voices in the West? By and large, perplexity, astonishment, and mistrust. The Russian bear is treacherous, we hear, and so it's best to be prudent and wary, and not impetuously start spending "peace dividends" on social programs. People find it simply impossible to imagine a world without "the enemy" somewhere. Certain newspapers tirelessly cite Moscow's enhanced capabilities for an invasion, and its psychological war of false information. The Soviet Union is hellbent on victory, just as in the past, we are told—only, this time, it intends to win without the trouble of going to war. The real question, however, is whether we are willing to remain caught in the prevailing impasse, based on total mutual mistrust, or rather operate on a new basis of trust—with bilateral controls—and welcome and endorse Gorbachev's vision. Meanwhile, the West has no political figures of Gorbachev's quality, stature, and dynamism, who might join him in his march to the future.

After his visit to Moscow on the occasion of the celebration of a thousand years of Christianity in Russia, Cardinal Franz König of Vienna endorsed efforts for further progress, encouraging trust and confidence. Another witness — scarcely a Communist sympathizer — Bavarian Premier Franz Josef Strauss, wrote, after his talks in Moscow at the end of 1987:

> If the Soviet Union is prepared to continue along this new route of disarmament, and especially if it makes good on its announced withdrawal from Afghanistan, then we stand at a turning point for humanity. We stand at the beginning of a springtime of the peoples such as humanity in this or any other century has never seen. . . .
>
> There was agreement that war can and must no longer be used as a tool of politics in our times. There was agreement that historical developments and decisions can and must be taken no longer at the barricades of revolution or on the battlefields of war, but in scientific and technological development, and in economic competition. This broad agreement, and especially my personal impression of General Secretary Gorbachev, have made me more confident that we are indeed on the threshold of a new political age, an age no longer under the rule of Mars, the god of war, but of Mercury, the god of commerce and economics.[5]

Many of us today are simply astonished at this phenomenon of a Gorbachev. We feel a sympathetic reaction to him. He has reintroduced movement into the stagnation of world politics. His new ideas and initiatives take us by surprise ever and again. I would go so far as to dare to imagine God addressing the following words to Gorbachev: "I have called you by name, even if you know me not. I know you, and I am using you to implement my plan for humanity."

I first expressed my positive appraisal of the Gorbachev phenomenon in September 1987, at a meeting for high school religion teachers from all over West Germany, held in Limburg/Lahn. Afterwards the person in charge of the meeting told me privately that he regarded my view as premature. I answered that this was what I liked to do — keep ahead of things a bit, and not wait until they become obvious to come out and say them; and I think events since 1987 — both those inside the Soviet Union and those in the Warsaw Pact nations — have more than borne out my optimism.

A number of times in this book I have called for prophets — people who will leave the beaten path and attempt to introduce some change into our petrified structures. In Mikhail Gorbachev, a political prophet has apparently arisen who inspires us with hope that the unhappy East-West conflict is now at an end, that war will be banned for good and all, and that thus we shall "beat our swords into plowshares" (see Isa. 2:4). Thirty years ago a prophet arose in the church — one John XXIII, who, like Gorbachev, used a special word to designate what he foresaw and strove for. He called for an *aggiornamento,* a "today-ing," an updating, of the church. He was expressing the same hope for the church as *glasnost* and *perestroika* express for the state. He too used the comparison of opening windows as if to air a stuffy room. Specifically, he sought to further his plans for reform through the convocation of Vatican Council II. Now would be the perfect time for an economic prophet to arise somewhere in a Western industrialized nation and introduce some movement into the structures of world trade. This could resolve the North-South conflict as well.

Then the threshold of the third millennium could well be the threshold of a new phase in history. Then would the visions of Isaiah, the promises of Marx, the expectations of all humanity, all become reality. That God would call a pioneer like Gorbachev precisely from a system and an ideology where this sort of prophet would least be expected to arise ought to give Christian politicians pause. Has a secularized person not outstripped them in their efforts to achieve good? Why not? God's ways are inscrutable, and our God is the God of all the world. The secularized world is not the devil's after all!

If we speak of peace, and cite the Gorbachev-event in that connection, we must not omit mention of little Francis of Assisi (1182–1226), who not only lived a heavenly peace with God, but radiated a paradise of peace all around, creating it with his spontaneous initiatives and enchanting power — peace with creation, calling the sun and moon, water and fire, flowers and trees, birds and lambs, "brother" and "sister," and taming the ravenous wolf of Gubbio; peace with the outcast, in a life of solidarity with the poor, as he bore bread and wine to the robbers in the forest so that they would no longer have to steal, embracing lepers and caring for them; peace with enemies, strictly forbidding all who wished to live in his spirit to bear arms, and actually paying a visit to the archenemy of Christianity, the Sultan al-Kamil, who had laid siege to the crusaders in Egypt and sought to crush them there — actually striking a friendship with him, the first Christian ever to have encountered him not as an enemy but as a brother. Francis also showed respect for the dignity and freedom of conscience of each and every individual. When good Brother Leo said to him, "Brother Francis, you are very ill. Tell me what I am to do after your death," he did not enjoin him this or that, but simply prescribed: "In whatever way seems to you most likely to please the Lord God, do, with God's blessing and in obedience to me." All these ideas and attitudes of Francis had the effect of promoting a nonviolent revolution in his day, and they are still completely "up-to-date" in our own.

The Franciscan movement seeks to achieve its contribution to peace today in the spirit of its founder. Several years ago, the International Peace Center in Assisi sent delegations to Moscow and Washington, respectively, with a message to the current leadership of these superpowers and an invitation to a meet in Assisi. In November 1987, the same center launched another peace campaign, sending delegations of three or four men and women apiece to the capitals of Europe and conveying to the governments there a message of peace from the city of Saint Francis. Thereupon, from August 6 to 12, 1988, in Assisi, a meeting was held of over six hundred representatives from Christian groups in Europe committed to justice, peace, and the environment—to pray, to study the Bible, and thereby to contribute to the postconciliar process a project of spiritual preparation and accompaniment, while contributing as well to the ecumenical endeavors of the World Convocation on Justice, Peace, and the Integrity of Creation.

I earnestly endorse the words of Reinhold Schneider, who calls Francis the Western Christian par excellence, and who believes:

> This saint's hour has returned, and perhaps in a still higher and more proper sense than of old. . . . In this question [of the proscription of bearing arms] I incline to this most humble, and—for me—most exalted, authority to have appeared in postapostolic times. That authority has higher standing with me than all of the attenuations propounded since then by a suspect "radicalism."[6]

All who love Francis will swell the ranks of the peacemakers, then, to stride from dreams and "ifs" and "buts" to deeds. They will no longer cast their eyes heavenwards and dreamily say: "If Jesus were alive on earth today, things would be more peaceful here below." For Jesus lived in Francis, and brought us peace through him. Nor let us say any longer: "If Francis were alive today, we should be living as brothers and sisters in our land." For Francis is alive—in you and me. Let us reach out a hand to one another, and to all who live together on the face of our earth.

9

You Will Make the Earth a Paradise

Ecology and Eschatology

The beginning and end of each of our lives lie largely shrouded from us—in unfathomable wisdom God mysteriously cloaks our beginning and end in our unconscious. The newborn infant awakens to the brightness of consciousness only gradually. And when we come to die, we usually fall back into the dark of unconsciousness before the final moment. It is as if the human being encountered the properly human not as his or her own doing, but as God's gift and surprise.

Of the beginning and end of the world, too—of protology and eschatology—we know precious little. With all our science, we are still speechless in this area. We can speak only in mythological language here. Thus, working from some ingenious sketches in the Bible and from our own daydreams, we project that the beginning of all was a paradise. This paradise, as human beings have so long imagined it, simply never existed. The appearance of the first human beings on earth was far more humble, vague, and unsensational than this. Yahweh's promises to the people of God, and thereby to the whole of humanity, were calculated to appeal not to a vain nostalgia for a return to a lost paradise, but to the accomplishment of the coming paradise—the messianic age of peace, prosperity, a ripe old age, bountiful harvests, and an abundance of children, together with a creation so harmonious that calves would graze with lions, and children and serpents would play together in peace.

Whether this will occur in history, or only in a new heaven and on a new earth—in the world beyond history—remains shrouded in the mists of uncertainty even today. On the basis of Jesus' words to the good thief, "Today you will be with me in paradise" (Luke 23:43), Christian tradition has tended to locate "paradise" primarily in the world to come, and has sung, at once in sorrow and hope, in the Liturgy of the Departed: "May the angels lead you to paradise. . . ." But Christian theology and spirituality today prefer an "anticipated eschatology": the actualization of our present

124

hope does not exclude hope in an absolute future in and with God "in heaven," but is to be an anticipatory experience of the same, and thereby one which precisely endows it with credibility.[1]

Following upon the apocalyptic experience of World War II, especially that of the atom bombs that burst over Hiroshima and Nagasaki, the soaring hopes of the early postwar decades—that humankind would build a world of freedom, prosperity, and boundless progress for all peoples—gave way only too soon to shock and disillusionment. Humanity is scarcely reeling in an orgy of prosperity. We are more like someone waking from a beautiful dream and standing before the ruins of the Tower of Babel. Obviously we had thought we could "get away with something." We had set our sights exclusively on material prosperity. However, in the West our materialism-in-practice has been no more noble than the materialism practiced under the Communist ideology. We forgot that the human being does not live by bread alone—that we are not only an *ens sociale,* a social being, an *ens oeconomicum,* an economic being, and an *ens technicum,* a technological being, but an *ens mysticum,* a mystical being, a spiritual being, as well, a being whose orientation is toward God, on the basis of our most profound constitution. And so, in biblical categories, God has intervened to bring human beings to their senses once more.

One of the alarms that stirred us to a rude awakening was the publication in 1972 of a report by the Club of Rome. Earlier, in 1960, J. Walter Thompson had explained that Americans would have to increase their consumption by $16 billion every year in order to maintain their rate of production—with human beings in the service of the economy, then, rather than the other way around. But in the 1972 report we heard that we were destroying our biosphere, in which we live and breathe—that we were hacking to pieces the raft on which we were floating through the universe:

> If the current increase in world population, industrialization, pollution of the environment, and exhaustion of our raw materials continues, we shall suddenly find ourselves faced with our absolute growth limit, and shall have to accept catastrophic restrictions on our lifestyle simply in order to survive.[2]

Since then, Cassandra's cries have grown in both number and volume. "If we go on living for the next thirty years as we have for the last thirty, we shall be digging our children's mass grave" (Roger Garaudy). "Only if we are pessimistic enough to recognize the entire extent of the danger, shall we have the slightest chance of averting it" (W. Röpke).

We are waging a reckless war of conquest against a nature we have disarmed. We are exhausting in decades what it has taken nature millions of years to construct. Our forests are dying. The desert is encroaching everywhere. Our air is being contaminated. Our waters are turning to sewers. Technological humanity's total war on nature is ending in its own complete self-annihilation [H. Gruhl].

People in coming centuries will wipe out more and more plant and animal species, and finally exterminate themselves from the face of the planet they have devastated [T. Löbsack].

We might add F. Renner's definition of "postfuturology": the science of life on earth after the death of humanity.

The mounting quantities of gases poured into the air by factories, automobiles, aircraft, and heating installations create acid rain, which—together with the fertilization of farmland with hog manure and chemical poisons—is killing off our lakes along with their fish. In some countries, purification plants have been of moderate help, but the situation is far from in hand. For some years now the dramatic new catastrophe lurking in the wings has been the death of our forests, with a consequent erosion of the soil so that the land no longer stores up rainfall, and flooding occurs; further, when the forests disappear there is nothing left to contain the snowpacks, and avalanches occur which threaten the existence of whole villages. In a short while we shall be speaking of the death of the soil. Earth, humus, is not just "dirt." Soil is a unique miracle of creation. In a handful of earth, we learn, a gigantic host of living beings is at work—mites, microbes, bacteria—a magnificent biochemical factory which helps the grasses and other vegetation, the flowers and trees, to transform inorganic materials into organic ones. If this countless host of unsalaried proletariat are now to be killed off with poison rain, what will be left will indeed be only dirt—lifeless, sterile dirt. We already observe the bitter result in terms of human mortality. Responsible physicians are sounding the alarm: we are seeing an increase in cases of cancer, anemia, emphysema, and birth defects. Even buildings and monuments that have survived for centuries are now being pitted and eaten away. The Cologne cathedral, for example, has undergone more decay in the last thirty years than in the previous three hundred. As early as 1985, the Federal Republic of Germany invested 10 percent of its gross national product in efforts to correct the ecological and social harm done by economic growth. When will the same amount, or more, be invested to prevent this harm, instead of merely attempting to heal it?

Thus we have a series of problems affecting not only the Western industrialized world, but just as much, if not more, the Communist countries of Eastern Europe, and the third world, the latter especially through the draining of its raw materials to the dregs and its deforestation to the point of causing catastrophic climatic disturbances and the gradual disappearance of the earth's oxygen supply. The tropical rain forest is shrinking at the rate of 25 million acres annually, as land is cleared for pasture and timber is felled for our fancy furniture. For the three great forest countries of the world—Brazil, Zaire, and Indonesia—this brings in short-term income, but long-term misery. These countries are being used, and abused.[3]

How many plagues, then, threaten to visit not just the Egypt of biblical times, but whole continents, indeed the entire earth? One of these scourges is the process of "Saharization"—the gradual desert-izing of fertile soil, year after year. Another is the "nuclear winter," of which I have already spoken. A third is the "greenhouse effect," whereby gases—primarily carbon dioxide—trap the sun's radiant energy in the lower atmosphere and warm the air near the earth's surface; this, it is believed, will lead to the melting of both polar icecaps, and then to the swelling of oceans, the eventual inundation of our coasts, and the submergence of our coastal cities in floods of salt water. A fourth is the destruction of the ozone layer of the upper atmosphere by escaping hydrofluorocarbons used as propellants in spray cans and as coolants in air conditioners and refrigerators, so that our protection from the lethal ultraviolet rays of the sun becomes less and less adequate. And so on and on.

The ecological question is rapidly becoming problem number one of our century. Not that we lack the knowledge to avert the approaching catastrophe. What we lack is a willingness to change our behavior. Significantly, a study commissioned by President Carter, *Global 2000*, which painted such a gloomy ecological picture, was simply stuffed in a drawer by the Reagan administration, which continued to push for economic growth as if nothing had happened. We seem to want to race over the edge of the precipice as fast as our little legs will carry us, instead of purposefully dismantling the irresponsible lifestyle we have built up over the last decades. No one dares intrude on our "car consciousness," for example. We are "mobile on the street, immobile in the head" (K. Nientiedt). Year after year, our hesitation allows the harm to grow, and lays its burden on the shoulders of generations to come, who will one day curse both legacy and testators.

Ecological groups have long been a voice crying in the wilderness, warning us of the danger of this increasingly lethal state of affairs. Meanwhile, environmental protection has become a plank in every party platform. But is this not done lest any votes be lost to the "Greenies"? Is it a sign of any real readiness for conversion? Surely not.

In Switzerland, the question was debated in the Federal Parliament in the spring of 1987. Two years earlier, the Federal Council had been charged with the task of commissioning a study to clarify the state of things in this area. Now the study was proposed for discussion, and it was unassailable. Its description of the threat to our quality of life was correct beyond the shadow of a doubt. But when it proposed concrete steps to bring the level of air pollution down to the 1960 rate by 1995, a general panic ensued. Private interest lobbies killed off every measure that looked as if it had a chance of passing. And the legislators simply gave the excuse that the people would never live up to any of this! A few innocuous proposals were adopted, far from adequate to the need. How will the people ever be willing to be converted if their politicians behave so timidly, tossing the most urgent problems back and forth like hot potatoes? The Zürich *Tages-Anzeiger* for March 17, 1987, rightly commented: "The National Assembly has sent out no signals. Thereby it has missed an important opportunity." In the fall of 1988, a four-year information campaign was launched, with posters and slogans, to provoke, not confrontation, but cooperation—not to castigate anyone, but to call for responsible behavior on the part of all.

The same political ostrich tactics of delay and tergiversation are practiced throughout the European and North American community. A one-year span during 1987–88 was declared a European Environment Year. But when it comes to mandating a reduction in the manufacture of hydrofluorocarbons, adopting guidelines for the export of extremely dangerous insecticides and pesticides to the third world, establishing a responsible radiation ceiling for foodstuffs, setting air-pollution standards for Italian, French, and German automotive plants, or reducing the sulfur dioxide content of factory and power plant emissions, progress is very laborious. Private economic interests apply enormous pressure to prevent the adoption of any but token measures. The Max Planck Institute is right in styling these token measures "deathbed therapy." The Berlin-based International Institute for Environment and Society is likewise correct: the European Environment Year was "a year of unsatisfactory compromises and a year of impotence," and "made it clear how hopeless environmental politics really is."[4] And in this atmosphere of European disunity, the industries of individual countries make sure to be on hand to keep any radical measures from raising the costs of their products too high to remain competitive. And the vicious circle intensifies with each revolution.

Even if our present hopes come true, then, and the world never goes up in a puff of smoke, annihilated in a nuclear war, we are still faced with its creeping annihilation, not in virtue of the law of entropy—the leveling of all energy levels and the cessation of the sun's warmth over the course of billions of years—but as a consequence of the prompt results of the harm we do to our own environment. We are like drug addicts who may know perfectly well that they must break their habit, but fail to summon the strength to do so. Not only in the church, then, but in the world, as well, we see the tragic gulf between solemn proclamations and concrete action.

A book has appeared in the United States on the "alternative futures" facing the world and society. The first alternative is the "ideal future"—a utopia in which creative imagination generates alternative concepts, in which the Human Rights Charter is translated into reality, in which a decision is made for an alternative lifestyle out of love for the environment. But the experts give this possibility only 30 percent likelihood of ever being implemented. The second alternative would be the "plausible" future, constructed and organized by the technocrats, who claim to have a solution for everything and are convinced that even the rocky narrows of the economic and ecological crisis can be negotiated. This possibility gets a score of 50 percent. Third comes the "probable" future, with everything continuing as it has up to the present, without any cuts in our consumerism, with quantity continuing to take precedence over quality, with an attitude of eat, drink, and be merry, and with our eyes on the rearview mirror rather than on what lies ahead. This "future" is given a 70 percent chance for realization.[5] The winner, then, is basically a future without a future. Human beings seem to behave no longer as intelligent beings, but have become like animals, mere creatures of instinct — or worse than animals, since instinct tells animals exactly what is suitable for them and what is not. Reinhold Schneider's remark comes to mind: "No catastrophe occurs that has not failed to heed a prophet."

Here the churches are challenged to perform a role. If the politicians cannot speak out, and if the captains of industry are unwilling to behave in a way consistent with the common good, then it is all the more up to the churches to call out to people's consciences: "You shall not destroy God's creation!" As in the area of justice and peace, so in ecological matters, as well, we shall never be able to bestir ourselves to do what is to be done, to change the course of things, without religious motivation. In holy scripture we read: "Be fertile and multiply; fill the earth and subdue it. Have dominion over the fish of the sea, the birds of the air, and all the living things that move on the earth" (Gen. 1:28). But this cannot mean recklessly exploiting the earth after the manner of a usurper. It must mean caring for it lovingly as its steward, as Chief Seattle, for instance, or the Melanesian sage Papalardi express it in their famous *pronunciamentí* — but as Christians, past and present, unfortunately have failed to live.[6]

I should like to propose the following modernization, then, of the first chapter of the Book of Genesis:

History of the Creation
and Destruction of the World

In the beginning, I saw that all was good, and very good. Today I see all things are in a bad state, a very bad state. On the first day I created light, the sun for the day and the moon for the night. But you darken the day with your smoke clouds, and shatter the still of the night with your neon lights and electric signs. On the second day I divided the water from the dry land, and gave you water as your refreshment and land teeming with fruit. But you have contaminated the brooks, lakes, and seas, infecting the earth with your poisons. On the third day I caused new shoots to sprout, with every kind of plant and tree. But you allow fields and forests to die from your acid rain. Then I created water creatures, little and great, and feathered birds of every kind. But you annihilate masses of fish with your oil spills, and butterflies and songbirds with your chemicals. Then I created all manner of animals, both creeping and leaping. But you wickedly tear them from their habitats, to grant them melancholy survival in your zoos, where they may be gawked at and mocked. Last of all I created you, the human being, male and female, my own self-portrait, and set you over the whole of creation. But you are unprofitable stewards, for you destroy the work of my hands. On the seventh day I rested, and bade you, too, rest on this day. But you spend your weekends racing from pleasure to pleasure, listening to one record after another; and you lose all sense of things. Turn, my people, to me, your God, and to yourselves, and remember your progeny, to whom this earth of mine will belong as much as it has to you.

Thus it would be altogether permissible, in sermons and instructions, to castigate certain individual sins less dramatically, and concentrate instead upon these sins against creation. We may recommend a consumer asceticism, an alternative lifestyle, as a necessity and a virtue. A theology of renunciation and environmental protection must be developed. A. Tévoédjrè has written an important book under the title *Poverty, Wealth of Mankind.* He would encourage, not misery, either for Africa or for the North, but a meaningful, worthy poverty for everyone. This poverty would mean the dismantling of much of what is superfluous, and the substitution of a life that can be enjoyed once more.

Various bishops' conferences have published appropriate texts. But their voice lacks urgency. Their accent is not yet sufficiently emphatic, and actual church practice still too inconsistent. Only utopian-seeming proposals can now do justice to the challenge of ecological reality. When, in our cities, will the bishop and the mayor launch a joint campaign to replace cars with bicycles, and set the example by biking around town themselves? The strongest pastoral letter in this spirit has come from the bishops of the Philippines, in March 1988:

> Our fields, forests, and streams fairly cry out to us. They are being poisoned, stripped, and polluted.... Our country is in the gravest danger. The whole ecological system, on our soil as in the seas around us, is being recklessly exploited. The harm has already gone far, and, sad to say, is often beyond repair....

And the bishops urge that, together with efforts on the part of the government and individual citizens (and doubtless to the chagrin of certain "devout Catholics"), "a concern for service to the earth become a pervasive element of liturgy and catechesis."

The balance sheet lies open before our eyes. Things cannot go on as they are. And we are seized with a feeling of helplessness. What are we to do now? Well, as we say in our land, "When many little persons in many little places do many little things, they can change the face of the earth." We must simply begin to live more ecologically. We must conserve energy, take the bus and the train, stop using our cars for long trips alone or to pick up the morning paper, use less heat and more insulation, take the stairs instead of the elevator, compact our trash, build compost heaps, use fewer chemicals in our garden or field, buy biodegradable laundry and dishwashing detergents, and so on. We shall soon learn: to live simply is no simple matter. But if we join with others, and form groups, we can encourage one another, and thereby redouble our effectiveness. Yes, if many individuals do this and many other things, they can change the situation a bit.

Then too, we can exert more public pressure. We can subject campaigning politicians to some kind of ecological litmus test. We can hit the streets and the front page with the slogan "Ecology Is Good Economics." After all, this is the simple truth, at least in the long run. We can call for a search for alternative sources of energy—the sun, the wind—even with oil prices temporarily down. We can demand an end to our reliance on nuclear energy. And so forth.

In 1978, in Rome, a nuclear energy expert gave a talk to personnel from the general curias of the religious orders, hoping to convince us that nuclear energy was the "cleanest" form of energy, while admitting that it was not completely clean since of course there was radioactive waste to be disposed of. In the course of the ensuing discussion, I asked whether, instead of consuming more and more energy, we ought perhaps to encourage people to use less. The answer was: "Scientists don't preach. We only solve problems." Of course, that is just the point: the problems are not being solved. We need only think of the fallout from Windscale, in England, in 1957, from the Three Mile Island accident, and from Chernobyl in the Soviet Union in 1986—not to mention the many hushed-up near-catastrophes! Or we could think of the disposal and transport scandals, with trucks and ships carrying thousands of tons of toxic and nuclear waste to Eastern Europe or the third world, dumping it there for a pittance, and leaving the coming catastrophes to the unsuspecting, helpless populations of the region.[7] The countries of the European community produce 250 million tons of toxic waste annually, of which only some one-quarter is properly disposed of—an expensive proposition—while the remainder is just dumped, a gigantic time bomb waiting to explode somewhere.

In May of 1988, North American, European, Soviet, and Japanese scientists working at the Max Planck Institute launched a common search for a new source of nuclear energy—nuclear fusion, which, unlike nuclear fission, is supposed to be "clean." Although there is now increasing research in this area, it appears that it will be years before we know whether atomic fusion will be commercially viable as an energy source. Until then we have the problem of the disposal of atomic waste. Until that problem is solved, there can be no responsible commercial use of nuclear energy on a large scale. This thesis is posited by atomic physicist Carl Friedrich von Weizsäcker, as well as by ethicist Alfons Auer.[8]

Ordinary folk, too, feel the growing urgency of the problem. In 1987,

Italians voted against further work on nuclear energy plants. In Austria, as early as 1978, a bare majority of 50.4 percent voted against completion of the Zwentendorf nuclear facility; no politician has so much as dared to broach the subject since. In Switzerland, the Federal Council halted all work on the Kaiseraugst facility in 1988. In a number of places in the United States, proposals for new nuclear power plants have been turned down and in other places construction of plants has been brought to a halt. Of course, now people must be consistent. They must now vote no, in word and deed, not only to fear, but to their society of consumerism, profit, and disposables. In the course of a conversation about these matters in a house of our order a young confrere remarked, in all Franciscan idealism: "I don't get it. I just say to this flower, 'Good morning! How are you?' And I'm just glad about the flower." I replied: "Fine. But if that's the *only* thing you do, you won't be able to say good morning to that flower much longer."

Once more, we may hope that the ongoing process of Christian reconciliation will help create the public awareness needed in this area as well, and thus make still another contribution to the shaping of a new image of the world. Let us hope that economic growth, full employment at high wages, and international competition will no longer be our sacrosanct values. Absolute priority must be accorded a strategy for survival. Then we may rejoice in the hope of a survival worthy of the dignity of a human being—and without a recurrence of this menace to our existence.

Without the contribution of a pair of additional factors, we shall scarcely manage to leap unscathed from this runaway train in its headlong plunge to destruction. The first is a series of prophets—not hair-tearing screamers, but professional persons of the highest competence—who will draft a new concept for braking the economy in a way that people might actually be expected to tolerate. Then we could avert the worst. In days gone by, Adam Smith (1723–90) endowed the industrial revolution, and thereby "the wealth of nations"—the title of his great work—with a theoretical justification. Let these latter-day prophets do the same, with a new revolution, one whose be-all and end-all, this time, will be not more goods, but higher values, a more humane outlook, and an authentic quality of life. The second element we need will be something more than flashing red lights and warning signals. These we have in abundance. We need to be warned, alas, through actual catastrophes. Nothing less will shock us, move us to shake off our apathy, and force us to take the necessary, painful steps. We must actually wish for such catastrophes to occur, and as soon as possible. After all, we stand on the brink of the abyss.

Now the fact flies in our face: God's "old" Ten Commandments, the object of our self-accusation in the traditional confessional, and the "new" Ten Commandments now proclaimed to us by God via the signs of the times, are endowed with different degrees of urgency. Not that the former should be trivialized. They still call us to personal conversion, even as a prerequisite for a better world. But all too often, they remain in the private, the individual, the religious realm. The "new" Ten Commandments call us to a conversion to the world—the world of human beings, the world of God. They call us to cooperate in the history God is making with the creature known as the human being. They call us to actualize the universal, comprehensive salvation that God seeks to bestow on humanity. Will human beings throw themselves into their task mightily, with all of their creative powers? Or will they wretchedly fail in it, and prefer to demonstrate their power and their impotence, and so actually poison their own joy in creation—and then, when all is said and done, die in their own stench, cursed by their progeny, a new ilk that will sicken and die like its progenitors?

But enough of these dismal predictions. The churches will never tire of giving us hope, of inspiring in us the courage we shall need to mold this world to a world worthy of human beings and God after all. When Communists have forgotten their promised Marxian paradise; when Chairman Mao's *Little Red Book,* which thirty years ago was inundating the West itself, has been trampled underfoot as its author's statues have been quietly removed from their pedestals; when Oswald Spengler's *The Decline of the West* is appropriately updated with a new prognostication, that of a decline of the world itself; in sum, when a paradise according to the human heart never materializes—the churches will yet be instilling within our hearts the hope of a paradise according to the heart of God. Then shall God become our savior again, and human beings' fate be in the divine hands for good and all. When and how this will occur, we know not. We are not under any obligation whatsoever to "figure it out" and whisper it in God's ear. God has it already "figured out." And it will be precisely the divine surprise. It will be God's gift, and all will end well. All will be consummated. And we shall only be able to say: This is ever so much more than we had dared hope for!

The original paradise was myth, then. The paradise of earth may remain forever utopia. But the eschatological paradise is promised and guaranteed. O mystery of faith! The climax of human history is thus a tragedy of decline and fall, but beyond that lies the ultimate mighty deed of God—rescue! Redemption. Calderón's *The Great Theater of the World* should be rewritten to this story line, and produced.

10

You Will Encounter the God of History

Spirituality and Politics

Having thus far considered the first nine of the "new" Ten Commandments of God, we may well have a question. Have we not heard too much talk of the world here, of economics, of politics, and too little of piety, of the edifying, of faith? Has not all our talk been tantamount to a profanation of the temple, a contempt for the afterlife, a distortion of the Christian proclamation?

The first "new" commandment called on us to "allow common sense to prevail." Now the moment has come to complement common sense with inspiration, with spirituality. Our spirituality will still bear a relation to politics, however. After all, politics and mysticism are not simply without interconnection. Nor do they coincide merely in their object. They compenetrate, they merge. They animate mutually. It is the task of spirituality to enlighten politics as to its ultimate meaning, motivate it, and engage it in the authentic welfare of human beings. Politics will always have the task of admonishing spirituality to discern its God not just in the heights of heaven, but in history, as well—along the highways and byways of earth.

That the "new" Ten Commandments, instead of beginning with spirituality, end with the same, is only an outgrowth of the so-called anthropological shift. In the past, one simply began with divine revelation, with the eternal truths, with the supernatural order, from which there was no appeal, and before which one only bowed one's head in docility. But the primacy of the supernatural no longer comes as standard equipment in the majority of modern women and men. The Enlightenment has cast doubt on so many of our pat answers! Today we feel drawn precisely to questions of justice, peace, and the preservation of creation, and therefore to the secularized human being, who is generally more involved with these questions than are the majority of devout churchgoers. In a word, today's human being prefers to begin with human beings, analyzing their ultimate constitution, their glimmering surmises, their longings and their expectations, both theologically (especially since Karl Rahner) and psychologically (for example, with Carl Jung, B. Stähelin, Paul Tournier, and Viktor Frankl). Then we are forced to the conclusion that these human beings, for good or ill, are grounded upon, and orientated toward, a further reality—an ultimate meaning for their lives, a primordial mystery—which we call God. Faith, then, comes as a final answer precisely to one's actual, real questions. Faith is no longer rote formula. Faith is now the joy of existential fulfill-ment. Faith is no longer a "must," but a "may." What we finally believe is what we have always longed for. Religion is not alienation, then, but ulti-mate, existential self-identification. Does such an understanding mire us in the horizontal, our gaze fixed on ourselves and along the plane of the earth? No. Rather it means that, at the appropriate time, we raise our eyes toward God in order to interpret the human being and the world as God's human being and God's world.

One who dares not take this leap of faith will sooner or later suffer the pain of "feelings of meaninglessness," fall victim to an "existential vacuum" (Frankl), lead "the life of the eternal vagabond" (Tournier), lose his or her primordial trust and ultimate security (Stähelin). But those who have found their home in a religion thus understood can readily see that, as long as men and women walk this earth, an invincible hope in an absolute future, called God, will always be. The very phenomenon of skepticism evinces this:

> [The skeptics are those] who decline to think their existence through to the end, who journey they know not whither, and who actually constitute the only real alternative to absolute Christian hope. It is simply inconceivable that this Christian proclamation should ever be transcended, should ever become outmoded, and as such replaced and displaced by a new religion or by the demise of all religion.[1]

To encounter this God, in mystical experience, is more precious than all else beside. Here is the pearl of great price, for which we shall gladly sacrifice everything else in the world (Matt. 13:46). It is good to leave the scene of activity for a moment—ideally an hour a day, a day a month, a week a year—to withdraw into the "desert," naked and poor, hungering and thirsting for justice (Mark 5:5), alone before our God, to raise our antennae toward God, to listen to God, to belong to God. Of course, one ought not expect "experiences of God by summary procedure" (K. G. Rey), or attempt to build "a sure way out of the darkness of the pilgrimage into the light of what we shall then appear to be" (J. Sudbrack). The more spontaneously, the more disinterestedly, selflessly, and generously we bestow our time on God, the more God can bestow the gift of the divine Self upon us, in the stillness of peace and joy—perhaps even (doubtless very rarely) in a sudden interior illumination and comprehension, like the one experienced by a friend of mine, who wrote me about it: "Suddenly you discover a kind of physical contact with the Ineffable, the Unspeakable, be it only for a split second. With oases like that, how can the desert be called suffering?" This will be the exception. The rule is still sober faith. The crucial thing is love and surrender, not feeling.

God can of course always manage exceptions and surprises, and will select great souls, as well as — by predilection — little ones, and draw them near, into the divine light and blessed happiness. I was asked to write a book about blessed Ulrika Nisch, a nun who died of tuberculosis in 1913 at the age of thirty-one, and I was happy to do so. In the short years of her religious life this humble little sister, from a poor family, poorly educated, and in fragile health, was granted an almost incredible experience of God. She spent all her free time, including every evening until 10:00 p.m., in the chapel . . . with God. When unexpectedly called to perform some service, she responded at once, but almost as if she were sleepwalking. How painful it was for her to return to the world! I wrote of Sister Ulrika most sympathetically, although, of course, not altogether uncritically. Not a few of my readers expressed their surprise that I would go out on a limb with a book about a simple nun. But I felt I knew exactly what I was doing. My intent was to place the spiritual and mystical dimension of the Christian life side by side with the political. Of course, this is precisely where Sister Ulrika's life comes in for some criticism. Not that she failed to practice a tireless love of neighbor. On the contrary, she performed her work as scullery sister with the utmost fidelity and devotion, and prayed unceasingly for the conversion of sinners and unbelievers. But she showed no sensitivity whatever for the social questions of her time, not even when it came to a living wage for the scullery maids. And she certainly had no sense of a Christian obligation to criticize the church, however flagrant the shortcomings of that church may have been. No, all her pondering bore on the world to come. Her only desire was to die as soon as death might be granted her, in order to be with her Jesus. Her other-worldly, individualistic piety was, of course, only a mirror image of the general attitude of her time, which we today know must be complemented.

I knew an old brother, in my community in Arth, who was attached to the same sort of contemplative life. For decades, he rose at 4:00 a.m., repaired to our little upstairs chapel, and began to pray. First he recited a number of vocal prayers. Then he made the Stations of the Cross. Then he said the rosary and a number of litanies. All the while, his soul strove to maintain an interior, prayerful attitude in keeping with these outward prayers. Then came Mass, breakfast, and work. But even in the course of his workday, whenever he was free, he would spend some hours in his little corner in the chapel. And he did this day after day, year after year. He told me once:

My prayer used to be dry. It was so miserable, so pitiful. But I didn't give up. Now it's not tiresome. Just the opposite. Time goes by so fast! It's like when you light a fire. First you put twigs on top of one another. Those are the prayers you get going with. Then all at once the whole thing just flares up and burns all by itself. And I just start saying, "Jesus, I love you. Only let me die for love of you." I just feel that God loves me so much that he just doesn't pay any attention to my faults and sins.

Today we tend to regard such persons as one-sided Christians. And quite a number of them may well find it painful to hear of "new" commandments of God, and will urgently remind us at every turn of the "one thing needful" (Luke 10:42). I envied that brother. I had to admit that I was just a clumsy beginner alongside him. But I consoled myself with the thought that I, too, had received charisms from God—after all, there are different gifts, but all come from the same Spirit, to complement one another (1 Cor. 12:4).

Basically, spirituality and politics go together. They are two sides of the same coin. They are the twin aspects of God's one salvific plan. In itself, that plan is serene, eternally undisturbed, an incomprehensible mystery. But it mounted its first invasion in the "Big Bang"—a mystery for the greatest scientists even today—which sent the cosmos hurtling down the path of evolution, that act of creation still in process. And it mounted its second invasion in the Incarnation—again, a mystery even today, this time for the greatest theologians—in which God dispatched the eternal Son into the midst of human history, an inconceivable "interference" in the world. Thus the God of eternity became the God of time and history. The living, palpable God of the mystical encounter became the God who practices politics with the chosen people. God's movement forth to the world has become our primal, everlastingly valid image of love.

We have the classic example in Moses. Moses was granted an astonishing experience of God on Mount Horeb. There he beheld a bush that burned without being consumed. And he said to himself, "I shall go and see this strange apparition." He would have liked to loll in this mystical experience, to tarry in it. But the Lord wrested him from it, without ado, and imposed upon him the task of a mission: "Come no nearer.... Rather, go! I send you to Pharaoh. Lead my people, the Israelites, out of Egypt.... I am with you. I have sent you" (Exod. 3). No clearer expression of the intrinsic connection between vocation and mission, between call and sending, between spirituality and politics, could be wished for.

The call and mission of Isaiah (Isa. 6), Jeremiah (Jer. 1), indeed of most of the prophets, occurred in this same manner—to be radicalized in Jesus, who, in his nights alone on the mountain, experienced an inconceivably profound inward presence of God, while by day he spent himself to the point that he no longer had either the time or the desire to take any nourishment (John 4:6; Mark 3:20). So also were his disciples called. They were summoned in order to be sent. "Come, follow me. I will make you fishers of men" (Mark 1:17). "Then the Lord chose seventy-two others and sent them in pairs into every town and village where he himself was to come" (Luke 10:1).

Finally, the same holds true for the church, and for all in the church. As with the apostles, Jesus enjoins all in the church to pray (Luke 11:1), but likewise sends them to proclaim, to heal, and to deliver the world from the powers of evil (Mark 16:14–15; Matt. 28:17–20). We often hear it remarked that in the course of the conversion process, for example during a retreat, we should not be too quick to speak to exercitants of their worldly duty as Christians, lest we distract them from the "business at hand"— their relationship with God. Let us remember, however, that a conversion to God is always a conversion to a God concerned for human beings, a God who has intervened in history, and who always calls men and women to a mission.

Not only biblically, but empirically as well, spirituality and politics enjoy a mutual reference. Spirituality without politics would be a cheap, surely not altogether godly, lounging in self-satisfied piety. Politics without spirituality, at the other extreme, could become a reckless careerism, a brutal economic exploitation of the weak, a mighty nation state in which the powerful lord it over the others. As Johannes Metz says, "A head-in-the-clouds type spirituality, bearing on the redemption of the individual soul, will never do. The only valid spirituality will be a spirituality of brotherhood, and will bear on the liberation of the entire world."[2] Individual Christians can accent various dimensions of this kind of spirituality, in accordance with the various charisms they have received, as I have said. Depending on the case, then, Christians should be counseled, not piously to withdraw from the world, but perhaps to shut out a bit of the noise of the world now and then.

In Europe, too many of the pious seem too unpolitical, and too many politicians seem wanting in piety. Thus we should have to call the former unpolitical Christians, and the latter un-Christian politicians. Both are deficient. In Latin America, a harmony is gradually arising, from the base, from the grassroots, and, as I mentioned above, Gustavo Gutiérrez feels that he can claim with justification that the first (genuinely) Christian generation is growing up there after four hundred years of Christianity. Michael Zulehner would like to see the same happen in the North. People are "political *because* they are spiritual," Zulehner says. "The more spiritual they are, the more political they are."

Those who follow the ideal rule we have cited above, and who withdraw from time to time from action to contemplation, will eventually stand a good chance of no longer having to practice these components alternately. They will be able to exercise them in compenetration. For such Christians, "contemplation on the street" (Jacques Maritain) will become a reality, and politics will receive its effective stimulus from spirituality. Now politics will become continuous creation—God's salvific project with the human creature at last. Francis of Assisi was fond of saying that his cell, his place of contemplation, was his body, and his monastery the world.

I have already spoken of my friend Meinrad Hengartner (chap. 2). Over the course of three decades, Meinrad communicated an enormous pastoral impulse to the church in Switzerland. How did he manage to have that much influence? He had no special training. He had only his natural talent. The answer, then, is very simple. His abilities in these matters came from the Holy Spirit. We need only read some of Meinrad's many attestations to this effect. For example:

> It comes down to this. We must be among those who have eyes to see—who allow the words of Luke 4:18 to affect them, who believe that these words were intended for us too: "The Spirit of the Lord is upon me. He has sent me. . . ." May we ever apply this to ourselves, so that we set the imprisoned free, and proclaim the Lord's year of jubilee. . . . I pray to the Holy Spirit every day. . . . We can look back at our Mission Year as on a year of grace and strength, a year of the invisible working of the Holy Spirit. . . . When the Holy Spirit of God, and our own holy spirit, work hand in hand, superhuman things happen. . . .

In this new image of the world, which can excite the hearts even of today's youth, there is no longer a divorce between spirituality and politics—between above and below, between God and human beings—but harmony. The Holy Spirit and common sense go wonderfully hand in hand. From the former come human intuitions; from the latter, divine inspirations. The two form a unity, as bow and stern, soul and body, path and goal.

PART 3

Reflections on the New Future

The Church on the Way to the Third Millennium

THREE MILLENIAL TURNING POINTS

Soon we shall cross the threshold of the third millennium. What will await us on the other side? The question of the shape of tomorrow demands that we consider our interpretation of what is happening today. Over the past decades, a new, epochal framework has crystallized around us, one whose effects are almost beyond imagining, and one that we can list among the few really great turning points of Christian history.

The beginning, the "Christian Big Bang," was the Jesus-event. Jesus was the human being who once upon a time rendered the love of God, and thereby God's very self, visible and palpable on this earth. The turning point in history we know as *Jesus* inaugurated a new phase in salvation history, and world history would later be rightly divided into the time before and after Christ. The second great turning point in Western history was that which we call *Constantinian*. In the year 313, the Emperor Constantine recognized the Christian church, and what began under him was normative for that church well up into the twentieth century. Admittedly the following assertion bears nuancing, but basically we can say: With the Constantinian turning point in history, a persecuted church became the persecutor, proclamation became institution, meekness became power, the people of God was supplanted by a hierarchy, a church freely embraced became a church inherited from the preceding generation, the Reign of God became Christendom, and the gospel was replaced by canon law.

Now we are in a position to gauge the impact of the third great notch in church history. I like to call it the *Johannine turning point.* I refer to the event of Pope John XXIII and his council, Vatican II. Our best insight into the uniqueness of his life and his pontificate will be afforded by a consideration of his firm belief in the Holy Spirit's inspiration of human beings and God's sovereignty over history. John's notion that he might call a new council, resulting in his altogether unexpected announcement of January 25, 1959, had been a sudden inspiration of the Holy Spirit, as he later repeatedly insisted. In the person and the council of this pope, a "Johannine springtime" burst upon church and world alike. A kind of new Exodus transpired. A veritable messianic hope stirred. John and his council inaugurated "the privileged age of the Holy Spirit," of which his successor, Paul VI, spoke in *Evangelii Nuntiandi* (no. 75). With John—with this little old fat man of whom it had been said almost apologetically that he had been elected as a "transition pope"—occurred the church's transition indeed: from the second to the third millennium, from the Constantinian era and its "inherited church" to the age of the Holy Spirit and its "conscience church." With the council's overtures to the laity, to our fellow Christians, to non-Christians, and to the world, an erstwhile introverted church—which for a thousand and more years had shot its barbs and excommunications at Jew, heathen, and heretic—was genuinely transformed and accoutered for the coming millennium. Do we not stand at an epochal turning point in history? Are we not living in an extraordinarily momentous time in the history of the church? And do we not therefore speak too much of the church's crises and too little of its opportunities?

It can all be summed up in one statement: The age of dialogue is upon us. In the second millennium, one ecclesial class, the hierarchy, spoke for the people. Churches condemned one another. The various religions throughout the world held one another in contempt. Nation made war on nation. One continent exploited others. In the third millennium, mutual respect, dialogue, and common solutions will be the watchword, as will befit the age of the Holy Spirit. For the Spirit will pour out its gift of tongues once more, enabling us to overcome all historical exclusivism and to feel at home in a conversion to the breadth of God. The way has been prepared by Vatican Council II, which will prove to have been the council of the third millennium. The "Johannine spring" will not have been just a beautiful episode, then, nor the "Johannine turning point," a door ajar only for a moment, promptly to close again. No, this new age will be a long one, like the Constantinian era itself.

THE ACTUAL SITUATION OF THE CHURCH TODAY

It would be neither honest nor realistic, after the foregoing macrocosmic contemplation, with its so many hopeful visions and expectations, to fail to complement the same with an existential reflection on the microcosm of the concrete, everyday situation in the church. That situation looks less optimistic. But we must take a position toward it.

Anyone involved in the Catholic church, and having the eyes to see, must be deeply concerned for that church—for its base, which is obviously crumbling, as well as for its structures, which so often prove to be a hindrance instead of a help. In the Federal Republic of Germany, statistics tell us (and approximately the same will hold for the other countries of Europe), in 1965 55 percent of Catholics attended church on Sundays, in 1975 35 percent, and in 1985 25 percent. In 1985 attendance ranged from 50 percent to 5 percent depending on the region. As for Protestants: an average of roughly 5 percent attend church on Sunday. Who can assure us that this trend will not continue, and that Catholics, too, twenty years from now, will not be down to a 5 percent average? The elderly, who have "remained true," are dying off, and few among the young are taking their place. In many cities the number of those who formally leave the church already exceeds that of those who enter it through baptism.

Then there is the fact that the clergy, once the backbone of the Catholic church, are older, fewer, and more overwhelmed by the year. The shortage of priests that we have been watching develop for more than ten years has now entered into its acute stage. Ever more rapidly, parishes are combined and priests become harried dispensers of the sacraments and religious instruction, living all alone in their great rectories — scarcely an attractive prospect for the "new blood" that might have been hoped for. And not a few of these priests suddenly say, "I've had it," and walk away.

Worse still, parents, who now must step in and fulfill their responsibility for the religious upbringing of their children, are often no longer very sure of themselves when it comes to their faith, and do not "know what to say," so that for the first time we must fear for the handing on of the faith to the coming generation. Parents do not want to teach the faith to their children in the way and manner in which they themselves had their religion drilled into them once upon a time. But when it comes to going about it in a new way, they do not have the needed help and instruction — if indeed they "feel like" doing anything along these lines at all. Often they simply lack interest. "It's not so terrible not to go to church," they say, as if having made some surprising new discovery. In particular, they fail to see any meaningful connection between official church teachings or Roman decrees, on the one hand, and human reality and daily experience, on the other. Many parents state this outright when they are asked about religious education.[1] Once more, a poll in Germany has determined that only 23 percent of Catholics still regard Roman decrees as important and binding. If this situation, and these tendencies, continue, the future of the church between now and the year 2000 looks far less rosy than we might have thought. We hear of an unsensational, but ultimately disastrous, "evaporation of Christianity."

All of these symptoms betoken an ecclesial condition that we can describe only as an emergency. And we anxiously ask what will happen next. Especially, what are we ourselves to do? Emergency situations call for emergency measures. To be sure, these will generally fall massively short of the ideal, and they can never be anything more than partial solutions. But these emergencies also offer new, elementary opportunities. Perhaps they are moments of "first aid from the Holy Spirit" (K. Koch).

There are various ways of reacting to an emergency. In the case of the Catholic church, the supreme authority is the Vatican, and it is well aware of its responsibilities, and intervenes in the ordinary course of affairs more than would be needed or desirable in normal times. One cannot begrudge the bearer of Peter's commission his efforts to strengthen in faith his brothers and sisters as he sees fit (see Luke 22:32). But as things are now, the opinion seems to prevail in the Vatican, with all respect for the principles of the council itself, that the postconciliar years have occasioned a great deal of harm in the church: a mass exodus of priests and religious, confusion in theological teaching, insubordination among the laity, an erasure of the boundaries between Catholicism and Protestantism or even non-Christian religions, and finally, an absorption into the secularized world. And the conclusion is drawn that this world is in need of a "contrasting society" possessing a loud voice and proclaiming a message immune from casuistry and nit-picking.

The fine-honed tool for the implementation of the above-mentioned strategy is the new Code of Canon Law, now in force throughout the world. The official church hopes that the code will help confine the raging torrent of freedom and independence once more within its banks. Even the generals of religious orders, even the bishops' synods, are now helpless against it. All questions and suggestions, however worthy in themselves, ricochet off "the code." At the turn of the century, Alfred Loisy declared: "Jesus prayed for the coming of the Reign of God, and the church came instead." I should like to reformulate Loisy's insight for our day: Jesus left the gospel, and the church is guided by the Code of Canon Law. How readily exceptions to the gospel are tolerated, and even created! But exceptions to the code, never.

Examples? In the gospel we read: "Do not swear at all. . . . Say, 'Yes' when you mean 'Yes' and 'No' when you mean 'No.' Anything beyond that is from the evil one" (Matt. 5:34–37). But the index to the code lists precisely thirty references under "Oath." Again, in the gospel we read: "Avoid the title 'Rabbi.' One among you is your teacher, the rest are learners" (Matt. 23:8). But in Rome, day after day, we still find all the old medieval nomenclature, for example in the *Osservatore Romano:* "Venerable Sisters, Reverend Fathers, Very Reverend Superiors General, Very Reverend and Right Reverend Monsignori, Most Reverend Bishops, their Most Reverend Excellencies the Lord Cardinals." The laity alone are without titles. Once more, in the gospel we read: "When a person strikes you on the right cheek, turn and offer that person the other cheek. . . . Let the person with two coats give to one who has none" (Matt. 5:39; Luke 3:11). And no one seems to take any account of the fact that only saints or fools actually do these things.

Instead, Rome hammers on *Humanae Vitae,* overlooking the fact that the majority of even sincere married Christians no longer find its concepts helpful; Rome focuses on individual confession versus penance services, seemingly forgetting that in 589 the Council of Toledo condemned auricular confession—then being popularized by monks—as an "execrable presumption" and "most foul manner of dispensing penance" (*execrabilis praesumptio, foedissime paenitentiam agere*); and Rome hammers on the prohibition against dispensing the Eucharist to the divorced and remarried, who are reminded that they can attend church without receiving communion, be reconciled with God, and lead a Christian life—thereby completely evacuating the meaning of the sacraments. Rome is currently interfering repeatedly in discussions of the AIDS epidemic, pillorying both the U.S. Bishops Conference and the Italian government for publicly confessing, with all insistence on fidelity to the marriage bond and continence outside that bond, that not every human being can hold to the Christian ideal of marriage, and recommending birth control for emergencies. Rome is desperately swimming against the tide. As if afflicted by some sort of color-blindness, it confuses the "signs of the times" with the bad old world. It stubbornly clings to positions that can no longer be maintained. And so the history of missed chances (or less euphemistically, lost wars), from the days of Pius IX to our own, continues apace.

But Rome clings rigidly to the official line, and seeks to impose that line on others by appointing bishops of unquestioned loyalty to Rome. Any nominee who may ever have expressed himself in other than completely Roman terms on *Humanae Vitae,* priestly celibacy, women's ordination, and so on — and the Vatican computerizes all such transgressions — is automatically dropped from consideration, whatever other qualities he might have to recommend him. And so one region of the world after another is brought under the control of such trustworthy abiders by the law.

But the people no longer go along with all this. We refer not to right-wing groups who cannot proclaim loudly enough their loyalty to Rome and the pope, nor, surely, to the excellent people who wish only to pray and save their souls and who are vexed at all of this new conflict in their church, but to the wide-awake, mature laity, priests, religious, and bishops who are of the stuff that the council wished the church to be. These persons represent the genuine, gratifying fruit of Vatican II. And they suffer from the fact that they mean so little, that they are passed over, and that they must now oppose the church they love.

It is easy to see why Catholic theology teachers should protest this manner of appointing bishops, this censorship of theology teachers, and this distorting interpretation of *Humanae Vitae,* and 170 of them did so in the "Cologne Declaration" of January 6, 1989. The presidents of the German-speaking bishops conferences expressed reservations about the manner in which the protesters voiced these complaints, questioning whether those complaints should have been immediately communicated to the press, but they could scarcely fault the substance of the complaints. Subsequently, groups of Italian and Brazilian theology teachers expressed themselves in a similar vein.

The hierarchy is still guided by a principle it has received from feudalism. The great and mighty lord knows best. He must not be criticized, for he rules by divine right. But this uncritical attitude generates infantile human beings, and only such individuals filter to the top in the prevailing ecclesiastical system. Hence the difficulty encountered by this system in dealing with independently thinking men and women. But the majority of persons today belong to this latter category. We have no wish to render a moral judgment on the individuals of the Roman curia. We are only raising the epochal question: Do these persons notice that a new era has come? Do they recognize the "signs of the times"?

It is not far from heresy to hold, or to behave in practice as if one held, that the laity and the local churches do not possess the Holy Spirit too. The pope has the obligation of attending to the operation of the Holy Spirit among the people of the church. Instead, narrow-mindedness and fear prevail—let us call it by the name of "anxiety," which is connected with the Latin *angustia,* meaning "narrowness," or the condition of feeling oneself to be in dire "straits." To see certain members of the Vatican Curia, one would get the impression that they believe neither in the Holy Spirit nor in Jesus, and that this is why they imagine that it is up to themselves to save the church, by hook or by crook.

When we observe the overall strategy with which Rome reacts to the emergency situation in the church, we are struck by how obviously the bark of Peter is being steered back onto its old course, thus "correcting" the new direction given it by Vatican II. The council's reorientation is regarded as a mistake. Vatican I had given the church a strong central government, with the dogmas of papal infallibility and universal papal jurisdiction as a theological basis. Vatican II then complemented this theology with an emphasis on the episcopate, the local churches, and leadership in collegiality. But never before in history has the church been ruled with the centralism with which it is governed today. Vatican II took the "new theology" that had always met with such resistance on the part of Rome and integrated it into the church. Today, however, as in days gone by, only a Roman scholastic theology is allowed to be taught, and bishops true to the party line are enlisted in a world project to install a conservatism such as never before seen. Vatican II, taking its cue from Pope John XXIII and his *Mater et Magistra,* shifted the accent to the maternal function of the church—that of offering human beings understanding and pastoral succor along the course of their pilgrimage. Rome, however, currently practices an absolutely unprecedented legalism, hammering on orthodoxy at all cost, church law at all cost.

We must draw up the mournful tally. All of the expectations awakened by Vatican II for a genuine co-responsibility on the part of the people of God, for a genuine competency on the part of local bishops, have been rendered null and void. All democratic structures—from local parish councils to the bishops' synod of the Catholic world church—have collapsed like a house of cards. It has all been a mirage.

The much-touted new "co-thinking and co-deciding" have become parroting and trotting at the heel. Rome makes the rules in all matters of concrete importance. You have to give Rome credit: there are no better tacticians in the world. In the twenty-five years since the council, one step ahead of everyone else, Rome has cunningly scooped everything back into its own hands. The whole world church dangles like a puppet on a stage, jiggling and dancing on a string.

This judgment was presented in the opening pages of this book. It seemed like such a hard one at the time. Now it is abundantly clear. We have seen the painful facts in chapter after chapter. There is no more joy in the community of the church—only helplessness in the face of the colossus.

BUILDING A "CHURCH OF CONSCIENCE"

How should we react to this situation in the church? Not a few Catholics simply sever ties. "The church hurt me all those years. Well, that's all in the past now. I just don't care any more." The others—the better part of the laity, priests, even bishops—are spontaneously developing a different emergency tactic from that employed in Rome, and say to themselves: This centralistic church law, which is supposed to be valid for the whole world church, cannot do justice to situations that differ so radically from country to country and from case to case. It must therefore be interpreted generously, and applied with flexibility. The main thing is to deal sensibly—less in the spirit of law than in that of the gospel, less after the model of the church as teacher than after the other model, the church as mother. In other words, what is crucial is to proceed in a pastoral fashion, according to common sense, according to conscience, according to the Holy Spirit.

This is what Jesus did. Jesus can scarcely be reproached with making light of the Sabbath. And yet he actually sought an opportunity to heal on the Sabbath, in order to make the legalistic Pharisees aware that the Sabbath was for human beings, and that human beings were not made for the Sabbath (Mark 2:27–28). Accordingly, the women and men who follow him may, for the sake of those human beings, legitimately regard themselves as above the law. Church law itself, strict as it is, makes that very admission: in the last canon of the code, church law admits that the salvation of souls, of human beings, must be the supreme law in the church.

How good it is to see, in the Lateran Museum in Rome, the oldest existing representation of Jesus, preserved since the third century: the statue of the youthful good shepherd, who, in Jesus' parable, seizes every possible initiative for the rescue of the lost sheep, and thereupon—a deliberate oriental exaggeration—summons all his friends and neighbors to celebrate his joy (Luke 15:4–7). The prophet Ezekiel portrayed the shepherdly love of God in a similar way:

I myself will look after and tend my sheep. As a shepherd tends his flock when he finds himself among his scattered sheep, so will I tend my sheep. I will rescue them from every place where they were scattered when it was cloudy and dark. . . . In good pastures will I pasture them, and on the mountain heights of Israel shall be their grazing ground. There they shall lie down on good grazing ground. . . . I myself will pasture my sheep; I myself will give them rest, says the Lord [Ezek. 34:11–15].

Only in later centuries, when the church had adapted to the power structures of the state, did the mosaics of Christus Pantokrator, Imperator, Kyrios, Christ the Almighty, the Sovereign, the Lord, appear in the apses of the basilicas, to be revered and feared, instead of trusted, as the good shepherd had been. Those who discharge the task of shepherd today, then, may, in good conscience, perform their task after the model of Jesus as good shepherd and the church as mother.

This will apply first of all to bishops. It is they who are really the shepherds of their churches, who are really responsible for them. This is how Vatican II regarded the bishops — it did not see them simply as the executive instances of a Roman authority. Granted, they have an obligation to take church law and Roman decrees seriously. But they must decide, on their own responsibility, the right thing to do in their pastoral emergencies, and hold to that decision even in the face of opposition. They have a greater obligation to their pastoral sense and to their conscience than to the Code of Canon Law.

Furthermore, they are obliged to speak out, and in prophetic fashion, whether their auditors be other, less courageous bishops, or even Rome itself. They must heed their responsibility, as a college of bishops, for the implementation of Vatican II. Thus they must not simply accept this centralism, this conservatism, this legalism. True, some are forthright enough to make certain statements on the occasion of their *ad limina* visits or in the bishops' synods. But they fail to make their point. After all, they are on the short end of the teeter-totter. They are made to feel the overwhelming power of the curia, which allows them to speak and to criticize — thus giving the appearance of freedom of speech — but then pays no attention to what they have said. More and more often, bishops are out and out humiliated, run over roughshod, by Rome. What we now need are tacticians — prelates who know just how to move, not in order to mount a palace revolution, but simply to close ranks and offer organized resistance to this anticonciliar system. But hope dwindles year by year. The chance is almost gone. Bishops "loyal to Rome" already are in the majority in most places. The bishops will have to be encouraged to have more courage, precisely. Else they will have to hear the reproach of Isaiah as addressed to themselves:

> They are all dumb dogs,
>   they cannot bark;
> Dreaming as they lie there,
>   loving their sleep [Isa. 56:10].

. . . Loving their sleep of a conflict-less dependency.

If the bishops are less than totally successful in this task, the pastoral base will have to fill in the gaps. In an emergency, there is not always time to await instructions from superiors. One must take action as promptly and as purposefully as possible. During the two World Wars, on the fronts and in the trenches, Protestants and Catholics celebrated Christmas and Easter together, long before there was any official talk of "ecumenism." In the African rain forest, or the Peruvian Andes, a great deal is done in less than complete conformity with the letter of church law, but altogether in conformity with the given situation. Surely, responsible priests and laity in our own countries may proceed in this way, whether the principle of moral theology they invoke to justify their behavior be that of *epikeia,* or pastoral solutions, or situation ethics, or autonomous morality. To be sure, such procedures must always be accompanied by respect for the demands of prudence and love, as Paul himself recommends in the Letter to the Corinthians (1 Cor. 8:13), in order to aggravate as little as possible any untoward polarization within the community. A careful pedagogy, calculated to enable the community to accept the responsibility of a mature Christian life, will be a great boon in this area.

In an emergency, one may and should expound generally acknowledged principles generously, and then translate them concretely into deed. For example, the universal priesthood of all the baptized and the equal worth of all believers are clearly set forth in holy scripture, by the council, and again in the bishops' synod on the laity in 1987. Now is surely the time to implement such theoretical pronouncements in practice, in the warp and woof of daily life, through the invention of pastoral tactics that will bring this equality-in-principle down to brass tacks rather than belying it once more with timid acts of retrenchment.

The gospel is far more generous than is church law in this regard. Jesus dispatched "the Twelve" as his special deputies (Mark 6:7). But he also sent the seventy-two disciples with the same commission (Luke 10:1) — ordinary men, perhaps women as well, who had been struck by his teaching and would be eager to carry it to village and city. Again, Jesus tells the apostle for whom he intends a special role: "You are 'Rock.' . . . Whatever you [sg.] declare bound on earth shall be bound in heaven; whatever you declare loosed on earth shall be loosed in heaven" (Matt. 16:18). But shortly thereafter he says to his disciples: "I assure you [pl.], whatever you declare bound on earth shall be held bound in heaven, and whatever you declare loosed on earth shall be held loosed in heaven" (Matt. 18:18). This latter logion appears as part of the "community rule," in which Jesus apprises the community, or the communities, even small groups, indeed, families as domestic churches, of their full responsibility to decide their daily questions independently, in good conscience and in the Holy Spirit. This "both . . . and," this emphasis on an individual together with a recognition of many, must not be retroactively restricted to an elite, exclusive group. All who believe in Jesus, and who belong to his community, should be not simply passive beneficiaries, but active administrators, of the power of binding and loosing. In the sacramental area, the church has made the determination that this power will be reserved to those holding church offices. But in the nonsacramental area, all of Jesus' disciples, women and men alike, may and should appeal to the plenary authority he has conferred upon them.[2]

Concretely, this will be spelled out in applications like the following. If pupils happen to confide more in their teachers than in their pastor, if women and men reveal their personal problems more to a physician who takes the needed time, and who shows the needed understanding, than they do to a priest, if the dying suddenly make a sort of general confession to the hospice nurse—these "confessors" should take their "priestly office" seriously, assure their "penitents" of the remission of their sins in God's name, and seek to encourage them for the journey ahead. We should remember that, until the ninth century, in monastic communities, the *starets*, or elder, who manifested special charisms as a spiritual director, functioned as a "spiritual father," and heard the monks' confessions without benefit of priestly ordination.[3]

Again: when pastoral ministers, together with an open-minded priest, hold a eucharistic celebration for small groups of children or for other small groups, they should be permitted a great deal of freedom in the choosing of texts and the invention of "rubrics" that will make the celebration not only understandable, but actually attractive and inviting.

Again: In former times, any exemption from the law had to be obtained from proper authority. If a farmer wanted to harvest on Sunday, he had to ask the pastor. If an elderly priest wanted to say Mass seated, he had to ask the apostolic nuncio for a dispensation. Today, parishes, even individuals, implement their evangelical authority of binding and loosing. When Christians have reasonable grounds for omitting attendance at church on a given Sunday, or for expressing their marital love with certain precautions, or when the partners of a mixed marriage wish to receive Holy Communion together, they may dispense themselves from the norm, and in good conscience. Recently Cardinal Ratzinger declared that priests suffering from alcoholism may celebrate the Eucharist by using unfermented grape juice instead of wine. But in the same breath he cautioned that the dispensation to do so must be obtained from Rome. Really, one fails to see why, in such individual cases, one should trouble the highest ecclesial instance. The bishop, religious superior, or confessor should be able to grant such a dispensation—and now should simply do so, when licitness alone, and not validity, is in question.

Here I have touched on a point that ought to be spelled out somewhat more in detail: the significance of the decision taken in conscience. As early as 1922, Romano Guardini began his famous book, *Vom Sinn der Kirche*, with: "A religious event of incalculable consequence is now under way. The church is awakening in souls." He recognized the "signs of the times," and thus could anticipate the insights of the council. Guardini was saying: Genuine, renewed Christians no longer experience the church first and foremost as exterior structure and hierarchy, but regard themselves as church, as the people of God. I should like to recast his formula thus: The church is awakening in consciences.

In times past, particular personages in state and church, members of the nobility and clergy, made decisions for the masses, while the masses—apart from, for example, the slave uprising of ancient Rome and the rebellions of serfs in medieval times—bowed their heads in obedience. Since those times, however, it has been discovered that all human beings are persons. Persons are now taken seriously as such. They have been convalidated: their objective worth has been recognized and acknowledged. They now seek to share in thinking, in speaking, in deciding, and in many instances they wish to make their decisions themselves. Thus we stand today before the fait accompli that the majority of Christians no longer practice "blind obedience" toward outward authority, but, as we have already observed, simply seek to behave sensibly, in accordance with common sense, according to the dictates of their conscience, according to the inspirations of the Holy Spirit. Whether the authorities look kindly on this state of affairs or not does not, of course, alter the state of affairs. The council acknowledged it, and *Dignitatis Humanae* (the Declaration on Religious Freedom), which met with considerable resistance, but which was finally adopted by an overwhelming majority, decreed that human beings' proper worth consists in the fact that they are not simply the executors of the orders of other instances, but can and "should act on their own judgment, enjoying and making use of a responsible freedom" (no. 1). Karl Rahner had the foresight to predict, in those days, that this would surely be the richest and most pregnant decree of the council. And indeed we see its consequences grow by the year. Christian freedom is being exercised far more extensively than ever before.

To be sure, freedom of conscience entails dangers. It can be abused in the spirit of libertinism, in which one may blissfully believe that one may simply do whatever one wishes. This is not what freedom of conscience means. Freedom of conscience actually presupposes more personal responsibility, not less, than "blind obedience" does. I must take the norms of the gospel, and the church's norms, into consideration, and then confront them with the concrete case before me—with the question of its moral permissibility or impermissibility—and in the last instance decide what I am to do. Thus the process moves not along the bipolarity of law and absolute obedience, but along the triangle of law, individual situation, and decision of conscience in cognizance of cause.

Thus, church law remains a factor in my decision of conscience. Only, it is no longer simply the ultimate norm of my behavior. Nor must we idealize the conscience as if most Christians now practice it in a perfect manner. Here too we are still *in via,* and must improve with age. In the meantime, failures and sins are far from being out of the question, and we should openly admit that we are not honestly up to all that we ought to do.

Responsibility will be a key topic in discussions with young and adult Christians alike.

A second danger lies in a calcified polarization. Integralists, rightists, conservatives, also appeal to their conviction, and their conscience, and very stubbornly. Thus both groups are hardened in their positions, the one swearing by the law, the other by liberty. Side by side with the movement toward freedom of conscience, a countertrend is already in the making. There are those who "want to know the score" once more, and who are issuing a new call for absolute authority and uniformity in the church. They lack the courage for personal decision.

Fragile though it be, freedom of conscience is here to stay. "Human beings are mature to the extent that they take their distance from those who have led them to maturity" (F. Pöggeler). Or:

> The personal Christian conscience must be capable, in particular situations, of transcending the letter of a particular law and actualizing the basic meaning of all law, love, in the manner that may be called for at a given moment. "I was only following orders" is not a valid excuse [A. J. Novak].

We recall Dostoevsky's Grand Inquisitor, who is burning heretics by droves in sixteenth-century Spain "to the greater glory of God." One day he comes upon Jesus going about working miracles again, and making his proclamation of love and liberty. He immediately has him arrested as a dangerous person, and, the whole night through, attempts to explain to him why freedom of faith is dangerous. The masses cannot deal with freedom, he explains. They are happy when they have bread. The church must see to law and order, and must do so with divine authority, bringing consciences under the yoke of obedience and suppressing the frenzied vertigo of freedom. "But you have come to bother us. You have made men upstarts, like boys conspiring in the schoolroom and chasing the master about." Soon, however, the celebration will be at an end, and the foolish boys will have to pay dearly. "If anyone alive deserves our stake more than all heretics together, it is you. Tomorrow I shall have you burned." Jesus is silent, all night long. And when the Grand Inquisitor has done screaming his lesson, Jesus kisses him on his bloodless lips. The Grand Inquisitor is shattered. He throws open the prison gate: "Leave this place and never return! Never return, never, never!"

But Jesus has returned, with his proclamation of love and freedom, and today we hear more than ever of freedom of conscience, of the "courage for conscience," of the "insurrection of conscience," of "decisions of conscience as encouragement to the deed. They demand courage, but they inspire courage, as well."[4]

A church like this — a church of decision and conscience, even a remnant church, in small, convinced groups — will have more weight in the sight of

God and human beings, and will develop more power of witness, than did the old, hereditary church. In particular, it will testify to the Reign of God, which extends far beyond the church. God causes the Reign, like the sun, to rise over good and wicked alike, and the divine love to fall like rain over righteous and unrighteous—precisely because God is the Parent of all, whose harbinger, whose credible personification, we Christians are to be in the world.

Of course, the road to freedom of conscience can also generate—and here is the third danger—an atomized mist of individual Christians and small groups who are no longer a church, which of course is not what is wanted, and which would not be helpful to people. The individual has no voice in the world. In particular, the individual is helpless before structures. What is needed, then, is a church, the community of all of the women and men who follow Jesus, endowed with a certain institutional mass and possessing a powerful voice. Surely it is to be hoped that the people of the church will pursue their path of freedom of conscience unerringly. But it is to be hoped as well that the pinnacle of the church will chime in before it is too late and cease its attempt to control Christians with authoritarian measures, which repel them instead of uniting them. Rather, in the style of a church of siblings (in the style, for example, of the churches of not a few bishops in Latin America), let those at the pinnacle inspire trust, let them be able to listen and learn, let them begin to animate and motivate, and thus bring Christian individuals once more to a sense of "we," a sense of church, and thereby as well to coordinated action as church in the world.

Such a "church of conscience" would be far closer to the primitive model of the church than the hereditary church has been—although, today, we ought to be not born "again" in a kind of reincarnation of the primitive church, but born "anew," as a credible church for the coming third millennium, a church no longer marked by the Constantinian turning point in history with all its power structures, but a church that will bring the Johannine turning point, with all its fascination with freedom and love, to full blossom.

Now we can once more stand in wonder at the special promptings of the Holy Spirit. Has it not prompted—instead of the hereditary church, where fine Christians "practiced their religion" as if that went without saying and was all one had to do—a new church, the conscience church of mature Christians, *in petto?* And will this not be a church, also, that will be able to stand tall in the secular world of the third millennium? Does the Spirit not tolerate the present authoritarian, unendurable ecclesiastical regime precisely in order that it may create a church of conscience by way of reaction, while the old church itself gradually isolates itself until it finally crazes like a piece of old china, eventually to disintegrate? Would not old Spirit-inspired John XXIII smile at all of this, and here again, as in his opening address at the council, when he spoke of the confusion of his own era, invite us to "see a hidden plan of divine providence, that through the course of the ages and through the deeds of human beings pursues its own goal"?

For the moment, the hereditary church is still with us, and the church of conscience has not yet come. We still await the "skinning" of the old medieval church. When will this occur? This is the insecurity of our time. We are in the midst of the painful birth pangs of a new age, and we must persevere, in the hope that the Holy Spirit will transform chaos to cosmos once more. For it is the *Creator Spiritus,* who, ever and again, has the power to sweep down upon the church and upon humanity with unexpected, unforeseeable solutions to things.

Observing that the Roman curia's preparation for the council was proceeding in a very conservative spirit, Pope John XXIII remained optimistic, and told himself inwardly: "The council will take things in hand, and all will be well." And so it happened. One of the first things the council fathers did was to reject the prepared schemata, start again from scratch, and work through to a happy conclusion. For the moment, we cannot look to another council to snatch us from our confusion. But we may still say, in the logic of the council: the people of God will take things in hand, and all will be well. Thus, in this joyless time of transition, we are permitted to glimpse, with John XXIII, "a hidden plan of divine providence," and to remain optimistic.

SUMMARY

Let me draw up a balance sheet for this entire book. In part 1, I called the reader's attention to three main themes, and indicated that they would run all through the book. The first is a hope that, in these difficult times of ours, prophets will be sent to us, to show us the way, and courageously lead our people out of exile. In the domain of world politics, in this era of a single humanity, we may be allowed to place a great deal of hope in the only two giants of the present day—open to criticism though they may be— Pope John Paul II, and President Mikhail Gorbachev. While the former wields only a moral authority, the latter has at his disposition the political means to see his good plans through to their gradual accomplishment. It seems to me that the implications of the December 1989 meeting between these leaders will make that meeting the event of the century for church politics. In the area of a more just world economy, or more effective environmental protection, we still lack figures of the stature of these two personages. We must pray the harder, then. And if we lack "great prophets," all the more must we ourselves become "little prophets," and speak and act in such a way as to bring these ends to their accomplishment.

My second theme is the tension between documents and deeds, and we have encountered it at every step of our way. It is wearisome, it is depressing, it is downright crippling to see what we have to see. We are drowning in documents. We thirst for deeds. The council forthrightly proclaims, and the pope proclaims, unabashedly and at every opportunity, the autonomy of the sciences, the convalidation of the laity, the urgency of ecumenism, the legitimacy of a theological, liturgical, and disciplinary pluralism, and so much more that would constitute an appropriate response to the "signs of the times." But woe to the one who behaves accordingly. Theologians and bishops are promptly whistled to heel, to be chastised and humiliated, with painful measures if need be. Many a time we have heard of commissions, professional opinions, or honest proposals, all calculated to help the church move forward, being rejected by Rome — this rejection is scarcely by way of exception, then, but is the mournful rule. Rome, with its imperturbable self-assurance, simply goes its traditional way, thereby — my third theme — extending the pernicious concatenation of by-passed opportunities.

We can change nothing of this concrete situation for the moment. And things will worsen. In Europe and North America our last hope is assailed by analyses of the state of the church, and of Christianity. But where need is greatest, God's help is nearest. Hope is the last thing we may surrender. Furthermore, precisely along the two horizons where religion seemed most to founder, a new morn dawns. Scientists, who have derided our faith for a hundred years, today stand in astonishment at the inexplicable puzzles they have recently encountered, and invite us of "little faith" to share their awe at the ultimate mysteries and wonders of creation and its Creator. Marxists, who for a hundred years have striven by every possible means to storm the fortress of religion, are today on the point of acknowledging not only religion's inalienable rights, but its significance for culture and humanity. Both of these phenomena will have their effects on the future of religion. Furthermore, even in Europe and North America, once the time is ripe, why may we not experience an invasion of the same Holy Spirit who has turned so much to the good over the last twenty years in Latin America, Africa, and Asia? If I speak of the Holy Spirit, of course, that does not mean that we should sit on our hands waiting for a little "coup d'état of the Holy Spirit." On the contrary, the Holy Spirit takes us all very seriously, and encourages us to undertake great deeds. The hour of truth is striking. No longer can we point the finger of blame at the pinnacle of the church — at the "others." No longer do we ourselves get off scot-free. Now we must take the great declarations of the council seriously. The council has said that we are the church, that *you* and *I* are the church. All criticism of the church, then, all church reform, all hope for the church, must begin with you and me. Let a few hundred, a few million individual Christian "I's" utter prophetic speech and practice prophetic behavior, implement the conciliar documents step by step, seize opportunities large and small by the nape of the neck and use them for all they are worth, and — despite all — things will be at least a little better in the world and the church.

The Holy Spirit, who has given us eyes to see, fashions within us a heart to act, as well. Nothing is hopeless, then, so long as we ourselves do not collapse in hopelessness. "Fear not, it is I!" is the motto on our Christian escutcheon.

Notes

PART 1
INTRODUCING A NEW CONSTELLATION OF WORLD FORCES

One World and a World Church

1. The figures are taken from the *Annuarium Statisticum Ecclesiae 1985* (Ex Urbe Vaticana, 1987).
2. J. B. Metz, "Im Aufbruch zu einer kulturell polyzentrischen Weltkirche," in *Zeitschrift für Missionswissenschaft* (Münster in W., 1986), pp. 140–53, esp. 140.
3. K. Rahner, "Theologische Bedeutung der Position der Christen in der modernen Welt," in *Sendung und Gnade*, rev. ed. (Innsbruck, 1966), pp. 13–47.
4. In this regard see H. Schüngel-Straumann, *Der Dekalog—Gebot Gottes?* (Stuttgart, 1973); F. L. Hassfeld, *Der Dekalog. Seine späteren Fassungen, die originelle Komposition und seine Vorstufen* (Göttingen, 1982); F. Furger, *Die zehn Gebote, Spielregeln des Lebens* (Fribourg, 1983); A. Exeler, *In Gottes Freiheit leben. Die zehn Gebote*, 3d ed. (Fribourg in Breisgau, 1985); J. Fuchs, "Christliche Moral. Biblische Orientierung und menschliche Wertung," in *Stimmen der Zeit* (October 1987), pp. 671–84.

PART 2
THE "NEW" TEN COMMANDMENTS OF GOD:
A DECALOGUE BASED ON THE SIGNS OF THE TIMES

1. You Will Allow Common Sense To Prevail: Autonomy of the Sciences

1. H. Küng, *Theologie im Aufbruch* (Munich, 1987), pp. 224f. Eng. trans.: *Theology for the Third Millennium* (New York, 1988).
2. F. Dessauer and X. von Hornstein, *Seele im Bannkreis der Technik* (Olten, 1945).
3. Further developed in my book *Leben—Sterben—Leben*, 2d ed. (Graz, 1987), pp. 37–72. See also H. P. Dürr, ed., *Physik und Transzendenz. Die grossen Physiker unseres Jahrhunderts über ihre Begegnung mit dem Wunderbaren*, 4th ed. (Bern, 1987); H. A. Müller, ed., *Naturwissenschaft und Glaube* (Munich, 1988).
4. L. Kaufmann, *Ein ungelöster Kirchenkonflikt. Der Fall Pfürtner* (Fribourg, 1987).
5. Further developed in Kaufmann, *Ein ungelöster Kirchenkonflikt*, pp. 40–59.
6. Club of Rome, *Das menschliche Dilemma. Zukunft und Lernen* (Munich, 1979). In English, see the various volumes of the Club of Rome's Project on the Predicament of Mankind.

2. You Will Take Yourselves Seriously as People of God: The Laity in the Church

1. U. Ruh, in *Herder Korrespondenz* (December 1987), p. 565.

2. P. Beyerhaus, *Die Selbständigkeit der jungen Kirchen als missionarisches Problem* (Wuppertal, 1956).

3. For these latter, see W. Ludin, Th. Seiterich, and P. M. Zulehner, eds., *Wir Kirchenträumer. Basisgemeinschaften im deutschsprachigen Raum* (Olten, 1987).

4. E. Klee, *Gottesmänner und ihre Frauen* (Frankfurt, 1979), p. 47.

5. See, e.g., Solidaritätsgruppe engagierter Christen in Österreich, *Gottes Töchter und seine mächtigen Söhne* (Salzburg, 1981); W. Beinert, ed., *Frauenbefreiung und Kirche* (Regensdorf, 1987); E. Cutting, *Offensive gegen den Patriarchalismus* (Fribourg in Breisgau, 1987).

6. U. Ranke-Heinemann, *Eunuchen für das Himmelreich* (Hamburg, 1988).

3. You Will Extend Your Hand to Your Fellow Christians: Ecumenism

1. H. Fries and O. H. Pesch, *Streiten für die eine Kirche* (Munich, 1987), pp. 150–71.

2. H. Fries and K. Rahner, *Einigung der Kirchen — eine reale Möglichkeit* (Fribourg in Breisgau, 1983).

3. K. Lehmann and W. Pannenberg, eds., *Lehrverurteilungen — kirchentrennend?* (Fribourg in Breisgau, 1986). See also Fries and Pesch, *Streiten für die eine Kirche,* pp. 85–134.

4. O. Cullmann, *Einheit durch Vielfalt* (Tübingen, 1986), p. 22. Eng. trans.: *Unity through Diversity* (Minneapolis, 1988).

4. You Will Take Sides with the Poor: Justice in Latin America

1. W. Brandt, *Der organisierte Wahnsinn* (Cologne, 1985).

2. L. R. Brown, *Zur Lage der Welt 87/88. Daten für das Überleben unseres Planeten* (Frankfurt, 1987).

3. C. F. von Weizsäcker, *Die Zeit drängt* (Munich, 1986), p. 28.

4. N. Lohfink, *Der Geschmack der Hoffnung,* (Fribourg in Breisau, 1983), p. 117.

5. U.S. Bishops, *Economic Justice for All: Social Teaching and the U.S. Economy.* For the full text see *Origins* 16, no. 24 (Nov. 27, 1986).

6. E.g., in his book *Saint Francis: A Model for Human Liberation* (Maryknoll, N.Y., 1982).

7. Hélder Câmara, *Die Bekehrung eines Bischofs* (Wuppertal, 1978).

8. See A. Longchamps, A. Perrot, and S. de Pury, *L'honneur perdu des évêques argentins* (Geneva, 1987).

9. English translations of many books in the series are being published in the United States by Orbis Books and in Great Britain by Burns and Oates.

10. Leonardo Boff, *Trinity and Society* (Maryknoll, N.Y., and Tunbridge Wells, 1988).

11. José Comblin, *The Holy Spirit and Liberation* (Maryknoll, N.Y., and Tunbridge Wells, 1989).

12. See the documents from the Pontifical Justice and Peace Commission.

13. V. Cosmao, *Dossier nouvel de l'ordre mondial. Les chrétiens provoqués par le développement* (Chalet, 1978).

5. You Will Wonder at the Breadth of the Creator: Inculturation in Africa

1. C. F. von Weizsäcker, *Zum Weltbild der Physik* (Zurich, 1954).

2. See H. Fischedick, *Von einem, der auszog, das Leben zu lernen. Glaube und Selbstwerdung* (Munich, 1987), pp. 165f.

3. M. Hay, *Failure in the Far East* (London, 1957).

4. A beginning of this kind has been made by J. G. Healey, *A Fifth Gospel: The Experience of Black Christian Values* (Maryknoll, N.Y., 1981).

6. You Will Acknowledge That the "I Am Here" Is Present among All Peoples: Dialogue with the Religions of Asia

1. Announcing the establishment of the Secretariat for Non-Christians, on Pentecost of 1964, Paul VI spoke of the "council's atmosphere of oneness and understanding among all believers"(!). The document published by this same secretariat in 1984 on dialogue and mission spoke, in an early draft, of "believers of other religions," but was changed—obviously under pressure—to "followers of other religions." The Secretariat has since been renamed the Pontifical Council on Interreligious Dialogue.

2. Further developed in my book *Wenn Gott zu allen Menschen geht. Für eine neue Erfahrung der Auserwählung* (Fribourg in Breisgau, 1981).

3. On this point see the works of Raimundo Panikkar.

4. Further developed in H. Küng, *Theologie im Aufbruch* (Munich, 1987), pp. 298–306. Eng. trans.: *Theology for the Third Millennium* (New York, 1988).

5. P. Puthanangady, ed., *Sharing Worship: Communicatio in sacris* (Bangalore, 1988). See J. Neuner's report on this seminar in *Zeitschrift für Missionswissenschaft und Religionswissenschaft* (Munster, 1988), pp. 240–48.

6. H. Bürkle, "Die Rolle des Vatermotivs in den Gottesvorstellungen des neuern Hinduismus," in A. Falaturi, ed., *Universale Vaterschaft Gottes und Begegnung mit den Religionen* (Fribourg in Breisgau, 1987), pp. 115–33.

7. See G. Evers, "Ist Christus der einzige Weg?" *Publik Forum* (January 1988), pp. 29f.

7. You Will Accompany Religious Nomads: Secularization in Euramerica

1. K. Rahner, "Theologische Bedeutung der Position der Christen in der modernen Welt," in *Sendung und Gnade*, rev. ed. (Innsbruck, 1966), pp. 13–47.

2. Missionszentrale der Franziskaner, ed., *Pastorale und franziskanische Prioritäten im Kontext der Ortskirchen Asiens, Lateinamerikas und Europas* (Bonn, 1988), pp. 13f.

3. L. A. Elchinger, *Sät die Kirche auf Beton?* (Fribourg in Breisgau, 1988).

4. J. Sudbrack, *Neue Religiosität. Herausforderung für die Christen* (Mainz, 1987); M. Kehl, *New Age oder Neuer Bund? Christen im Gespräch mit Esoterik, Okkultismus, Wendezeit* (Mainz, 1988).

5. J. Paillard, *Christ unter Atheisten* (Frankfurt, 1971); W. Kerber, ed., *Säkularisierung und Wertewandel* (Munich, 1987).

6. See K. Rahner, *Schriften zur Theologie* (Zurich, 1978, 1980), XIII, pp. 226–51; XIV, p. 236. Eng. trans.: *Theological Investigations* (New York, 1974–83).

7. H. Lübbe, *Religion nach der Aufklärung* (Graz, 1986), p. 14.

8. R. Malek and M. Plate, eds., *Chinas Katholiken suchen neue Wege* (Fribourg in Breisgau, 1987).

9. Further developed on the basis of biblical, patristic, and medieval theology, and the modern experience in H. U. von Balthasar, *Was dürfen wir hoffen?* (Einsiedeln, 1986). Eng. trans.: *Dare We Hope "That All Men Be Saved"?* (New York, 1988).

8. You Will Swell the Ranks of the Peacemakers: Justice and Peace

1. See F. Alt, *Liebe ist möglich. Die Bergpredigt im Atomzeitalter* (Munich, 1985).

2. Th. Later, *Ziviler Ungehorsam* (Baden-Baden, 1986).

3. See M. Gorbachev, *Perestroika: New Thinking for Our Country and the World* (New York, 1987); cf. Schmid-Häuer, *Michail Gorbatschow*, 5th ed. (Munich, 1987).

4. Reprinted in *Frankfurter Rundschau* (September 1987), p. 24.

5. F. J. Strauss, "Sowjetunion—quo vadis?" in *Bulletin des Schweizerischen Bankmagazin* (March 1988), pp. 11–13.

6. R. Schneider, *Gesammelte Werke* (Frankfurt on Main, n.d.), VIII, pp. 449, 374.

9. You Will Make the Earth a Paradise: Ecology and Eschatology

1. Developed in exemplary fashion in M. Kehl, *Eschatologie* (Würzburg, 1986).

2. D. Meadow, *Die Grenzen des Wachstums* (Stuttgart, 1972). In English, see the 1972 report by the Club of Rome.

3. M. Wöhlcke, *Umweltzerstörung in der Dritten Welt* (Munich, 1987).

4. See F. Vorholz, "Mehr Schmutz als Schutz. Die Verantwortlichen in Brüssel blockieren einen wirksamen Umweltschutz," *Die Zeit* (Hamburg, January 29, 1988).

5. C. Overmann, *Four Alternative Futures* (Washington, D.C., 1980).

6. See, e.g., the rather pessimistic book by C. Amery, *Das Ende der Vorsehung. Die gnadenlosen Folgen des Christentums* (Hamburg, 1972).

7. K. Traube, et al., *Der Atom-Skandal* (Munich, 1988).

8. A. Auer, *Umweltethik* (Dusseldorf, 1984), esp. p. 134.

10. You Will Encounter the God of History: Spirituality and Politics

1. K. Rahner, *Schriften zur Theologie* (Zurich, 1983), XV, pp. 177f. Eng. trans.: *Theological Investigations* (New York, 1974–83). See also B. Stähelin, *Urvertrauenund*

162 *Notes*

zweite Wirklichkeit (Zurich, 1973); P. Tournier, *Geborgenheit—Sehnsucht des Menschen* (Fribourg in Breisgau, 1971); V. E. Frankl, *Die Sinnfrage in der Psychologie* (Munich, 1981).

2. In E. Schillebeeckx, ed., *Mystik und Politik. Festschrift J. B. Metz* (Mainz, 1988).

PART 3
REFLECTIONS ON THE NEW FUTURE

The Church on the Way to the Third Millennium

1. Pastoralsoziologisches Institut, *Junge Eltern reden über Religion und Kirche* (Zurich, 1986).

2. See H. Vorgrimmler, *Busse und Krankensalbung,* fasc. 3, vol. IV: *Handbuch der Dogmengeschichte* (Fribourg in Breisgau, 1978), pp. 16f.

3. I. Smolitsch, *Leben und Lehre der Starzen* (Fribourg in Breisgau, 1988).

4. H. Windisch, ed., *Mut zum Gewissen. Einladung zu einer riskanten Seelsorge* (Regensburg, 1987); A. J. Novak, *Gewissen und Gewissensbildung heute in tiefenpsychologischer Sicht* (Vienna, 1978).

CHRISTIAN MISSION IN A PLURALISTIC WORLD

by John Patrick Brennan

Are the different religions many ways to the one goal? Should Christian missionaries continue to proclaim the Good News of Jesus Christ to people of other faiths? In the pluralistic world in which we live is the Christian mission still viable? How must the Church relate to the contemporary world? These are some of the questions confronting the Church and her missionaries today.

John Patrick Brennan, at the close of the second Christian millennium, examines the questions and argues that the modern situation, far from diminishing the urgency of the Christian mission, helps to underline its centrality within Christianity as a whole.

He sees the contemporary situation as a challenge to the Church, evermore profoundly the servant in the world in which she lives. This is her *raison d'être*. More than ever the Church must be the "Light of the world" – but she must be so in a truly Christian way – the way of humble, loving service.

JOHN PATRICK BRENNAN *was born in 1944 in Co. Mayo, Ireland; in 1968 he was ordained priest in the Society of African Missions (SMA). He did his doctoral studies in Rome in 1969-1979, and from 1981 is a Seminary Professor in Nigeria.*

136 pages   ISBN 085439 326 9   £6.50

IN SEARCH OF UNITY

Ecumenical Principles and Prospects
by Edward Yarnold

"Ecumenical principles and prospects" in the light of the past two decades of Anglican-Roman Catholic dialogue, is the theme of this new book by one of Britain's foremost theologians. In many ways the gap between Canterbury and Rome seems wider now than when it all began. The road to unity is harder to map than was imagined in the post-Vatican II ecumenical optimism. And yet the ecumenical commitment remains: there is no turning back.

Fr Yarnold here outlines the challenges that confront, at every turn, the efforts towards unity, showing how to overcome some of the apparently insurmountable difficulties and how to break new grounds in Christ's footsteps.

EDWARD YARNOLD *is tutor at Campion Hall and Chairman of the Oxford University Faculty of Theology. He is the author of several books such as* The Theology of Original Sin, The Awe-inspiring Rites of Initiation, The Second Gift *and numerous articles.*

132 pages   ISBN 085439 309 9   £5.75

LOVE IN THE ECONOMY

by Christopher McOustra

Love in the economy summarizes the last hundred years of Catholic teaching on the role of the individual in modern economy, covering topics such as housing and shared ownership, the "social mortgage", pay and profit, and the rights and responsibilities of men and women in business, at work and in Trade Unions. The Vatican Council, Popes and bishops repeatedly present a social doctrine based on Christian love. In the words of Pope John XXIII "love is the driving force of the economy" and the hallmark of the Christian social doctrine. The author, sifting through the main documents of the Church – from Pope Leo XIII's *Rerum Novarum* (1891) to Pope John Paul II's *Christifideles Laici* (1988) – identifies the specific character of the Church's teaching on social issues. An anthology and guide book for all Christians, especially priests and teachers, workers and students, members of Trade Unions and businessmen, who care for peace and progress in a society often motivated by sheer profit and power.

CHRISTOPHER McOUSTRA, *Master of Arts at Christ's College, Cambridge, trained as a lawyer, and from 1959 to 1982 worked in British Industry.*

222 pages   ISBN 085439 324 2   £7.95

EVANGELIZATION TODAY

by Bernard Häring

Inspired by the proclamation of 1990's as the "decade of Evangelization" Fr Häring revisits the subject of evangelization in today's world and explores its two inseparable aspects: the morals of evangelization and the evangelization of morals. For it is only if we are evangelized ourselves that we can evangelize others.

In this process the prime agent of transformation is grace, not morals: grace meets and leavens the existing morals of every culture. And the "law of grace", to which faith is the response, is dynamic and liberating, in the sense that it frees from sin, it frees from merely cultural norms and it liberates the already existing good.

Fr Häring faces the difficulties with a religion of incarnation, which has constantly to immerse itself in cultures and disentangle itself from them if they become arrogant and threaten to supersede the gospel itself. Any cultural values, dynamism and liberation themselves, may become idols, so that in relation to both past and present, to both western and other cultures, we need education in discernment as well as in reconciliation. It is towards this education that the present book offers guidance and support.

BERNARD HÄRING, *now retired after fifty years in the active ministry, is considered one of the most outstanding moral theologians of the RC Church. He is the author of several books, some of which have been published in English by St Paul Publications.*

184 pages   ISBN 085439 338 2   £6.95

CHURCH, ECUMENISM
& POLITICS

by Joseph Ratzinger

"The articles and papers collected here form a kind of
second volume to the ecclesiological essays which I published in 1969 under the title *Das neue Volk Gottes*. The basic
issues have remained the same: the question of the nature
of the Church, its structure, the ecumenical scene, the
relationship of the Church and the world. But in many cases
the emphasis has shifted and new evaluations have become
necessary.
The debate about Christian ecumenism and efforts to
achieve the right relationship of faith and politics occupy the
foreground of the reflections that make up this volume.
Some of the contributions reprinted here aroused vigorous
debate when they were first published, and I have tried to
do justice to this debate either in additional footnotes or in
newly added postscripts. I hope that in this way it will
become clear that these essays are meant as a contribution
to dialogue with the aim that by listening to each other we
shall be able to hear more clearly Him who in His person
is the word and truth."

JOSEPH RATZINGER, *born in 1927; Professor of Theology in
the Universities of Bonn, Münster, Tübingen and Regensburg;*
peritus *at the Second Vatican Council; Archbishop of Munich
(1977); since 1981 Prefect of the Sacred Congregation for
the Doctrine of Faith.*

278 pages   ISBN 085439 267 X   £9.95